PENGUIN BOOKS
BBC BOOKS

# THE FIFTY YEARS WAR
## ISRAEL AND THE ARABS

Ahron Bregman was born in Israel. He studied at the Hebrew University, Jerusalem, and worked for three years in the Knesset as a parliamentary assistant. He holds a Ph.D. from Kings College, London, has taught at institutions of higher education and has written for various academic journals. He also writes for the *Daily Telegraph*. His books *War and Israeli Society 1948–1990s* and *A History of Israel* are Forthcoming.

Jihan El-Tahri was born in Beirut, the daughter of an Egyptian diplomat. She holds degrees from the American University in Cairo. She has been a journalist since 1984 and worked for four years with Reuters in Egypt before going to Tunisia, where she worked for *US News and World Report*, the *Washington Post* and the *Financial Times*. Since 1990 she has been working in Paris for *US News and World Report*. She is co-author of *Les Sept Vies de Yasser Arafat*.

# THE FIFTY YEARS WAR
## Israel and the Arabs

**Ahron Bregman**

**Jihan El-Tahri**

PENGUIN BOOKS
BBC BOOKS

PENGUIN BOOKS
BBC BOOKS

This book is published to accompany the television series *The Fifty Years War:
Israel and the Arabs*, which was first broadcast in spring 1998. The series was
produced for BBC Television by Brian Lapping Associates Ltd

Executive Producer: Brian Lapping
Series Producer: Norma Percy
Producers and Directors: David Ash, Dai Richards,
Michael Simkin and Charlie Smith

Published by the Penguin Group and BBC Worldwide Ltd

Penguin Books Ltd, 27 Wrights Lane, London W8 5TZ, England
Penguin Putnam Inc., 375 Hudson Street, New York, New York 10014, USA
Penguin Books Australia Ltd, Ringwood, Victoria, Australia
Penguin Books Canada Ltd, 10 Alcorn Avenue, Toronto, Ontario, Canada M4V 3B2
Penguin Books (NZ) Ltd, 182–190 Wairau Road, Auckland 10, New Zealand

Penguin Books Ltd, Registered Offices: Harmondsworth, Middlesex, England

First published by Penguin Books and BBC Books,
an imprint of BBC Worldwide Ltd, 1998
1 3 5 7 9 10 8 6 4 2

Text copyright © Ahron Bregman, Jihan El-Tahri, 1998
Preface and research material © Brian Lapping Associates Ltd, 1998
All rights reserved

The moral right of the authors has been asserted

Maps by Line + Line

B B C

The BBC logo is a trademark and is used under licence

Set in 10/11 pt Sabon
Typeset by Keystroke
Printed in Great Britain by Clays Ltd, St Ives plc

*To our children Daniel, Maya and Inès*
*with much love*

*May you share a lasting peace*

# Contents

# Acknowledgements

Our biggest thanks go to Brian Lapping, Executive Producer of *The Fifty Years War: Israel and the Arabs,* and Norma Percy, Series Producer, for inviting us to work on this extraordinary project and write this accompanying book. Brian's generous support and patience throughout was invaluable, and Norma's obsession with collecting every scrap of information provided us with huge amounts of material to sieve through. We are grateful to the documentary team and directors whose rapidly expanding knowledge of the details of the Arab-Israeli conflict encouraged us to keep on researching in order to stay in the lead! They are: David Ash, Dai Richards, Michael Simkin and Charlie Smith. Thanks to the production managers Casper Norman and Jacqui Loton and especially to production researcher, David Alter, whose charm and unlimited willingness to help made life much easier for us. Thanks, too, to Lawrence Freedman for his generous help.

At BBC Books we would like to thank Editorial Director Sheila Ableman who commissioned this book, Project Editor Lara Speicher, and Picture Researchers David Cottingham and Sarah Houghton for the photographs.

We were fortunate to have Barbara Nash as our editor. Barbara's vast experience, efficiency, advice and unfailing encouragement proved of great value in the writing of this book.

Thanks must go to our guardian angels in the Middle East: Nava Mizrahi in Jerusalem, Mariana al-Farr in Amman and Bouthaina Shaban in Damascus. Their wisdom, charm of persuasion and persistence opened doors for us to interview Presidents, Prime Ministers, Generals and many others, thus turning the television series and this book into a first-hand account.

Last, but certainly not least, our love and thanks go to our companions, Dana and Benoit, who bore with us so patiently throughout the long and difficult period of writing – and to Nermine El-Tahri. Without their patience, understanding and willingness to take over all day-to-day family responsibilities, this book would not have been completed.

It is to our children – two of whom were born during the writing period – that this book is dedicated.

**Ahron Bregman and Jihan El-Tahri**
**London and Paris**
**November 1997**

# Preface

This book results from a suggestion made by Michael Jackson, then Controller of BBC 2. Fortunately for us, he liked our previous six-part television series, *The Death of Yugoslavia*, so he suggested that we choose Israel's relations with the Arabs as our next theme. When Norma Percy, the series producer, and I began assembling a team for the Middle East, we decided that we must include two full-time specialists: an Israeli and an Arab. The two we eventually selected were Ahron (Ronnie) Bregman and Jihan El-Tahri. Ahron had written an impressive thesis entitled *Civil-Military Relations in Israel*; Jihan was joint author of a newly published book on Yasser Arafat. Both showed a firm grasp of reality in examining the myth-filled recent history of the area.

When our production team went on their research trips to Egypt, Israel, Jordan, Lebanon, Syria and the territories under the control of the Palestinian authority, Ahron and Jihan played a key role both in helping to organize the interviews and in conducting many of them. They then helped Norma and the team plan the programmes. When, after filming, the team began to edit the programmes, Ahron and Jihan settled down to write this book, making extensive use of the transcripts of the recorded interviews.

By then, it had already become clear that this Israeli and Arab could work together. They both disagreed at various points with other members of the production team or with Norma or with me, but there was no consistent pattern to their disagreement with each other. They both proved dispassionate in their pursuit of accurate evidence. Once, at a party in Jerusalem after Jihan and Ronnie had been arguing about some point in dispute for most of the day, the team were surprised to see them bopping enthusiastically together.

The BBC television series and this book have unearthed significant new insights of behind-the-scenes negotiations and intrigues. For example, an extract from the conversation between

King Hussein of Jordan and Prime Minister Golda Meir, taped by the Israelis ten days before the 1973 War, is published for the first time. In this, Hussein warns Golda Meir that his Arab brothers – Syria and Egypt – are preparing to attack Israel.

Secret talks between the representative of Egypt's President, Gamal Abdel Nasser, and the representative of Israel's Prime Minister, Moshe Sharett, are here authenticated for the first time. Our team has interviewed both Abdel Rahman Sadeq (Nasser's man) and Ziamah Divon (Sharett's man) enabling the book and the series to reveal remarkable details – for example of Nasser's request that Israel help him in dealing with the Americans.

The series and this book contradict the familiar picture of implacable hostility on the part of the entire Arab world against Israel. They reveal an unexpectedly high number of peaceful encounters across the offical battle-lines, of which this one between Egypt and Israel in the early 1950s is the first.

Another scoop of this book and the series is our interview with Egypt's Minister of War in 1967, Shams Badran. When our team asked about him in Egypt, they were told nobody knew whether he was still alive. He had been imprisoned after the 1967 War and had then vanished. But the team tracked him down and he gave many illuminating insights into top Egyptian decision-making in the run-up to the Six Day War, including the biggest mystery of that war, the role of the Russians in provoking it.

Likewise, in the peace talks between Israel and Syria, and those between the Israelis and Palestinians in Oslo, the major participants on all sides as well as the American mediators told us, in exclusive interviews, several unpublished stories of moments of crisis in the negotiations.

Also included are first-hand accounts – never before published – by CIA, Mossad and PLO representatives, and military Chiefs of Staff of the countries involved in the Middle East conflict and peace negotiations; and the hot-line exchange in 1967 between US President Lyndon B. Johnson and USSR Prime Minister Alexei Kosygin.

If our television series and this accompanying book have any merits, perhaps it is the revelation that honest and fair-minded people from opposite sides of the divide, like Ahron Bregman and Jihan El-Tahri, can agree about a great deal of the contentious and inflammatory information that flashes out of the Middle East. They have agreed what are political lies to be ignored. They have agreed what is demonstrably true and worth including. In that respect, this book is, I believe, both original and refreshing.

When I suggested the title *The Fifty Years War* for the television series on which this book is based, I was, of course, referring back to the Hundred Years' War that ravaged Europe in the fourteenth and fifteenth centuries. The two wars have much in common. In both, the states of a region were establishing their national identities and borders; in both, the war was seen at the time as a succession of separate, short wars; in both, the perspective of history identifies a single continuity.

The Arab-Israel conflict is usually seen as five main wars: the 1948 War that followed Israel's independence; the Suez War of 1956; the Six Day War of 1967; the War of 1973 (known as the October War by the Arabs and the Yom Kippur War by the Jews); and the Israeli invasion of Lebanon in 1982. But between these major outbreaks, tension was continuous.

Neither this book nor the television series attempts a comprehensive history. Both concentrate on those episodes which detailed questioning of participants can illumine; both offer, wherever possible, a many-sided story of key moments of decision. That, the makers of the series believe, is the best way television can contribute to history. It also makes for a book – and a research archive – full of new insights.

The fifty years war has been fought over an area known variously as Palestine, the Holy Land and Israel. Described in the Bible as a land of milk and honey, it is in reality a barren place. Set on the north-western edge of the great Arabian desert, it forms part of the fertile crescent, the only route between mankind's earliest civilizations, Mesopotamia (now Iraq) and

13

Egypt. The desert being all but impassable, all trade went through the crescent: from Egypt, north through Palestine and Lebanon, then east through Syria, and south again down the Tigris and Euphrates rivers to Babylon and Sumer.

But Palestine was more than part of a trade route. It nurtured three of the most important religions in history. Judaism and Christianity had their origins here, and Muslims treasure Jerusalem as the place from which the prophet Muhammad ascended to heaven. Both Christians and Jews travelled thousands of miles – Christians in the Crusades, Jews in the Zionist movement – overcoming obstacles they should have considered insurmountable, to recover this rocky land. No other territory on earth has aroused such passion.

Throughout its history, Palestine tended to fall under the control of the most powerful state in the Middle East, in turn Persia, Egypt, Rome, Byzantium, the Arabs. For four centuries, until 1917, control lay with the Ottoman Empire.

Then as the Ottoman Empire disintegrated, British troops took over. Desperately seeking allies during the First World War, Britain offered deals to both the Jews and the Arabs. Both thought they had been promised Palestine. Britain's purpose was to secure the territory for British use, as a bastion to protect Egypt, which it then controlled.

But Palestine proved to be the British Empire's most disastrous mistake. Not even the mismanagement of the American colonies by King George III and Lord North brought Britain such total humiliation or such total absence of gain.

In the small print of the Balfour Declaration and of the MacMahon-Hussein letters (in which the incompatible promises were made) British officials inserted well-drafted get-out clauses. But these did no good. Both Arabs and Jews felt betrayed, fostered resentment, and turned against Britain.

Before the British conquest, a Jewish movement called Zionism, born out of the pogroms in Eastern Europe, had been buying land in Palestine to enable Jews to return to their biblical home. A brilliant English Jew, named Chaim Weizmann, managed to persuade first the British government and then the League of Nations that backing Zionism should be the policy of British rule.

The League of Nations had a say in the matter because the then President of the United States of America, Woodrow Wilson, disapproved of empires. He did not want to see the British empire enlarged. But he could not remove from his allies the fruits of their victories. So the League of Nations introduced a new label and called the conquered lands 'mandated territories'. The new rulers signed undertakings to advance the welfare of the conquered people. Whether these 'mandates' were really to be trusts for the inhabitants, as Woodrow Wilson intended, or colonies by another name, as most British assumed, the mandate documents all placed first emphasis on leading the inhabitants towards self-government – all, that is, except the mandate for Palestine. This gave first priority to 'the establishment of the Jewish national home' and instructed the British government to 'facilitate Jewish immigration and encourage settlement by Jews on the land'.

But the vast majority of the inhabitants of Palestine were Arabs. They quickly began to fear that increased Jewish immigration would swamp them. Nevertheless, for a few years, the British encouraged Jews to settle in Palestine. The British even appointed a Jew and Zionist, Herbert Samuel, as their first Governor of Palestine. Arab protests and demonstrations turned violent. Many Jews were killed.

The British hit back, at first, against the Arabs. But this policy merely increased Arab anger and turned it against the British. From 1936 to 1939, Arab rebellion caused some 5,000 deaths. The main leader of the Palestinian Arabs, Haj Amin al-Husseini, the Mufti of Jerusalem, joined Britain's enemies and, during the Second World War, threw in his lot with Hitler and Nazi Germany.

By then, the British had decided that Jewish immigration into Palestine had to be cut to a trickle. Britain needed the Arab states as allies to secure the route to India and the Far East through the

Suez Canal, to maintain bases in Jordan, Iraq and Egypt, and to keep Arab oil flowing.

The British decision to woo the Arab states by cutting Jewish immigration to Palestine was badly timed. Hitler and his allies were beginning to expel and murder Jews by the million. Thousands of Central European Jews gave their life's savings for berths on ships that promised passage to Palestine, the only place of refuge they thought likely to admit them. Britain did all it could to stop the ships sailing or, if they reached Palestine, turned the Jews away. But many ships carrying illegal Jewish immigrants landed at remote beaches, enabling tens of thousands of Jews to by-pass British rule.

By the end of the Second World War, Britain's Palestine policy was in ruins. When the Nazi concentration camps were opened, few Jews survived in central Europe. The number begging to be allowed to go to Palestine was approximately 100,000. But Britain had made promises to the Arabs and continued to restrict Jewish immigration. To fair-minded observers, Britain seemed to be adding to the horrors that the Jews in Europe had suffered. The view that the Jews had a right to a state of their own in their ancient homeland gained ground.

The Jews in Palestine left the British government in no doubt that they supported this view. Jewish terrorists blew up bridges, raided British military camps, destroyed railways. On 22 July 1946, the headquarters of the British administration and armed forces, which was in the southern wing of the King David Hotel, Jerusalem, was blown up by Irgun, a Jewish terrorist group. Ninety-one people were killed.

Sir Alan Cunningham, the top British official in Palestine, complained 'of the inability of the army to protect even themselves'. The British were still the rulers, but in fear. They withdrew into wired security compounds and sent thousands of staff and families home to Britain. At one point they had 100,000 soldiers in Palestine trying to keep control of 600,000 Jews. They could not do it.

The British ordered their troops and staff not to leave their compounds unless they were in groups of four or more with armed escorts. Even that did not work. Two British sergeants went out, unarmed, to a café and were caught by Irgun terrorists who hanged them, leaving their bodies on display.

After that, the British threw in the towel. They asked the United Nations to advise what should be done and then, when the UN advised partition – and produced a partition scheme with a map – the British declined to implement it. The British cabinet saw the scheme as unfair to the Arabs and impossible to impose except by the overwhelming use of force, which it was neither willing nor able to employ.

So the British announced a departure date, 15 May 1948. They ran down their manpower, emptied the offices, put the keys under the mat, and, amidst growing Arab-Jewish violence, kept their heads down and left.

**Brian Lapping**
**Executive Producer**
*The Fifty Years War: Israel and the Arabs*

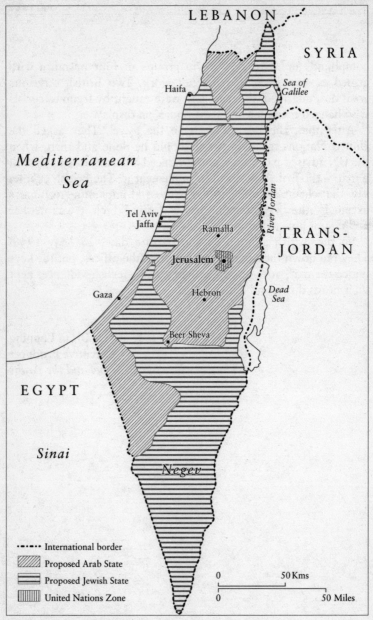

Map 1: The United Nations Partition plan for Palestine, 1947.

Territories occupied by
Israel during the 1967 War

The Sinai desert was returned to
Egypt after the signing of the
Israeli-Egyptian peace treaty
of 1979.

Gaza Strip and parts of the West
Bank came under Palestinian self-rule
in 1994 following the signing of the
Oslo and Gaza-Jericho First agreements.

LEBANON   Damascus

Kiriat
Shmona   SYRIA

Kuneitra
GOLAN
HEIGHTS

Naharia

Haifa   *Sea of
Galilee*

*Mediterranean
Sea*

Jenin

Nablus   Ajloun   Mafrak

WEST   Jarash
BANK

Tel Aviv
Jaffa   Salt

Ramalla   Amman
Jericho   Karameh

**Jerusalem**

Gaza   Hebron

**GAZA
STRIP**   *Dead
Sea*

Beer Sheva

Port Said

*Suez Canal*

**ISRAEL**

Ismailia

*Negev*   **JORDAN**

Suez   *Giddi Pass*

*Mitla Pass*

**EGYPT**

*Sinai*

*Gulf of
Suez*   **SAUDI
ARABIA**

*Gulf
of
Aqaba*

*Straits of
Tiran*

0   Kms   50

0   Miles   50

Sharm el-Sheikh   *Red Sea*

River Jordan

Map 2

# 1 PALESTINE, EGYPT AND THE NEW STATE OF ISRAEL

## Introduction

On 18 February 1947, Britain's Foreign Secretary, Ernest Bevin, declared: 'His Majesty's government have of themselves no power to award the country [Palestine, which it had administered since the San Remo conference of 24 April 1920] either to the Arabs or to the Jews, or even to partition it between them. We have, therefore, reached the conclusion that the only course open to us is to submit the problem to the judgment of the United Nations.'

Britain announced its intention to withdraw its forces from Palestine on 15 May 1948. Thus, before this deadline the newly-established United Nations (UN) would have to find a solution that would satisfy both the Arab and Jewish inhabitants of Palestine. During this period, two proposals dominated the scene. Partition: whereby Palestine would be divided into two separate Jewish and Arab (Palestinian) states – the solution favoured by the Jewish community and rejected by the Arabs. A Unified State: whereby a single state would be established in Palestine with proportional representation for the different indigenous communities (Muslims, Christians and Jews). This idea, favoured by the Arabs, was rejected by the Jews.

In May 1947, the United Nations appointed an eleven-member[1] Special Committee on Palestine (UNSCOP) with a mission to study the problem and present its recommendation on which of the above proposals should be adopted.

UNSCOP, headed by Swedish judge Emil Sandström, went to the Middle East to start its survey. It solicited the help of both the Jewish Agency – which was formed in 1929 as the main body representing the Jews of Palestine – and the Arab Higher Committee – which was formed in 1936 to represent the Arabs. While the Jewish representatives gladly co-operated – hoping to illustrate the merits of Partition – the Arab representatives boycotted the UN mission. They did this because they did not think the UN had the moral right to surrender any portion of Palestine to the Jews; and because the Jewish community only constituted one-third of the total population in Palestine and owned about eight per cent of the land, yet would receive over half of the land under Partition.

The task of UNSCOP seemed daunting: how to resolve the struggle of two peoples to control one land in a way that would avoid bloodshed. At an early meeting, Emil Sandström polled the committee members as follows: 'Does anyone favour an Arab state in all of Palestine?' No reply. 'Does anyone favour a Jewish state in all of Palestine?' No reply. At a later date, however, eight members of the committee advocated Partition, and three the Unified State.

On 1 September 1947, UNSCOP released its report stating, 'only by means of Partition can these conflicting national aspirations [of Arabs and Jews] find substantial expression and qualify both peoples to their places as independent nations in the international community and in the United Nations'. The UNSCOP report was accompanied by a map allocating Eastern Galilee, the coastal strip and the Negev desert to the Jewish community. The Arabs were allocated Upper and Western Galilee, the West Bank and the Gaza Strip. Each state would be composed of three parts linked by roads. However, the Holy City of Jerusalem – being sacred for Muslims, Christians and Jews – would be *corpus separatum* under UN control.

The Jewish community was delighted by the recommendations while their Arab counterparts were devastated. Both now had their hopes pinned on the outcome of the UN General Assembly session to be held on 29 November 1947 which would either adopt or reject the Partition plan (see chapter one).

The civil war that followed its adoption did not stifle the birth of a nation: Israel. But it was US recognition of the new independent state which rescued it from stillbirth. However, as five Arab armies – Egypt, Syria, Lebanon, Jordan and Iraq – marched on to the borders of previously Mandate Palestine only hours after the departure of the British troops on 15 May 1948, Israel had to fend for itself. The first Arab-Israeli war had begun.

The following decade would be one of violence and confrontation. As the neighbouring Arab countries rid themselves of colonial rule, Israel became their main enemy. Arab rhetoric to crush the newly-established state fed the flames of the angry masses. However, behind the scenes, secret contacts between Egypt and Israel – that have never before been revealed – were timidly attempting to find common ground on which they could build peace. These efforts came too soon.

*Chapter 1*

# The vote for partition

In September 1947, Abba Eban, a young Jewish Agency[2] liaison officer, had just arrived in London after hovering in the corridor outside a session of the United Nations Special Committee on Palestine (UNSCOP). The committee had decided to recommend the partitioning of Palestine into two states – Jewish and Arab – a proposal, which would now have to win a two-thirds majority vote at a UN General Assembly if it were to be endorsed.

Now, in the Dorchester Hotel, London, Eban was waiting to report to Zionist leader Chaim Weizmann. Eban was excited. If the proposal were endorsed, the creation of a Jewish state would fulfil the dream of many Jews worldwide – a dream that Weizmann, a founding father of Zionism, had been for over thirty years struggling to make a reality. (Zionism began as a political movement for the establishment and support of a national homeland for Jews in Palestine. Later, it was concerned chiefly with the development of the modern state of Israel. The name is derived from Zion, the hill on which the city of Jerusalem stands.) Weizmann had started his career as a chemistry lecturer in Manchester. Now – although nearly blind and in poor health – he moved in top political circles. Known as the 'supreme persuader', his success in getting Zionism on to the British political agenda was described by Sir Charles Webster, a British historian, as, 'The only victory in diplomatic history for persuasion without power'.[3]

Once Eban had reported the committee's decision to Weizmann, they started planning the Jewish strategy for persuading other countries to vote yes for partition.

Despite Eban's and Weizmann's initial euphoria about UNSCOP's decision to recommend partition, their meeting with a few colleagues was soon overshadowed by pessimism. 'We sat going through all the states,' Eban recalls, 'trying to predict how they would vote.' As Weizmann was going through the list, he stopped and said, "What about Paraguay and Uruguay? If anybody here says he knows where they are, I won't believe him."'

Weizmann was right – they knew little about how the UN functioned and, if they were going to win the day, they needed to learn about its procedures. So, Eban went to Foyles' bookshop, Charing Cross Road, and bought a copy of the UN Charter. In New York, where the voting would take place, he knew that persistence and lobbying would be required. The Jewish delegation took the map of the world and divided it into regions. Eban was allotted the four Scandinavian countries, France, and the three Benelux countries – Holland, Belgium and Luxembourg.

### The vote

On 27 November – under the glass dome of Flushing Meadows, an old skating rink, where the UN General Assembly held its plenary sessions – the members of the Jewish delegation were plunged in gloom. The day before, an *ad hoc* committee had met to conduct an unofficial vote. (It is usual before UN General Assemblies for preliminary *ad hoc* votes to be taken to ensure that a quorum can be reached. This pre-session activity also helps the parties involved to predict where they stand.) As a result, the Jews had counted on General Carlos Romulo, the Filipino delegate, but he just announced that he would vote against partition; then the Haitian government, which they had also counted on, ordered its UN delegation to vote no. Just prior to the session, Paraguayan officials told an *ad hoc* Jewish committee that, due to lack of instructions from their government, they would abstain. Greece was also abstaining.

But just as the Arab delegations were about to celebrate their victory, Jewish hopes were revived. Oswaldo Aranha, the Brazilian Chairman of the UN General Assembly – whom the Arabs believed to be a Jewish ally[4] and who had not attempted to obstruct the Jewish tactics to stall the vote – announced that as it was the American thanksgiving holiday he was postponing the vote for two days. The Jewish delegation used the time to convince undecided nations. Some of their last-minute methods were unorthodox. Harvey Firestone, the wealthy owner of a tyre manufacturing company, with huge plantations in Liberia, was threatened by Robert Nathan, an influential American, that Firestone products would be boycotted in the US unless he pressurized Liberia to vote for partition.[5] President Carlos Rojas of the Philippines – who was awaiting confirmation of a large US Congressional credit – was contacted by twenty-six senators and two Supreme Court judges urging him to reverse the vote of his UN delegation.[6] Such tactics didn't always work. Efforts to reverse the negative vote of Ethiopia only succeeded in securing its abstention. But it took no more than a promise of a five-million-dollar loan to alter Haiti's vote.[7]

On 29 November, the changes were apparent. A new delegate from the Philippines argued as fervently in favour of partition as the previous delegate had argued against.[8] Prince Wan, the Thai delegate, departed in order not to vote against partition.[9] Liberia and Haiti changed their votes to yes. The United States – despite its delegation's and the State Department's reluctance – voted yes. (President Truman, horrified by the Holocaust and stating that the 'survivors of Hitler's madness had a right to build new lives with a guarantee that such atrocities could never reoccur', had placed himself firmly behind the partition proposal, having made a 'yes' promise to Chaim Weizmann at a 19 November meeting.) The USSR also voted yes. When France's delegation also said 'Oui', there was an outbreak of applause on the Jewish side[10] and grim faces on the Arab. The Jewish delegation had won.

Abdul Rahman Azzam Pasha, the General Secretary of the Arab League, which was created on 22 March 1945 to defend the interests and co-ordinate the political position of the member states, led the Arab delegates out of the hall.[11] His last words were an ominous warning: 'The partition line will be nothing but a line of fire and blood'.

## Civil war in Palestine

Between 29 November 1947 – the date of the UN partition vote – and 15 May 1948 – the day the ruling British departed from Palestine – Palestine was a disaster waiting to happen. British rule dwindled into powerlessness. The tension that had been mounting for years between Arabs and Jews swelled into civil war.

The early battles – fought between the Jews and the Palestinian Arabs during the period before Britain announced its intention to leave and before the vote for partition – were to determine the outcome of the civil war. The battle for Jerusalem – a city which the UN had awarded an international status and not given to either side – was crucial. The main road from Tel Aviv to Jerusalem ran through Arab towns, an advantage that the Arab militia used to block access to the Holy City. By stopping convoys of food, they were able to place Jerusalem under siege. Neither the Arab majority within its walls nor the Jews who lived there, had any intention of abandoning Jerusalem. For months, the main task of the forces of Palestine's Jewish minority was the fight to get supplies into the besieged city.

For Uzi Narkiss, a young Palmach[12] officer, and his fellow Jewish fighters, there was no question of giving up. They believed that controlling the route to Jerusalem – and the Holy City itself – was vital for the state they hoped to establish when the British departed. Narkiss recalls: 'The Jerusalem-Tel Aviv road was essential for the defence of Jerusalem. Whoever captured Bab el Wad and Kastel on this road would secure Jerusalem from the west.'

Narkiss participated in the battle of Kastel. This village, which controlled the western entrance to Jerusalem, fell fairly easily to the Jews. When Palestinian Commander Abdel Kadir Husseini – who was in Damascus trying to acquire weapons from neighbouring Arab states – heard the news, he returned hastily. Gathering as many armed men as he could find – including some volunteers from neighbouring Arab countries[13] – he led his troops in the dead of night to the top of the hill where Kastel lay in the hands of the Palmach.

On 8 April 1948, Husseini's battle for Kastel raged for several hours, but the fate of this key village could not be reversed. The fighting resulted in many wounded but only one fatality – a death that was to prove disastrous for the Arabs. When Uzi Narkiss arrived to supply his troops with food and ammunition, he recalls: 'I asked how things were going. They told me everything is fine, morale is high. We've made the Arabs retreat and have no casualties. But there is one corpse down there. I went down, and, to this day, I can remember the corpse lying on its stomach in the field, dressed in a light brown suit. We didn't know who it was, but he had a Koran. I took the Koran and left.'

Later, the Arabs counter-attacked. They had returned to retrieve the corpse lying at the foot of the hills. The corpse was that of Commander Abdel Kadir Husseini, their legendary leader whose fame was built on military achievements. His charisma had also made him the only Arab leader in Palestine who commanded the full loyalty of the masses.

Husseini's death was a disaster for the Palestinian Arab community. Who would now command their troops in the civil war? Who would draw up a strategy for the conflict they were expecting after the British troops left? The Arabs of Palestine had no answers.

On 9 April 1948, the Arabs who had fought so hard to keep Kastel under Arab control abandoned their positions to attend Husseini's funeral.

That day also marked another Arab tragedy. A village called Deir Yassin – on high ground overlooking the key road to Jerusalem – was captured by the Jews. The fall of Deir Yassin – and the exaggeration of the atrocities that followed – triggered a mass exodus from Arab villages. The events of Deir Yassin remain controversial. Only five weeks before the British withdrew from Palestine, the fate of this village altered the destiny of both the Jewish and Arab communities.

### The truth about Deir Yassin
For the villagers of Deir Yassin, the fall of Kastel – only five kilometres away – signalled imminent danger. They counted on the support of Kastel and Ein Karem for protection. The threat,

however, did not come from the Palmach troops, but from two Jewish underground groups, Lehi and Irgun.[14]

The Lehi and Irgun commanders gathered to plan their attack. Ezra Yakhin, a clerk at the Jerusalem post office, and a clandestine member of Lehi, attended the meeting. 'When I got there,' he recalls, 'I found out that our next action was to conquer an Arab village. I felt electrified. Until then, we had only set explosives and run, or shot Arabs and escaped. This time we were going to conquer part of the land of our fathers.'

The meeting, presided over by a Lehi commander, code-named 'Dror' (Mordechai Ben-Uziahu), clarified the strategy of the raid. For its participation alongside Lehi, Irgun made it a condition that they use loudspeakers to evacuate the village and decrease deaths and casualties. Ezra Yakhin: 'We were confused when we heard that they wanted us to use loudspeakers before the attack. This meant we would lose the element of surprise on which the success of the operation depended. We accepted unwillingly.'

Shimon Moneta attended the same meeting. Unknown to his colleagues in Lehi, he was a Haganah[15] agent who had been assigned by Haganah to infiltrate Lehi. He remembers the plan and the instructions: 'Dror explained the points of departure, an eggs factory in Givat Shaul ... We were told how the Irgun would go into Deir Yassin – and the route of the lorry with the loudspeaker ... ' He also recalls one of the commanders saying, 'Our objective is looting.' Moneta: 'Jerusalem was under siege, and nothing could get through from the coast. Many of the Lehi fighters were local boys whose families lived in Jerusalem and they knew all about suffering. They were after oil, kerosene and flour.'

Ben Zion Cohen, a Jewish soldier who had previously fought in the British army, was in command of the Irgun forces at Deir Yassin. 'The Lehi,' he recalls, 'had a lot of explosives, and we had a lot of firearms and machine-guns. We gave them Bren-guns and they gave us explosives and bombs. The Lehi prepared the explosives for bombing the houses. Each bomb had about ten kilos of explosive which could be carried on your back with your weapon.'

Meir Pail, Commander of a Haganah Special Operations Unit, whose job was to fight all Haganah enemies – the Arabs, British and Jewish dissidents – first heard of the plan to attack Deir Yassin on 6 April through a friend who had left Palmach to join Lehi.[16] Sitting at a small Jerusalem café, he discovered that Lehi and Irgun had received permission from Haganah Commander David Shaltiel to attack the village. He was shocked. Convinced that there must be a misunderstanding, he raced off to see Shaltiel. Pail recalls the conversation: '"Is it true that you have given permission for an attack on Deir Yassin?" He said, "Yes". I asked, "Why – this village has an agreement with us?" [This agreement, authorized by the Haganah Intelligence Service in Jerusalem, stipulated that Haganah would not attack Deir Yassin if Deir Yassin did not attack neighbouring Jewish villages, for example Givat Shaul.] He said, "They [Lehi] came not to ask for permission, but just to let me know. They wanted to be synchronized". I asked again, "Why did you allow this?" He said, "What could I do? Jail them, shoot them, fight them? I have enough trouble as it is. I couldn't shoot them in the back – they are Jews, you know."'

In the event, Shaltiel not only allowed the Lehi and Irgun dissidents to attack Deir Yassin, but provided them with logistical support. His headquarters in the adjacent town of Givat Shaul monitored the operation.

Meanwhile, the villagers of Deir Yassin, worried about the battle raging in Kastel, rightly assumed that their turn would be next. Abu Mahmoud (Mahmoud Assad Yassini), a young villager who had been assigned guard duty, remembers: 'When we heard of Abdel Kadir Husseini's death, we were all very troubled and prepared ourselves. We held a meeting and decided that everyone should stand guard. We took special emergency measures'.

Ben Zion Cohen, who led the Irgun troops towards the village in the dead of the night, recalls: 'The hour of attack was four-thirty in the morning . . . The password [for identification purposes] we had decided on was *Ahdut Lohemet* [solidarity fighters]. One of the Arab village guards who had spotted some movement suddenly shouted, "*Mahmoud*" [the name of the above villager]. An Irgun fighter mistakenly thinking that a Jewish fighter had shouted "*Ahdut*" [solidarity], replied "*Lohemet*" [fighters]. The Arabs realized that Jewish forces were close by, fired a warning shot and shouted, "*Yahud, Yahud*" (Jews, Jews).'

Abu Mahmoud, who had left his guard post to make tea for his fellow fighters, heard the shot that signalled danger. (The village possessed only two Bren machine-guns and a few single-cartridge rifles bought in Egypt, and had strict instructions, on account of the shortage of ammunition, that no weapon should be fired except in extreme danger.) Abu Mahmoud recalls running out to join his fellow fighters: 'My cousin, who had seen the first group sneaking up from the eastern section towards the village centre, had fired the warning shot. Then shooting, fighting, killing broke out everywhere'.

The plan to send the loudspeakers ahead of the fighters had run into difficulty. Ezra Yakhin, who was told to accompany the armoured car on which the loudspeakers had been installed, recalls: 'The vehicle hit a ditch [the Arabs had dug trenches around the village some weeks earlier] and we had to fill this in before we could continue. Then there was a second ditch. And, at the entrance of the village, we reached a third ditch. We decided there was no point in going on.'

Abu Tawfik Yassini was stationed where he could see the vehicle attempting to cross. 'They crossed as far as the school where we had placed some rocks,' he recalls, 'and they couldn't go further. One of them came out of the car and started lifting the rocks. One of our guys fired and hit him. His companions pulled him back under the car and took him in.'

By then, it was daybreak and Ezra Yakhin decided to activate the loudspeaker from where the vehicle was stuck, to get the villagers to leave before the fighting became more intense. Abu Mahmoud: 'They tried to terrify us into leaving the village and running away. The loudspeaker kept saying, "Stop the fighting, retreat, run for your lives, put down your weapons."'

The use of the loudspeaker proved counter-productive. The villagers resisted with rifle fire and the Jewish fighters set about a house-to-house battle. Ezra Yakhin: 'It was impossible to advance without shooting back and throwing grenades into the houses – because that is where the firing was coming from. There was no choice . . . ' Ben Zion Cohen, the Irgun Commander, also provides an explanation for the high number of casualties that resulted: 'I gave the order that our fighters should not enter a single house without using explosives or throwing a grenade or two inside. That I guess caused the enemy many losses.'

Abu Mahmoud remembers: 'They threw a grenade into the Zahran family's house and it burnt with twenty-eight people inside. The whole family was killed on the spot'.

Largely thanks to one of their local heros, Kassem, the villagers managed to hold out. Kassem, along with other fighters, was stationed on the roof top of the Mukhtar's[17] house. Abu Mahmoud proudly remembers their efforts: 'Kassem and the others managed to resist the Jewish fighters and stop them from encircling us. If they had encircled the western sector, not one of us would have been left alive. But then they began firing mortars from Givat Shaul'.

As a result of the Arab resistance, the Lehi had decided to solicit the help of the Palmach. Shimon Moneta recalls: 'The commander told me that in Givat Shaul there was a squad of the Palmach, and I should run there and tell them they were needed to shoot a mortar at the Mukhtar's house. They shot a two-inch mortar. I don't think there were more than three shots in all, and that's how the battle ended'.

Moshe Wachman, a Palmach officer, recalls: 'We were given permission to go to Deir Yassin. We took a couple of primitive armoured cars and some new weapons – machine-guns and a two-inch mortar.'

The Arab fighters, overwhelmed by superior armaments, started pulling out of the village from the western side. This was the moment when the events that spawned the controversy of Deir Yassin occurred. Once the armed Arab fighters fled, the killing continued.

Abu Tawfik Yassini believes that it was a battle that deteriorated into a massacre. After the Arab resistance was over, he explained, the Jewish fighters killed civilians for no justifiable reason. He says he even saw a pregnant woman being shot. Abu Mahmoud adds, 'When we say massacre, we mean that the Jews shot indiscriminately at anyone who was running away. They also took fourteen people to the entrance on the eastern side, lined them up by the quarry and sprayed them with gunfire. Then they threw their bodies in the quarry. I saw this with my own eyes'.

Shimon Moneta gives a different account of the events. 'There was no shooting after the fighters left. The Lehi began going from door to door, ordering the inhabitants out. Then we began to loot the houses. Some of the Arabs were wealthy; we found gold coins in the bottom of jars . . . Then we loaded the Arabs on to lorries and drove them through Jerusalem.'

Meir Pail, the Commander of the Haganah Special Operations Unit, however, confirms the recollection of Abu Mahmoud: 'I saw twenty to twenty-five men stood up by the wall of the quarry and shot.'

Despite the discrepancy over the numbers killed – which was soon to become the cornerstone on which the Deir Yassin controversy was built – Pail confirms that the killings mainly happened once the village's fighters withdrew: 'Those who were left had no weapons or ammunition with which to fight. I went with my man from house to house and saw women murdered there. In the corner of one house, I saw a woman, two children and an old man dead. All of them killed by shots, nothing else'.

Once the shooting had died down, the Jewish forces proceeded to move the remaining Arabs out of the village. The survivors were loaded on to lorries and taken to Jerusalem. Shimon Moneta confirms: 'We took a lorry load of Arabs through the streets of Jerusalem, in order to display to the people of Jerusalem that Lehi had strength and power and knew what it was doing.' The group that was paraded through the streets was shot, the rest of the villagers were dumped near the Damascus gate.

The following morning the surviving villagers went to a meeting with the National Committee, the local Palestinian leadership in Jerusalem. It was up to the committee to decide how they should handle what had happened.[18] Abu Mahmoud remembers that the survivors were asked to exaggerate some aspects of the terrible events: 'When we arrived in Jerusalem, we were taken to a hotel near the Damascus gate. We started asking after each other who had been killed, who was alive? Then the leaders of the National Committee arrived, including Dr Hussein Fakhri Al-Khalidi [Head of the National Committee in Jerusalem]. He invited some of us to go to his headquarters. He [Khalidi] said: "We want you to say that the Jews slaughtered people, committed atrocities, raped and stole gold". He said you have to say this so that the Arab armies will finally make a move and come to liberate Palestine from the Jews"'.

Hazem Nusseibah, a senior programme assistant for the Palestine Broadcasting Corporation, was also contacted by the National Committee. 'Dr Hussein Khalidi,' he says, 'rang me and said we must alert the Arab countries to what is happening. I was sure there were no rapes, but we were shaken by the events.'

Ironically, it was Hazem Nusseibah's broadcast exaggerating the atrocities that triggered the mass exodus of Palestinians from their homes. He recalls: 'We transmitted Dr Hussein Fakhri El Khalidi's statement mentioning rape and this and that. It had a devastating impact on everyone in Palestine, and the exodus began . . . It was the biggest blunder that could have happened.'

Abu Tawfik and Abu Mahmoud resent the way these distortions of the truth led to Arabs fleeing their homes. Abu Mahmoud: 'Dr Hussein Fakhri Al-Khalidi was the one who caused the catastrophe. Instead of working in our favour, the propaganda worked in favour of the Jews. Whole villages and towns fled because of what they heard had happened in Deir Yassin.'

The National Committee's attempt to make Arab governments send troops to their aid allowed the events to be described as 'the myth of Deir Yassin'.

Shimon Moneta: 'The horrors done by the Jewish soldiers [at Deir Yassin] definitely caused the Arab population to run away every time they thought a Jewish soldier was coming near. Perhaps our leaders, Ben-Gurion at their head – even if they didn't know the term psychological warfare – used such tactics to help us then – and in all the battles that lay ahead . . . '

Some Haganah and Palmach leaders thought it imperative to evacuate as many Palestinian Arabs as possible. This evacuation would achieve a two-fold advantage. First, Jewish immigrants would be able to settle in the evacuated areas, thus protecting the Jewish territorial gains of the civil war. Second, when war with the Arab regular armies erupted – as was thought inevitable after the British troops departed on 14 May – the fighters would not have to worry about local enemies at their rear.

Yigal Allon, the Commander of the Palmach, described the means he adopted to achieve these objectives: 'I gathered all the Jewish Mukhtars who had contact with Arabs in different villages and asked them to whisper in the ears of Arabs that a great Jewish reinforcement had arrived in Galilee and that it was going to burn all the villages of the Huleh valley. They should, I said, suggest to these Arabs, as their friends, that the Arabs should escape while there was still time. The rumour that it was time to flee was then spread in all the areas of the Huleh valley. The flight that followed numbered myriads'.[19]

## Chapter 2

# Crisis in America

Across the Atlantic in the US, news of the civil war in Palestine was to lead to an extraordinary clash at the highest level of government. Secretary of State General George Marshall supported a new US Trusteeship proposal for Palestine. This proposal would delay a final decision about the future of Palestine, would give the UN the responsibility of administering the country, and would guarantee the rights of both communities. Besides, for strictly US national interests, Marshall argued, America *should* support the Arab camp which held the keys to the most strategic natural resource: oil. So, less than four months after the US delegation had voted yes for partition at the UN, the State Department instructed its delegation at the UN General Assembly, which reconvened on 19 March at Arab request to discuss Palestine, to reverse its position and opt for trusteeship.[20]

For President Truman, this reversal of his position undermined the promise he had given to Zionist leader Chaim Weizmann on 19 November 1947. On his calender for 19 March 1948, Truman wrote:

> *The State Department pulled the rug from under me today . . . The first I know about it is what I see in the paper! Isn't that hell? I am now in the position of a liar and a double-crosser. I've never felt so low in my life. There are people on the third and fourth level of the State Department who*

*have always wanted to cut my throat. They've succeeded in doing it.*

As the date approached for the British withdrawal, Truman remained incensed with the State Department, but he wanted to avoid a conflict with George Marshall. (In 1948, Truman was not highly regarded. He had assumed the presidency on the death of Roosevelt and was about to face his first presidential election in a few months. He needed the support of Marshall who was a popular war hero.)

Truman was convinced that if the US did not opt for partition – and recognize the Jewish state that he knew the Jews were going to declare upon the departure of the British from Palestine – then a golden opportunity would be lost forever. The Jews, after all their suffering in the Holocaust, would be left homeless and stateless. He decided that at his press conference on 13 May, the day before the British Mandate would end, he would announce his recognition of the Jewish state and thus secure its creation.

Truman telephoned George Marshall. When he had finished the call, he said to Clark Clifford, his administrative assistant, 'I am impressed with Marshall's argument against a hasty recognition of the Jewish state'. He then added, 'General Marshall and some of his assistants are coming over to present the case against recognition, and I want you to present the case in favour of recognition . . . I want you to attach the same importance to this as though you were going to make it an argument before the Supreme Court of the United States.'

The showdown took place at the oval office. Secretary of State Marshall arrived with his deputy, Robert Lovett, and two other State Department officials. Clifford: 'President Truman was sitting at his desk. On the left-hand corner was the sign saying "The Buck Stops Here". General Marshall gave his reasons why he thought that we should not assist the Jews in establishing their state. Lovett added points that strengthened Marshall's argument. President Truman listened attentively and then said, I would like to hear from Clark the other side of this problem. As I spoke, I looked at General Marshall, his face was getting redder and redder. When I finished, he exploded and said, "Mr President, I do not know what's going on here. I don't even know why

Clifford is attending this meeting". The President said quietly, "General, he's here because I invited him."'

Then Marshall threw a bombshell. He turned to President Truman and said, 'I'm obliged to tell you that if you should adopt the policy that is recommended by Clifford, I would be unable to vote for you in this coming November election'. There was, Clifford recalls, dead silence in the room, no-one had ever heard anybody threaten the President of the United States in that manner. Before Marshall could go any further, Truman ended the meeting. When the Secretary of State had left the room, Truman asked Clifford to find a way out of his dilemma.

Clifford and Marshall's deputy, Robert Lovett, tried to avoid a public break between the President and his Secretary of State. By 14 May, following a rush of calls back and forth, they found a formula. Truman would go ahead with recognizing the Jewish state, but he would not ask for Marshall's support on the issue. Marshall agreed not to oppose it.

## Declaration of the State of Israel

On 14 May 1948 at 4 p.m., in Tel Aviv, David Ben-Gurion, leader of the Jewish community in Palestine, rapped on the gravel to signal the beginning of the official ceremony to declare the independence of the Jewish state. The assembled Jewish leaders rose spontaneously and sang the *Hatikva*, the national anthem. Ben-Gurion then read the Scroll of Independence. Towards the end, he announced, 'We hereby proclaim the establishment of the Jewish State in Palestine, to be called *Medinath Yisrael* [The State of Israel]'.

In Washington, as the White House prepared its statement recognizing the 'Jewish state', news was brought in that the name was 'Israel'. In the official US statement, Truman himself crossed out the words 'Jewish state' and inserted 'Israel'.

At midnight, in Kibbutz Ma'aleh Ha'hamishah, only a few miles outside Jerusalem, the mood was sombre. The soldiers of Palmach, led by Yitzhak Rabin, were aware that Ben-Gurion's proclamation of the State of Israel would transform the civil war into a fully fledged war against five regular Arab armies – Egyptian, Iraqi, Syrian, Lebanese and Jordanian.

In Tel Aviv, Golda Meir – one of the few women at the executive level of the *Yishuv* (the Jewish community in Palestine), left the ceremony and returned to her hotel. A few minutes after midnight, the telephone rang: 'Golda? Are you listening? Truman has recognized us!'

Just before dawn, the next morning, Golda Meir – awakened by a sound – looked out of the hotel window. Four Egyptian Spitfires were attacking Tel Aviv. The Arabs were signalling their rejection of the State of Israel.

### Arab armies on the march

On the Arab front, there had been little preparation for war until early May 1948. Until then, the Arab leaders were far from unanimous about the necessity to go to war. Haj Amin Husseini, the Head of the Arab High Committee and the main Palestinian spokesman in exile, was fiercely opposed to the intervention of Arab regular armies. He favoured intensifying attacks by local fighters. He did not hide his anxiety that if the Arab armies entered Palestine, King Abdullah of Jordan would occupy Jerusalem and claim it as part of his kingdom.

The Egyptian Prime Minister, Mahmoud Fahmi El-Nokrashi Pasha, also opposed intervention. During a Parliamentary session held in Cairo on 25 April 1948, he argued that Egypt's primary objective was to persuade Britain to leave the Suez Canal zone rather than to enter into a costly war with the Zionists.

After extensive debate – during which no war preparations were undertaken – and barely a fortnight before 15 May – Egypt decided to abide by the Arab League members' decision to go to war. Azzam Pasha, now the main advocate for a concerted Arab attack, did not hide his unease about the lack of preparation. The Arab rulers, he was convinced, had totally underestimated the strength of the Jewish fighters. His appeals to start preparing the Arab armies – if only for the sake of credibility – continued to fall on deaf ears, and were only heeded when echoed by Sir Edward Spears, a high-ranking British general, who was considered one of the founders of Syrian and Lebanese independence. On a visit to Cairo during the first week of May 1948, a lunch was held in Spears's honour by the head of the Egyptian National Party. This lunch, attended by all the top Egyptian ministers, quickly turned into a discussion about the imminent war in Palestine. Adel Sabit,

Azzam Pasha's aide and a cousin of King Farouk, remembers the discussion: 'Spears said, "Gentlemen, are you going to war?" So they [the ministers] started discussing this and said, "Yes . . . no . . . you see," until, finally, he said, "Well, it seems to me you have decided to go to war", and they said, "Yes". So then he said, "Well, gentlemen, I have to tell you that two things will emerge. Either you will show your weakness and be defeated, or you will win. It is my opinion that you are going to be beaten"'.

Azzam Pasha asked Sabit to report to King Farouk what the respected British officer had said. He recalls: 'I did, but he said, "We have threatened war in the Arab League and at the United Nations. Our word has been engaged. We can't betray the Palestinians by withdrawing now. The honour of Egypt and the Egyptian army is engaged."'

Despite General Spears's pessimism, the Arab regular armies were not worried. Sabit describes the general attitude in Egypt only days before the war, 'We thought it was going to be a push-over, that the Jews were going to run away the moment they saw the Arab regular army moving in on them with bayonets and whatever. Therefore, we didn't really make any preparations'.

King Farouk gathered army representatives at his palace to announce his decision.

The lack of preparedness was most felt by the troops that were dispatched to Palestine with less than a week's notice. Zakaria Mohiedin, who would later become Egypt's Vice President, was studying at the military academy when he was ordered to go to war. He recalls: 'Orders came that we had to stop studying so that we could be distributed to units entering Palestine. There was not enough preparation – mentally or militarily. They said that we had to be ready within twenty-four hours. We could not object because, in the army, no one objects to supreme orders. But we were not thinking about the problems of Palestine. What we had in mind was how to get rid of the British colonization in Egypt.'

The 15,000 men sent from Egypt were the largest Arab League force. But they had no battle experience and no more than three days logistic supplies. They thought they could count on the backing of the other four invading Arab armies – the Iraqi, Syrian, Lebanese and Jordanian forces. And, anyway, how could the Jewish fighters stand up to the troops of five regular armies?

Within a month, the Egyptian attack was practically halted by the Jewish troops, and the Jews found they had little to fear from the Iraqi, Syrian and Lebanese troops who were few and badly equipped. The Arab Legion – Jordan's élite troops commanded by the British officer Glubb Pasha – was the best trained and equipped, and the most feared by their Jewish opponents. Indeed, the Arab Legion soon captured a section of Jerusalem which, according to the partition plan, was an international city.

The Jewish forces made rapid gains, but needed time and equipment to consolidate their hold on the country. So, the Jewish leadership poured its energy into trying to arrange for a cease-fire, which came into effect on 10 June. Although the truce terms specified that acquisition of weapons during this period was prohibited, both sides ignored the provision – and Israel managed to acquire a large shipment of arms from Czechoslovakia. Yitzhak Rabin said, 'Without the arms from Czechoslovakia . . . it is very doubtful whether we would have been able to conduct the war'.

## Attacks on Lydda and Ramla

The cease-fire lasted for almost a month. On 8 July, when some Arabs, refusing to accept defeat, resumed the fighting, Yigal Allon, Commander of the Central Sector, and Moshe Dayan, Commander of the 89th Mechanized Division, attacked the Arab village of Lydda (Lod) and Ramla to the east of Tel Aviv.

Under the terms of the partition plan, Lydda was awarded to the Arabs, so thousands of refugees had settled there over the previous months. Spear Monaier, one of the nurses at the local hospital, recalls that the town swelled from 22,000 residents to between 50 and 60,000, but there were few Palestinian fighters in the area because Lydda depended on the protection of the Jordanian troops. When the attack started, these troops held out for only a few hours.'

Since the renowned Arab Legion was defending this sector, Allon and Dayan had expected a fierce battle. Their fears proved groundless. Glubb Pasha, the Commander of the Arab Legion, decided not to defend that sector and hardly put up a fight. He argued that he did not have sufficient forces to hold on to the important area of Latrun, and simultaneously attempt to fight in

Ramla and Lydda. The skirmish between the Jewish forces and the Jordanian Army lasted barely a couple of hours.

By 4.30 p.m., on 11 July, Moshe Dayan and his troops had reached the centre of Lydda. The soldiers proceeded to gather all the inhabitants in the local mosque and the adjacent church. Spear Monaier remembers how his family was ordered to leave: 'Soldiers came to our house and said that, after fifteen minutes, they would come back and kill whoever they found in the house. They led us to the mosque which was full of people – men, women and children. When there was no room left, they took the women and children out, then said all the Christians should go to the church next door. The soldiers were on top of the wall of the mosque with their weapons aimed at us'.

Meanwhile Yigal Allon and Yitzhak Rabin, two of the Jewish commanders of the operation, were holding discussions with Prime Minister Ben-Gurion. They needed a clear decision about what should be done with the 50,000 Arab inhabitants of Lydda. In the formal meeting Ben-Gurion ignored the question. Yitzhak Rabin wrote down the details of this meeting, but the following quote was censored from his published memoirs:

> We walked outside [the operational headquarters], Ben-Gurion accompanying us. Allon repeated his question: "What is to be done with the population?" Ben-Gurion waved his hand in a gesture which said: "Drive them out!" Allon and I had a consultation. I agreed that it was essential to drive the inhabitants out. We took them on foot towards Bet Horon road . . . The population did not leave willingly. There was no way of avoiding the use of force and warning shots in order to make the inhabitants march the ten to fifteen miles to the point where they met with the Arab Legion.[21]

Spear Monaier remembers how the soldiers ordered people out of town, saying, 'Go to King Abdallah'. Monaier was one of the lucky 503 inhabitants who managed to remain in Lydda. The other 50,000 were driven out by force and marched away like a line of ants. George Habbash recalls: 'They directed us to a specific road . . . There were road blocks manned by Israeli soldiers every 100 metres or so to make sure that no one diverted until we arrived at the outskirts of Lydda. There, we found a large number of soldiers. They put us in rows and started body-searching each person . . . They kept moving us on and we didn't know where we were heading . . . Many families got separated. I will remember this day for as long as I live . . . '

The neighbouring town of Ramla fell with very little resistance. The Arab inhabitants had learned their lesson from watching the enforced departure of their neighbours. The exodus of the Arab inhabitants from their towns helped to solve one of the serious problems confronting the Israeli political leadership from the beginning of the war: What to do with the Palestinians?[22]

On 16 June 1948, thirteen ministers of Israel's provisional government met to decide what to do with the Arab population – those who had fled and those who remained. During this meeting, Foreign Minister Moshe Sharett started by commenting on the on-going Arab exodus. The flight of Palestinian refugees had increased in intensity since the events in Deir Yassin and the war had then accelerated the trend. For Moshe Sharett there was no hesitation. The Arab exodus was, 'A momentous event in world and Jewish history'. He added rhetorically, 'They are not returning, and that is our policy'.

Sharett's words expressed the desire of most of the Israeli leadership. It was a simple and radical solution. But could Israel deny 700,000 Arab inhabitants the right to return to their homes? In the 16 June Cabinet meeting, Ben-Gurion was clear enough: 'They [the Palestinians] lost and fled. Their return now must be prevented . . . And I will oppose their return also after the war'. This decision was endorsed by all thirteen members of the provisional government. The meeting sealed the fate of 700,000 Arabs to become permanent refugees.

### The Falouga Pocket

After the first truce – 10 June to 9 July – had ended, the Israeli forces won considerable ground. The 9th brigade of the Egyptian Army, between 4–5,000 soldiers, were encircled in the area of Falouga. This became known as 'The Falouga pocket'.

On 24 October, Yigal Allon, the Israeli commander at the front, decided to make direct contact with the encircled Egyptian officers. Zakaria Mohiedin: 'A jeep hoisting a white flag came. Inside was one of the military leaders with another officer from the Israeli army. They wanted to talk and brought some oranges which they gave to Gamal Abdel Nasser. They asked if they could bring religious men to collect the corpses of the Israelis. Nasser agreed.'

Twenty-four hours later at Kibbutz Gat, a kilometre and a half away from the Egyptian lines, the two commanders, Sayid Taha and Yigal Allon, accompanied by Gamal Abdel Nasser from the Egyptian side and Yitzhak Rabin and Yerouham Cohen from the Israeli side, met.

Allon: 'Your army is blocked by a hopeless war in the land of Israel. Your own country is controlled by the British army, which we managed to get rid of not so long ago. Don't you think that you are a victim of imperialism and their allies in Egypt?'

Taha: 'You succeeded in expelling the British. Soon we will get them out of Egypt!'

Allon: 'But how will you do that if your army is blocked here? Wouldn't it be best for you to return to Egypt to deal with your own problems rather than participate in an adventure in a country which is not yours?'

Gamal Abdel Nasser was listening attentively. Ironically, Allon was voicing the exact questions that he and his fellow Egyptian officers had been asking themselves while under seige.

The Egyptians and the Israelis shared dinner at the kibbutz. It was a rare moment that would not be repeated for three decades.

The war in Palestine was for all practical purposes over, and the Arab armies had been defeated. The official end of the war would be declared at negotiations on the Greek island of Rhodes in February 1949. Egypt agreed to sign an armistice agreement on condition that all the soldiers trapped in the Falouga pocket be released with their weapons. The international boundary separating Mandate Palestine from Egypt served as the armistice line between the Egyptian and Israeli armies. Within a few months, Jordan, Syria and Lebanon signed separate armistice agreements with Israel in Rhodes. Israel, having won the war, managed to retain some occupied areas – such as Ramla, Lydda and Beersheba – that had originally been part of the Arab sector of the partition plan.

The Arabs of Palestine were left with all their hopes dashed. After the war, they tried to salvage their aim to establish an independent Palestinian state by putting this to the Arab League Council. The Council members convened to decide whether it would be possible to proclaim an independent Palestinian state on land that Israel had not captured during the war – mainly the West Bank and Gaza – but they were thwarted from reaching a unanimous decision by King Abdallah of Jordan annexing the West Bank to his kingdom. Egypt, Syria and Iraq – exhausted by the war – had no desire to stir up a new confrontation – this time with Jordan, an Arab state. Thus the issue was dropped – and, at the time of writing, the Palestinian Arabs do not have their own state.

*Chapter 3*

# The winds of change

The Egyptian officers trapped in the Falouga pocket spent hours in the desert heat trying to understand the reasons for their humiliating defeat. Gamal Abdel Nasser, Zakaria Mohiedin, Salah Salem and a number of others, concluded that their own political leadership, mainly King Farouk, was responsible. Zakaria Mohiedin recalls that it was during conversations held in Falouga that the idea of carrying out a revolution in Egypt was hatched: 'The Palestine war was one of the reasons for our 23rd of July 1952 revolution. At the end of the Falouga period we established our organization [the Free Officers] . . . But it was not only a matter of the Palestinian war and the military, it was the whole political system in Egypt . . . We had to change the situation'.

King Farouk's weakness encouraged the Free Officers to move faster than they had intended. The idea of putting their military and social demands to the King was abandoned and they began plotting to overthrow the regime. 'We held a committee meeting,' Zakaria Mohiedin recalls, 'in which I was assigned to outline the military plan for the coup.'

Kamal edin Hussein, an artillery officer who was teaching at the military academy with Nasser and Mohiedin, was one of the inner circle who attended the meeting where the tasks were assigned. His role in leading the artillery would be crucial for the success of the coup. 'I met with my artillery officers in the house of a student,' he recalls. 'We divided into two groups, then gave the instructions for the revolution to start.'

The coup was almost foiled by one of Hussein's artillery students who told his mother of the planned revolution. She in turn told his brother, an air-force officer who had been dismissed and who thought that if he denounced the plot he would be reinstated. The Free Officers almost cancelled their plans but Gamal Abdel Nasser, the mastermind of the operation, instructed his colleagues to continue. Kamal edin Hussein recalls: 'When I told Nasser about the leak, he said we had to continue. So we moved from my house and went over to the Suez road. I then took my units to cut off the way to Suez . . . We placed artillery on the road to prevent any troops from moving, and an officer cut the phone lines to prevent any contact . . . Later we sent to [General] Muhammad Naguib telling him we had succeeded and asked him to come.'

The Free Officers named General Muhammad Naguib as President and secured control of the city. But they knew all would be in vain if they could not achieve King Farouk's abdication. Anwar Sadat, an army officer, was assigned to go and see the incumbent Prime Minister to demand the King's abdication: 'I delivered an ultimatum to him. He was shocked because, up to that moment, he didn't believe that we were going to de-throne the King. He said, "Are you powerful enough?" I said, "Yes. Go deliver it to the King. He must leave by six o'clock this evening"'.

King Farouk was escorted with his wife and baby son to the royal yacht, *The Mahrousa*, in Alexandria harbour. They sailed into exile.

The foremost concern of the Free Officers now was to root out corruption in the army and strengthen the military to serve as the back-bone of the regime. Only a strong army could expel the final remnants of British occupation and achieve the revolution's Six-Point Charter: ousting the king, ending colonization, strengthening the army, social equality, economic development and free education for all.

Ironically, although the seeds of the Free Officers' movement had been sown during the war in Palestine, their Charter and agenda – once they reached power – neither mentioned Palestine nor called for the uprooting of the new Israeli state. As far as the Free Officers were concerned, Israel was far from their thoughts. Kamal edin Hussein affirms: 'We had only one thing on our mind – Egypt. We didn't even notice that we hadn't mentioned Israel. It wasn't on our agenda'.

Israel did not feel threatened by the new regime in Egypt. The Israeli leadership rightly believed that the new junta was too involved in Egypt's internal affairs to pay any attention to the problems of their Palestinian Arab or Jewish neighbours. Israeli Prime Minister David Ben-Gurion hoped that the authors of the 'social revolution' in Egypt would be willing to talk to him, and made several attempts to contact them. One of his young lieutenants, Shimon Peres, suggested a safe channel. Peres recalls: 'We had a man, Sheike Dan, a paratrooper who had wonderful contacts in Yugoslavia. He took a letter from Ben-Gurion to President Tito[23], suggesting a meeting between him [Ben-Gurion] and Nasser to discuss the end of the state of war between us and Egypt . . . Nasser's answer was negative. His reply to Ben-Gurion was that he was afraid that this would mean the end of his life and regime.' Nasser could not yet afford to face the wrath of the surrounding Arab regimes. Besides, his priorities were clear: ameliorating social conditions and removing the British troops from their huge military base in the Canal Zone. The issue of Israel could wait.

It did not wait long. Within six months of the revolution, an opportunity to establish a direct link to the Prime Minister of Israel was presented to Nasser. The instrument was Abdel Rahman Sadeq, a young press attaché at the Egyptian embassy in Paris.

*Chapter 4*

# Secret contacts in Paris

Walking through Cairo's elegant Zamalek district, Abdel Rahman Sadeq approached the three-storey brick mansion used as the seat of government. His meeting with Colonel Gamal Abdel Nasser would either thwart months of preliminary contacts, or put the seal of approval on a top-level secret channel between Egypt and Israel. Either way, today was the crucial day. Sadeq remembers the details of the encounter: 'I went in and found Gamal Abdel Nasser standing in the middle of the room . . . He welcomed me and asked how is Paris? I answered. Then he said, "And how is your friend?" I asked him which of my friends he meant? "The one about whom you sent the letter", he said!'

Sadeq had sent a letter to an officer friend six months earlier, directly after the July 1952 revolution, and informed him that in 1951 in Paris he had met Ziamah Divon, an Israeli diplomat, who seemed keen on discussing ways in which their countries could seek peace. Since the Free Officers had not given any indication of their attitude towards Israel, Sadeq was worried that his contacts would get him into trouble. He had received no response to his letter. Now, Nasser's reference to the letter revealed that Nasser, the strong man of Egypt, knew about the secret contacts.

During their conversation, Sadeq explained how he had met his Israeli contact by chance during a UN conference: 'A young man came and sat next to me. We talked and then he said, "I am Jewish". I asked him, "Are you a Jew or an Israeli?" He said, "I am an Israeli whose dream is a peace agreement with Egypt"'.

Sadeq told Nasser about their subsequent meetings and how their friendship had developed: 'We used to meet in French cafés in the Etoile or the Opéra district. We spoke about culture, new books and became friends. Slowly we started speaking about our countries'. Sadeq recalls how Nasser asked him only one thing: '"Does he ask you any questions of a military nature?"

I answered that he did not, and that military names only ever came up when we talked about political matters. Nasser was quiet for a few moments, then he said, "You are now authorized by me to continue talking to Divon in Paris . . . But you should not give him any specific names . . . just say that the Revolutionary Command Council has authorized the contact. When he asks, tell him that you have found a similarity between his thoughts and yours, and that you will continue to contact him to look for the possibility of reaching a settlement without any bloodshed." '

Nasser insisted that the contacts should remain totally secret until an agreement seemed possible. He instructed Sadeq to send him detailed reports of developments, no matter how minor. Together, they devised a way of communicating. Sadeq would write his reports in the form of sealed letters labelled 'Eyes Only', and send them to Nasser via a diplomatic pouch. The reports would be enclosed in larger envelopes addressed either to Ali Sabri or Amin Shakir, Nasser's office directors. Nasser would then tell his aides that when they received a letter from Sadeq, they should deliver it to him by hand, unopened. In this way, for many months, Nasser personally controlled Sadeq's talks in Paris.

After the meeting, Sadeq flew back to Paris to launch the first of his official contacts with Divon. For Divon, the Egyptian seal of approval meant that he had finally achieved a goal he had been aiming at for four years. His mission in Paris had been ordered by Foreign Minister Moshe Sharett who had decided that it was time to break through the wall of hatred between the Arabs and Jews, and find Arab contacts. Divon recalls: 'We had no opportunities then to phone Arab ambassadors or approach them officially, and it seemed an almost impossible mission. Sharett made me join the UN delegation. There were more possibilities for success in such meetings than simply going out and looking for contacts. I remember telling a friend that I was going to Paris to meet Arabs, and he said: "Ziamah, what will you do? Go to the Place de la Concorde and start shouting, "I want to meet an Arab"?'

On 1 February 1953, Divon went to meet Sadeq, knowing that Sadeq had just returned from Cairo. Divon: 'This was an important meeting. We had finally reached the point of informal negotiations. That day, I sent a telex to Sharett, relaying a message from Sadeq. The first paragraph was the most important. It said that Abdel Rahman Sadeq was authorized by the Revolutionary Command Council to talk with me, based on the assumption that I, Ziamah Divon, was authorized by the Israeli government to carry out contacts with him.'

For Israel, the agenda of talks with their Egyptian neighbour consisted of topics that would lead to comprehensive negotiations: 'Mutual acceptance of the armistice lines as permanent borders; an immediate non-aggression pact; an agreement on the future of the Gaza Strip; efforts to solve the refugee problem in the Gaza Strip; the simultaneous use of Israeli influence to support Egyptian claims, and Egypt's influence in attaining Israel's acceptance by other Middle Eastern countries; efforts to obtain military and economic aid from the US and other sources; co-operation in regional security; co-ordination of their position and activities in the UN; establishing commercial ties between the two countries'.[24]

When Nasser authorized the continuation of the Sadeq-Divon talks, on the basis of these topics, he made it clear to Sadeq that negotiations could not be concluded until British forces left Egypt. Indeed, Nasser asked Sadeq to tell Divon that the goodwill of his government could be demonstrated by the Israelis helping Egypt to facilitate the evacuation. Sadeq promptly passed this message to Divon. The Israeli government's top priority was a settlement regarding waterways, especially safe passage of Israeli ships through the Suez Canal. Nasser's message to Israel, via Sadeq, was that if Israel through its good offices could help Egypt rid itself of British troops, then an agreement concerning the passage of Israel shipping through the Suez Canal could be discussed. If the evacuation happened without Israel's help, Egypt would still discuss Israel's passage through the Suez, but it would take longer. The two issues were not directly related, but the canal was used as an incentive for Israel to help Egypt.

Sadeq recalls how persistent Divon was about his government's demand: 'Each time he talked about the canal, I interrupted with, "We are waiting for the evacuation. When this occurs, then naturally your ships can pass through the canal, because we will have peace."'

Sadeq recalls: 'Divon often talked about drawing up a draft peace treaty . . . a document we could sit and sign. I said, "First we must settle our demands. Are you ready to take back the Palestinians who have been evacuated?" After consulting with Tel Aviv, he said, "We are willing to take some back". I asked, "How many – ninety per cent, eighty per cent, seventy per cent, and so on?" But he never gave me a specific answer.'

Sadeq had no more luck clarifying the issue of borders. Israel had never defined its borders and Prime Minister Ben-Gurion had repeatedly stated that Israel's borders were where the Israeli army reached. Although Divon could not provide any greater precision on this issue, Nasser told him to continue the attempts to find common ground. Through the Sadeq-Divon talks, both countries committed themselves to reducing – or trying to stop – their media attacks and aggressive rhetoric aimed at each other. Egypt also agreed to restrain Fedayeen attacks. The Fedayeen were an underground movement of Palestinian fighters. Between 1948–55, the movement consisted mainly of refugees conducting random raids to steal goods or bring back their belongings left behind in their Palestine homes during the 1948 conflict. From 1955 onwards, Egyptian intelligence sponsored the Fedayeen, and armed and trained them for organized military raids. The attacks that followed were not always targeted and conducted under Egyptian supervision, but there was no doubt that, from 1955, Egypt could control the group. Their attacks, which often led to skirmishes on the borders, were a constant source of tension for Israel.

The implementation of the tacit agreements reached by Sadeq and Divon in Paris represented a remarkable achievement for Israel and Egypt. For almost two years, goodwill was maintained, the aggressive rhetoric practically dried up, and the Fedayeen operations launched from Egyptian territory ceased. However, Fedayeen raids launched from other Arab countries did not stop.

## The Qibya raid
On the night of 13 October 1953, a Fedayeen raid on the village of Yahoud, near Tel-Aviv, left an Israeli mother and her two children dead. Israel immediately authorized a retaliatory commando raid on the village of Qibya in Jordan, led by a young commander, Ariel

Sharon. The Qibya raid left sixty-nine people dead. News of this disproportionate reprisal unleashed an international outcry.

Nasser was perplexed and disappointed by the news. Why would Israel resort to such an act? The initiator of the Sadeq-Divon talks, Foreign Minister Moshe Sharrett, had by now become Prime Minister. The Qibya raid seemed incompatible with his search for peace. Nasser, who had also become Prime Minister, had many questions and asked Sadeq to get some answers. Sadeq: 'I asked him [Divon] about the massacre at Qibya, and he told me that hardliners had carried out the raid. He said that they [the moderates] could not prevent the hardliners from committing such acts.'

The Qibya raid had been launched behind Prime Minister Moshe Sharett's back. The Prime Minister was less keen on military reprisals than his predecessor, David Ben-Gurion. Although Ben-Gurion had retired, he still had great influence as the founder of the nation and the leader of the great victories of 1948. Israel's military commanders still had close informal relations with him. Sharett was regarded as the main 'moderate' within the Israeli cabinet during this period. He believed that Israel's security would best be guaranteed if it achieved peace with its Arab neighbours. Those referred to as the hardliners in the cabinet, supported by Chief of Staff Moshe Dayan, held opposite views: only if Israel proved the extent of its power to its neighbours could it survive, be respected, and make peace. These two views in government were moving towards a collision course.

For the Sadeq-Divon channel to succeed, Sharett had to prevent incidents like the Qibya raid. The raid had deeply disturbed Nasser. Sadeq remembers Nasser's reaction: 'He discussed the matter of the Israeli hardliners and moderates in detail, then said, "I have decided to enter into the battle between the hardliners and the moderates". I asked him: "How can you enter into such a battle?" He said, "By coming out into the open. Tell the person you discuss such matters with that I am personally responsible for these talks."'

Time was working against an Egyptian-Israeli understanding. Sharett succeeded in obtaining a temporary agreement on the cessation of large-scale reprisal attacks by the Israel Defence Forces (IDF), but many in his government remained unconvinced about his policy of rapprochement with the neighbouring Arab governments.[25]

Unknown to Sharett and Divon, activities that would destroy their mediating efforts were about to be launched yet again behind their backs. An undercover operation to conduct sabotage against Western interests in Egypt had been authorized by Israeli Defence Minister Pinhas Lavon, and put into effect by Benjamin Givly, Israel's Director of Military Intelligence.

*Chapter 5*

# Sabotage in Egypt

Pinhas Lavon, a willowy sharp-witted man with prematurely greying hair, was Minister of Agriculture when he was handed the Defence Ministry, Israel's most sensitive job. Lavon's holding this office under Premier Moshe Sharett promised tension, since the two men had opposing views on how to deal with their Arab neighbours. Sharett, brought up in an Arab village, believed that peace could be reached through negotiations. Lavon was closer to Ben-Gurion who believed that their security depended on proving that attacks on Israel would cost their perpetrators dear.

In 1954, Lavon faced a pressing problem for which he solicited the help of Benjamin Givly, Israel's Director of Military Intelligence. The problem: Britain and Egypt had agreed plans to remove British troops from Egypt; how could Israel obstruct them? For Lavon, the British leaving the Suez Canal Zone would remove the military buffer between Egypt and Israel. The massive British military installations would be handed over to the Egyptian army, and, worse still, Egypt would become eligible for US military aid. Action had to be taken quickly. Givly proposed an undercover operation, using a unit which had been planted in the heart of Egyptian territory for four years.

Unit 131 had been created when Benjamin Givly had nominated a bright young agent, Avraham Dar to recruit local Jews to be ready for action behind enemy lines. Givly recalls: 'I gave Dar instructions to go to Egypt, to organize the best of the Jewish youth . . . We would then have them come to Israel for training and send them back to Egypt, with the intention of serving our needs when the time came.'

Avraham Dar, a veteran of Palmach's naval unit and experienced in running illegal Jewish immigrants through the British blockade, did not find the mission daunting. His western looks and mastery of Arabic facilitated his task. In April 1950, he left for Egypt under the name of John Darling to hand-pick recruits from among the Zionist youth in Cairo and Alexandria.

Marcel Ninio, a young Egyptian Jewish athlete, remembers her first meeting with Dar: 'I was twenty-one years old, naive, idealistic and full of admiration for Israel. For us, whoever came from Israel was like a god . . . I was ready to do whatever was needed to help Israel'. Ninio became the Unit's treasurer. Dar also recruited a dozen young Jewish men and taught them the tricks of the trade. Robert Dassa recalls the excitement of the initial phase: 'We rented a hut on the beach in Alexandria and carried out experiments with Vim canisters . . . to see how long it would take the explosive mixture placed inside them to ignite'.

The unit quickly perfected the art of making incendiary bombs with condoms. These were used as a timing device so that acid would only ignite once the chemical ruptured the condom. Dar recalls: 'When I taught them the trick with the condom and the acid, we tried out many examples. We spilt some in the bathroom, but had no water to clean up. Later Dassa sent a girl with pails of water to deal with the spills. When she saw the number of used condoms in there, she said to him, "Oh boy, you're some man!"'

Following Givly's proposal to use Unit 131, he and Lavon met to discuss how to proceed. Givly: 'The meeting was at Lavon's home in the centre of Tel Aviv . . . We talked about the fact that the British were about to leave Egypt, and Lavon said, "I would like us to activate the Unit in Egypt". During that talk we cooked up a plan to hit targets.'

The sabotage would achieve a double aim: first, by hitting American targets, the relations between Egypt and the US would be damaged; second, by targeting the British, Britain's withdrawal of its troops, and the instability that the Israelis feared would follow this, would be delayed.

Following the meeting between Lavon and Givly, the signal to activate the sabotage team was sent. 'We received a message written in invisible ink,' recalls Robert Dassa, 'informing us that someone would arrive that month. When he came at the end of June, the head of our cell asked: "When do you want us to begin?" He said: "Yesterday". We didn't understand the reason for the urgency . . . '

## Unit 131's bombings

Robert Dassa[26]: 'We met at an apartment in Mazareta [in Alexandria]. We put the explosive in the Vim canisters and prepared the condoms – two to a canister, set for a delay of half an hour . . . We wrapped it up in newspaper and on the outside of the package I wrote a name and address in Arabic. Then Philip Nathanson and myself went to the central post office.'

Dassa was proud of the success of his first operation. When the package exploded, the members of Unit 131 were reassured that their home-made bombs did function, and the blame was directed towards the Muslim Brotherhood which opposed Nasser's government in Egypt.[27] Only then could they start hitting the real targets.

On 14 July 1954, three incendiary devices were placed simultaneously in the United States Information Agency offices in both Cairo and Alexandria, and in a British-owned theatre. Who would suspect that undercover Israeli agents would sabotage American and European targets in Egypt? Again, Dassa carried out the operation. Dassa: 'They [in Israel] wanted the next operation to be more grandiose. We were told to act both in Alexandria and Cairo at the same time to create the impression that there were strong cells throughout the country. This time, instead of the Vim canisters, which weren't suitable for placing in the American Library, we used spectacle cases . . . We took a book off the shelf, put the bomb at the back of the shelf, and left.'

Dassa repeated the trick at western-owned cinemas in Cairo. The bombings succeeded in creating confusion within Egypt's security apparatus. Who was planting these bombs and why? The mystery was soon resolved. On 23 July, Philip Nathanson set out to plant an incendiary device at the Cinema Rio in Alexandria. But the timing device failed and the bomb detonated in his trouser pocket. Nathanson was taken to hospital and immediately inter-rogated. Dassa, who had carried out a parallel operation in Cairo, did not know of his friend's misfortune, nor did he know at the time that his own bomb had been discovered before it detonated.

Dassa was captured the following day. 'From the moment I got on the bus from Cairo to Alexandria,' he recalls, 'I felt I was being followed . . . felt I was in a trap. I hesitated about whether or not to go home and walked the streets of Alexandria, hoping to meet someone I knew. It was as though the city was empty of all my acquaintances. So, I went home . . . On the stairs up to my apartment, they caught me.'

Robert Dassa's brief career as an Israeli sabotage agent in Egypt had ended, and along with it one of the most extraordinary spy rings that Israel had managed to establish in the heart of an Arab country.

## A request for clemency

The news of the capture of an Israeli spy ring in Egypt came as a blow to Prime Minister Sharett. On 5 October 1954, Zakaria Mohiedin, Egypt's Interior Minister and Head of Intelligence, gave the details of the sabotage in a radio broadcast, and declared that the culprits would be tried in a military court. Gideon Rafael, a senior Foreign Ministry official, recalls how he broke the news to Sharett: 'My assistant in charge of monitoring Arab Radios came in and gave me the news. I said, "Is this propaganda or authentic?" Our Arab experts went over the Arabic text and said that it seemed authentic . . . So I went to Sharett and said, "Look, this is the communiqué from Cairo. What do you know about it?" He said, "No, no, this is not authentic. It can't be. It's impossible because I'm Prime Minister and I don't know anything about it. It can't be true."'

When he realized it was true, Sharett was shocked. This, however, was not the time to settle accounts within his government. First, Sharett had to try and save the lives of the Jewish saboteurs who were to be brought before a military trial in Egypt. Sharett decided to ask Ziamah Divon, his secret envoy, to appeal directly to Nasser to release the Jewish saboteurs. Divon recalls: 'Prime Minister Sharett said, "We want to do everything possible to prevent death sentences. Please find a way to send a message to

Nasser on this matter". I took a plane to Nicosia, Cyprus, went to the Central Post Office and phoned Abdel Rahman Sadeq.'

Sadeq had already heard the news through Zakaria Mohiedin's radio announcement and recalls how he immediately realized that his talks with Divon over the past two years were now in jeopardy. 'Divon said that he wanted to meet me, so I went to Nasser and told him. He said, "It's good that he has sent for you, because I was going to send you anyway . . ."' Sadeq also recalls: 'When I met Divon in Paris on 16 December 1954, he said that he was carrying a message from Prime Minister Sharett to President Nasser . . . telling him that the incidents in Egypt had taken place without his knowledge, and that those who had planned the sabotage were hardliners. He also said that Sharett was appealing personally to Nasser for clemency and that there should not be an execution verdict.' Divon – in accordance with Sharett's instructions – then added that there was a serious possibility that if death sentences were passed, it would cause fermentation and tension and affect the relationship between him and Sadeq. He was told that, to Nasser's deep regret, the President could do no more than make sure that the court in Cairo conducted a fair trial.

After this meeting, Nasser reassessed how he was going to deal with Israel. Could he afford to ignore the sabotage operations? For Nasser, the most important message that had come out of these was that Sharett was not strong enough to impose his will on the hardliners within his government. It was evident that trying to reach an agreement this way was futile.

Nasser explained to Sadeq his own interpretation of the sabotage operations in Egypt. Sadeq recalls Nasser's words: '"This operation [the sabotage] is very cunning. It serves several objectives. One: putting obstacles before the negotiations with Britain. Two: corrupting the relationship between us and the United States. Three: it also serves the hardliners' objective of putting obstacles before Sharett . . . They are sending us a message that the moderates are incapable of ruling Israel and that we should not depend on them . . . It is clear that they and not Sharett have the upper hand". Nasser concluded, "We should not continue with the secret negotiations until the moderates find solutions for their own internal problems."'

Soon, the military court in Egypt issued the verdicts on the saboteurs. These included two death sentences and several prison sentences. The executions were carried out almost immediately. Soon the Israeli public was calling for retaliation. Gideon Rafael: 'The Israeli public did not know about our involvement in this [sabotage]. They thought the whole thing was a staged political trial . . . Not knowing the background, the public reaction was: They're hanging Jews in Cairo and this is intolerable. We have to act. The army also wanted to retaliate. They wanted to show that one can't just execute Jews.'

## Chapter 6

# Confrontation

Following the sabotage operations in Egypt and the breakdown of the secret talks between Nasser and Sharett, Egypt's tacit agreement to control Fedayeen border incursions and the two countries agreement to avoid inflammatory rhetoric, collapsed. In Israel, after the court verdicts on the saboteurs were carried out, the media went wild with anti-Egyptian stories, while in Egypt the Palestinian Fedayeen pressured Nasser to give them a free rein to launch raids from Egyptian territory. The scene was set for a major clash.

On 23 February 1955, Egyptian spies broke into an Israeli military facility at Rishon le Zion, near Tel Aviv, and stole maps and documents. Two days later an Israeli cyclist was shot and killed.

On 28 February, Prime Minister Sharett's ability to argue against retaliation raids was undermined, and he reluctantly authorized an army raid against military installations in the Gaza Strip, then governed by Egypt. This confrontation unleashed a vicious spiral of events that would last for over twenty years.

Gideon Rafael recalls Sharett's reluctance to permit this raid: 'The military was pressing to act in Gaza, and Sharett gave them strict orders to avoid any major casualties. He told them they couldn't have more than ten casualties'.

Rafael tried, but failed to dissuade Sharett from imposing this condition: 'I said to him, "Moshe, this is not possible; do you think they can go in and count one, two, three . . . casualties, now finish, we have to go home". This is a battle and they will start shooting . . . There is no such thing as quotas in fighting'.

Command of the operation was assigned to Ariel Sharon who had conducted the raid on Qibya (see chapter four), which had caused an international outcry.

Sharon: 'We departed in the dark through Gaza, passing through the orange groves. My intention was to cross between two Egyptian posts in order to reach behind the Egyptian line and reach the outskirts of Gaza. After we had gone about one kilometre, maybe a bit more, we heard voices in Arabic, and then gunfire. Four Egyptian soldiers were dead, and it was clear to me that we had to proceed very quickly because there was no longer any element of surprise . . . We took over the camp and began to explode the buildings there.'

As Sharett had feared, the number of Egyptian soldiers killed was once again disproportionate. The retaliation for the killing of a single cyclist resulted in thirty-nine dead Egyptian soldiers. Sharett knew this would elicit an extreme reaction from Nasser.

Mohsen Abdel Khalek, a close associate of Nasser, recalls a meeting held in Nasser's office when he received the news of the Gaza raid: '"This has been done to humiliate Egypt, and it is unacceptable to a regime that is three years old and has great political, economic and social ambitions in Egypt. We have to find a solution. The UN Security Council is out of the question, because it will not do anything for us. So we have to find a source for weapons . . ." Thus, after the Gaza raid, we started to search for arms'.

The raid transformed the Egyptian regime into Israel's worst enemy. But Nasser dared not risk his army, still in tatters from the 1948 war. They needed sophisticated weapons. He accelerated the search for arms to bring the army up to standard, and relegated his regime's priorities for social and economic development.

For months, Egypt, which was then on good terms with the United States[28], had been pressing Washington for military aid, but had received no response. On 10 March 1955, Nasser called the American ambassador to his office. 'I have lost my voice asking you for arms,' Nasser reproached him. He then said that if Egypt could not get the arms it needed from the US, it would have to turn to other sources. The ruling military junta was unanimous. Mohsen Abdel Khalek remembers the prevalent attitude, 'Find weapons anywhere, even from the devil himself'.

The occasion to find the weapons from another source came in April 1955 at the Bandung Conference, the first Non-Aligned Summit.[29] Nasser knew that he had to turn to the Soviets, but did not want to become part of the Soviet camp.

In September 1955, Egypt announced that it had signed a major arms deal with the Soviet satellite state Czechoslovakia. But Soviet involvement in the deal could hardly be masked. The Czech arms deal came as a crushing blow to Israel. Abba Eban, the Israeli representative at the UN, recalls: 'By their very acquisition of jet aircraft, Egypt had rendered the Israeli air force with its propeller aircraft obsolete.'

Egypt had upset the balance of power in the region and had become part of the Cold War between the USA and USSR superpowers.

In Israel, the debate about the use of force against Egypt was now centre stage. Moshe Sharett and the Foreign Ministry preferred not to over-dramatize the Czech arms deal. But for David Ben-Gurion, who once again controlled the Defence Ministry, and his powerful Chief of Staff Moshe Dayan, it was out of the question to allow Egypt military parity – let alone air superiority. The challenge was how to strike at Egypt before it could digest and make use of the new weapons.

### The Suez War

On 26 July 1956, Nasser nationalized the Suez Canal.[30] This move took both Britain and France, major shareholders and operators of the canal, by surprise. They decided that the Egyptian revolutionary leader was getting too big for his boots. To cut him down to size, they solicited the help of Nasser's next-door enemy, Israel.

French Defence Minister Maurice Bourgès-Maunoury was assigned the task of co-ordinating a tripartite strike against Egypt. Only a day after the nationalization announcement, he summoned Shimon Peres, Director General of the Israeli Defence Ministry, and proposed the plan. Peres recalls: 'Bourges told me that a joint operation was being planned between France and England to maintain their rights in the Suez Canal . . . He asked me, if Israel participated, how long would it take the force to reach the canal?'

Peres returned to Israel with the plan for the tripartite strike. From that moment on, Israel prepared for war. On 30 September, 1956, a high-level delegation joined a French team at St Germain to discuss the details. For almost a month the intricacies of the military co-operation were hammered out in secret. Finally, on 22 October, the Israeli, British and French conspirators met in a private villa in Sèvres on the outskirts of Paris to give the final go-ahead for war. A week later, at 16.59 hours, Israel's 890 paratroop battalion, led by Rafael Eitan, was dropped at Parker's Memorial, just east of the Mitla Pass. The Suez War had begun.

Israel swept across the Egyptian border with little resistance and achieved a spectacular victory. But Ben-Gurion's speech declaring Israel's intention to remain in the Sinai came too soon. Within days of the first strike, other members of the international community spotted the tripartite plot and an ultimatum was issued by the UN to return to Egypt all the territory seized. Singled out as the aggressor, Israel was forced to relinquish its gains – a warning for the future to Israel's military commanders.

Egypt emerged from the aggression almost unscathed. The principal cost was that, after the cease-fire, Egypt was obliged to accept UN troops on its border with Israel. For the following eleven years, all was reasonably quiet between the two countries until, in 1967, the third total mobilization phase of the fifty years war erupted.

# 2 THE 1967 WAR

## Introduction

After the 1956 Suez War (in which Israel collaborated with Britain and France against President Nasser of Egypt), David Ben-Gurion, the Israeli Prime Minister, agreed to withdraw Israel's forces from the Sinai Peninsula which it had occupied during the war. This withdrawal, Ben-Gurion stipulated, was dependent on Israeli shipping being given freedom of navigation through the Straits of Tiran. The settlement held for eleven years. So, what caused the 1967 Six Day War?

The official Israeli version, still widely believed, places the blame on President Nasser, who, by his decision to close the Straits – which Israel had warned would be regarded as an act of war and resisted as a *casus belli* – left Israel with no alternative but to fight. Another version is that Nasser did not intend to go to war; indeed, he signalled a wish to send a senior envoy to Washington for secret talks to find a way out of the crisis. His threat was a political move to prove to fellow Arabs – the Jordanians, Saudis and Syrians – that he was still the champion of pan-Arabism and the most radical Middle East leader. It was an exercise in brinkmanship that went over the brink.

In May 1967, as Nasser deployed his troops in Sinai, Prime Minister Levi Eshkol initially resisted pressures to go to war. But on 5 June, Israel launched a pre-emptive strike against the Egyptian Air Force.

Once the fighting had begun, Israel also turned its guns on Jordan and Syria. In six days, Israel won a military victory that changed the face of the Middle East.

*Chapter 7*

# A storm is gathering

In May 1967, Levi Eshkol, Israel's Prime Minister, was completing his fourth year in office. In spite of his age – seventy-two – and severe health problems, he was also Defence Minister. In Israel, this post meant crucial power, and Eshkol – like his predecessor, David Ben-Gurion – had chosen to keep the job for himself.

There had been a general sigh of relief in Israel when Eshkol took over the Defence Ministry from the tough authoritative Ben-Gurion – and the change of face had been particularly welcomed by military personnel. Ben-Gurion had been very active in military affairs whereas Eshkol was happy to let them get on with their jobs. One problem for Eshkol, however, was that because he was more of a financial than a military expert, he had to rely on the advice of Yitzhak Rabin, his Chief of Staff, and he resented this.

People loved Eshkol. He was a warm-hearted man who would always try to find a compromise that would satisfy everybody. But, after four years in office, the honeymoon period was over and his standing had reached a low ebb. Israel's problems were causing increasing concern: the economy was going from bad to worse, the recession was biting and unemployment was rising. Eshkol's practice of seeking a compromise was now attributed to indecisiveness and had become the butt of many jokes. 'Coffee or tea, Mr Prime Minister?' was one of these; Eshkol, after a long pause, 'Better give me half and half'.

On 14 May 1967, as final preparations were being made for that night's military *Tattoo*, part of Israel's nineteenth Independence Day celebrations, Eshkol was on the balcony of his office catching strains of music coming from the municipal stadium just across the road. Alongside him was his wife, Miriam. Also present on the balcony was Rabin who, at forty-five, was regarded as one of the brightest Israeli-born military commanders. Rabin approached Eshkol and gave him some news. Shocked, Eshkol queried the words Rabin had spoken: 'Nasser has moved his forces into the Sinai?'[1]

## Urgent consultations

The next morning, May 15, Eshkol, Rabin and their aides met at the King David Hotel, Jerusalem, to assess the problem. They needed more information. All they knew was that two Egyptian divisions had crossed the Suez Canal and entered the Sinai. Even though the Egyptians had only crossed into their own territory, the movement of such a substantial force was unusual and alarming. From where they were now, the three Egyptian divisions could if ordered drive straight across the desert, past the UN buffer-zone forces that separated the Israeli and Egyptian forces, crush the few Israeli soldiers in their way and get to Beer Sheva and other Israeli cities.

Eshkol and Rabin had to calculate their next move. Should they call up more of their forces? This was not an ideal option: a counter-concentration of forces would, in itself, increase tension and could lead to a clash of arms. It was also expensive. The regular Israeli army was so small that bringing more forces to the front would mean calling up the reserve. And, if a total mobilization became necessary, all men aged between eighteen and fifty-five and also some women, would have to leave their jobs and join the army. The immediate effect would be a severe disruption of daily life. Eshkol and Rabin decided to wait. For the time being, they would put their military commanders on alert and monitor the situation. Just before leaving to watch the parade, however, Rabin said, 'If Nasser continues to send his forces into the Sinai, we will have to mobilize our forces. We can't risk leaving our southern border with only a few troops'.

## Parade and warnings

On the central stage in the stadium, not far from the route of the Independence Day march, Eshkol, President Zalman Shazar and ministers were sitting with their wives. Close to them was the top military brass. Distinctive in his light grey uniform was Mordechai (Motti) Hod who, since being appointed Commander in Chief of the Air Force, had worked his pilots day and night, preparing them for the possibility of war. Israeli military doctrine dictated that if war were imminent, Israel should pre-empt by using its air power to knock out the Arab air forces before they could take off. Hod and his pilots needed to know the minute details of the enemy's behaviour: the times they went out on patrol; their routes; when they were back at base; the position they parked their planes; and even the time the pilots took a break and had their meals. Above all, they had to know which routes would enable their planes to reach the enemy's airfields without being detected by radar. As he watched the parade, Hod had no way of knowing that just a few weeks later he and his pilots would be put to the test.

Yeshayahu (Sheike) Gavish, the Commander in Charge of Israeli Forces in the Sinai, was also informed that Nasser had moved his troops into the Sinai. The moment the parade ended, he rushed to his command post where latest intelligence reports confirmed that the Egyptians had indeed crossed the Suez Canal. 'I was puzzled and surprised,' he recalls. 'President Nasser had 70,000 of his best soldiers involved in a civil war in Yemen and we were not expecting war.'[2]

That evening, the traditional air force party which closes the Day of Independence celebrations, took place in Tel Nof, a military air force base not far from Tel Aviv. Almost everyone was there – politicians, veterans and young pilots with their wives and girl-friends. Miriam Eshkol joined her husband. 'The generals,' she said, 'were gathered in small groups. Everybody was speculating, "There will be war . . . There won't be war . . . ", and there was this strong smell of war in the air . . . One could feel the tension . . . could cut it with a knife . . . '[3]

Eshkol could not understand the motivation behind Nasser's actions, but he had good reasons to believe that Nasser was only putting on a show of strength. It was not, after all, the first time that such a situation had occurred. On 18 February 1960, after Israel had carried out a military operation against Syria at Tawfik, the Syrians had called for help and Nasser had responded – but only after the Israeli operation ended. Eshkol thought that, perhaps, Nasser was repeating this tactic, as tensions between Israel and Syria had increased alarmingly since 7 April when Israeli planes had shot down six Syrian Mig jets.

But on this evening, which closed the Independence Day celebrations, people could only speculate – nobody knew for sure why Nasser was sending his forces into the Sinai.

## A Soviet report and President Nasser's dilemma

In Cairo, on 13 May 1967, Anwar el-Sadat, Speaker of the National Assembly, just back from an official visit to Moscow, went straight to Nasser's home at Manshiet el-Bakri where the President was talking to Abd el-Hakim Amer, Deputy Supreme Commander of the Armed Forces. Sadat told the president of his conversation at Moscow Airport with Vladimir Semenov, the Soviet Deputy Foreign Minister. Semenov had told him that, 'Ten Israeli brigades were concentrating on the Syrian border'.[4]

Nasser and Amer were not surprised. They had already heard this from Soviet intelligence sources in Cairo. Not surprisingly, Nasser was worried – and also in a dilemma. He had a Mutual Defence Pact with Syria, which he had signed on 4 November 1966. This required Egypt to come to Syria's aid if Syria were attacked. Could Nasser turn his back again on the Syrians as he had when Israel shot down the Migs on 7 April? He had been criticized then for not reacting. Could he, who saw himself as the champion of the Arab world, decline to take a tough stance against the Israelis? The meeting between Nasser, Amer and Sadat went on well into the night. When it was over, Amer rang Chief of Staff Muhammed Fawzi and said, 'I want you to convene the military commanders early tomorrow morning'.

The top echelon of the Egyptian Army gathered the next day, 14 May, at Amer's office. Also present was Minister of War Shams el-din Badran. Amer opened the meeting, briefed the commanders, told them of the Israeli threats to attack Syria, and about the Soviet Intelligence report. He then turned to Chief of Staff Fawzi and said, 'I want you to start mobilizing our forces. Then go to Damascus and make sure the information we have received from the Soviets is correct'.

Fawzi issued the command to mobilize the Egyptian forces. His officers asked, 'What are our intentions? Are we actually going to start a war? Or are we just going to defend?' Fawzi did not know. Then, while Radio Cairo was playing triumphal nationalistic songs, Egyptian troops paraded through the streets of Cairo on their way to the Sinai. General Ahmed Fakher, then a young colonel in the Egyptian army, witnessed the march of the soldiers to the front. 'The streets of Cairo were full of military equipment and every sort of armament,' he said. 'There was no attempt at camouflage, and the troops were shouting: "We are off to Tel Aviv."'

While the Egyptian forces were pouring into the Sinai, General Fawzi was flying to Syria to see for himself the build-up of Israeli forces along the border with Syria. On arrival, he met with Minister of Defence Hafiz el-Assad and Chief of Staff Ahmed Suidani, and asked to be taken to the border with Israel. He was, as he explains, in for a shock: 'I was seeking confirmation about the Israeli troops, but when I arrived on the border I didn't find anything unusual . . . I looked at the latest aerial photos, but, again, I didn't find anything unusual'. Fawzi flew back to Cairo and wrote a report to Amer.

The Syrians who had also received a report from the Soviet Union, saying that Israeli troops were massing on their border, were also trying to verify the information. A Syrian general (who gave us a confidential interview, but cannot be named) recalls how the Syrian air force was sent out on reconnaissance, but 'they returned saying there were no Israeli forces massing on the border'. The Americans, who had also got wind of the Soviet report, dispatched their military attaché in Israel to check the story. He reported back that he had found no signs whatsoever of Israeli forces on the border. The Israelis themselves responded to the accusations, by saying that the only concentrations in the north 'are concentrations of tourists'.[5]

Israel had not concentrated any forces on its border with Syria. The Soviets, who had spread the rumour, knew this but had their own agenda. These were, after all, the days of the Cold War, days of competition between the superpowers, America and the USSR, for supremacy. And the Middle East was one of the regions where they were attempting to expand their influence.

Evgeny Pyrlin was Head of the Egypt Department in the Soviet Foreign Ministry when the false Soviet report was released. 'We believed then,' he recalls, 'that even if the war was not won by our side – the Egyptians – a war would be to our political advantage because the Egyptians would have demonstrated their ability to fight with *our* weapons and with *our* military and political support.'

A CIA agent was given another reason for the false report. 'The USSR,' he said, 'wanted to create another trouble spot for the

United States in addition to that already existing in Vietnam. The Soviet aim was to create a situation in which the US would become seriously involved economically, politically and possibly even militarily, and would suffer serious political reverses as a result of siding [with the Israelis] against the Arabs.'[6]

As far as the Middle East was concerned, the Soviets had succeeded in what they set out to do. They *had* stirred things up. Nasser had decided to mobilize his forces. Whether or not Nasser believed the Soviet report, in the light of his own Chief of Staff's report to the contrary is unclear. By that time, however, the situation had gained momentum and Nasser began to take actions which moved Egypt – and the whole region – towards the point of no return. To free himself from criticism by Arab radio – especially in Saudi Arabia, Jordan and Syria – that he was hiding behind the skirts of the United Nations Emergency Force (UNEF), he decided to remove UNEF from Sinai and tackle the Israelis.

### Getting rid of the UNEF

UNEF had been stationed along the Egyptian-Israeli border, and in Gaza and Sharm el-Sheikh, since the end of the 1956 War, and was operating on the Egyptian side of the border. (Israel had refused to have it on its soil, saying that problems along the border were a result of Fedayeen attacks from Egyptian soil and there was, therefore, no justification for a UNEF presence on its land.) The UNEF's role was to retain a buffer zone between Egypt and Israel and to monitor the border between the two countries. It was essentially a symbol of non-belligerence.

Nasser now instructed Amer to arrange for the UNEF to leave. Amer, in turn, passed the instructions to Fawzi who wrote a letter to Indir Jit Rikhye, the Commander of the UN forces in Sinai. This stated that Egypt was ready for action against Israel the moment Israel attacked 'any Arab country' and, therefore, for their own sake the UN soldiers should leave.

Egypt's initial intention was that only the UN forces between Gaza and Eilat should leave, but that those in Gaza and especially Sharm el-Sheikh should remain. Sharm el-Sheikh overlooked the Straits of Tiran (see map, page 19), Israel's only outlet to the Red Sea and its only link with the southern and eastern world. If the UN forces left Sharm el-Sheikh, it would no longer be a demilitarized zone, and Egyptian troops would replace them. If the Egyptian soldiers reacted to Israeli shipping passing through the Straits – and attempted to stop them – then the Israelis would take military action.

### A *casus belli*

Nasser called a crucial meeting of the Supreme Executive Committee. Around the table were Amer, Deputy Chief Commander of the Armed Forces, Sidqui Sulayman, Prime Minister, Zakaria Mohiedin, Second Vice President, Hussein el-Shafi, Member of the Arab Socialist Union's Executive Committee, Ali Sabri, Secretary General of the Arab Socialist Union, and Anwar el-Sadat, Speaker of the National Assembly. On the agenda: the Straits of Tiran.

If the meeting decided to block the Straits at the southern end of the Gulf of Aqaba to Israeli shipping, then half the world would be cut off for Israeli exports. Such a blockade would hit the Israeli economy hard, but it would also put a declaration of intent that Israel had made in 1956 to a crucial test. In the 1956 War, Israel had occupied Sharm el-Sheikh which controlled the Straits. Huge international pressure had forced Israel to withdraw. But, before doing so, Israel had declared that any future attempt to blockade the Straits to its shipping would be seen as an act of war that would be resisted. It was a *casus belli*.

Nasser, the champion of the 1956 War, must have known this when he opened the crucial meeting, but he went straight to the point. 'Now, with the concentration of our forces in Sinai, the chances of war are fifty-fifty. But if we close the Straits, war will be 100 per cent certain'.[7] Marshal Amer and other participants agreed that the Straits should be closed. Only Prime Minister Sidqui Sulayman queried the decision: 'Remember our economic situation and the ambitious development projects we are trying to carry through'.

Nasser paid no attention. He was determined to close the Straits and maintain his prestige within the Arab world. Minister of War Shams Badran recalls the pressures on Egypt to close the Straits: 'The Arab countries kept saying that we were allowing Israeli ships to go through Eilat, and that Eilat was the main port for Israeli exports. The attack against us – in Jordanian and Saudi propaganda

– was fierce, and showed us that we had to do something to stop the Israeli ships going through the Straits.'

The meeting ended. Nasser, accompanied by military commanders and top-ranking officials went to the Advanced Air Headquarters at Bir Gafgafa. There, he announced the decision to close the Straits of Tiran to Israeli shipping. 'Our armed forces have occupied Sharm el-Sheikh,' he said. 'We shall on no account allow the Israeli flag to pass through the Gulf of Tiran. The Jews are threatening to make war. We reply, *binqul lahum ahalan wa sahlan* (welcome we are ready for war), this water is ours.'

Upon receiving Fawzi's letter asking the UN forces to leave, Indir Jit Rikyhe, Commander of UN forces in Sinai, replied, 'I am a military man. I get my instructions from the UN, not from Egypt'.[8] He then referred the request to his superiors in the UN. The letter landed on the desk of the UN's Deputy Secretary General Brian Urquhart. 'I got a cable,' recalls Urquhart. 'It was a totally illiterate message asking us to remove UNEF. We realized that if this was serious, it meant war. So we called in the Egyptian ambassador. He was dressed for dinner – and very annoyed. He called Cairo from a phone in U Thant's office, came back and said, "Well, this seems to be right. This is serious."'

U Thant, the softly-spoken Burmese, who was Secretary General of the UN, acted quickly and apparently over-hastily. He informed the Egyptian government that its request for a *partial* withdrawal of UNEF was impossible. The UNEF force could not carry out its missions properly if it abandoned some of its positions. 'Such a request,' he told them, 'would be considered by me as tantamount to a request for the *complete* withdrawal of UNEF.' Nasser was cornered. If he backed down now, he would risk being mocked by all Arabs. His response was, 'Complete withdrawal'.

In a last-ditch attempt to sort out the mess, Paul Martin, the Canadian Foreign Minister, asked Gideon Rafael, the Israeli ambassador, to accept the UNEF forces on Israel's side of the border. Rafael refused. 'Ridiculous,' he said, 'Israel is not the Salvation Army and is not willing to accept UN discards from Egypt.'

'Well, this is starting to be much more serious . . . '

On the night that Nasser declared the closure of the Straits, Prime Minister Eshkol stayed at the Dan Hotel in Tel Aviv, and his wife, Miriam, came from Jerusalem to stay with him. The phone rang in the early hours of the morning. Yisrael Lior, Eshkol's aide-de-camp, was on the line. 'I need to talk to Eshkol,' he said to Miriam who had picked up the phone. 'Eshkol is sleeping,' Miriam replied. 'What's the matter?' 'Nasser has closed the Straits of Tiran . . . ' Lior answered. Miriam woke up the Prime Minister. He talked with Lior, then said to Miriam, 'Well, this is starting to be much more serious'. He got up, dressed and, when his bodyguards arrived, left immediately. Around that time the telephone at Rabin's also rang. His wife, Leah, recalls: 'Yitzhak dressed and left home running – literally running.'

Nasser's decision to close the Straits had hit Israel like a thunderbolt. Politicians, military men and every Israeli citizen knew what this meant. They had been told for years that closure of the Straits would equal war.[9]

On 23 May, full mobilization was ordered. By noon, Israel was at a standstill. The streets and beaches of Tel Aviv were deserted, shelters were cleared of rubbish, trenches dug, El Al flights were cancelled, car headlights were painted blue, donors queued at mobile blood banks, parks were closed to become emergency cemeteries, body-bags and more than 10,000 coffins were prepared, embassies advised their nationals to leave Israel, Jewish volunteers poured in to help in any way they could, rooms in hotels were booked by foreign correspondents, anything with four wheels was taken by the army.

Along the borders, the two armies had been concentrating their forces. The Egyptians had some 900 tanks, more than 200 war-planes and about 80,000 troops. Syria had deployed six brigades and 300 tanks. Hafiz Assad, Syria's Minister of Defence and Commander of the Air Force, declared, 'It is high time to launch the battle for the liberation of Palestine'. King Hussein of Jordan had deployed 300 tanks, put his small but capable air force on alert, and permitted the entry of Iraqi and Saudi troops into his territory close to the Israeli border. Even Lebanon had mobilized its tiny army. Facing these armies were some 275,000 Israeli troops, 1,093 tanks and 203 aeroplanes. The Middle East was a powder keg.

In Tel Aviv, consultations between the cabinet and the military leaders went on throughout the day. On his way to one of the meetings, Eshkol bumped into Meir Amit, Head of Mossad, who said, 'I have no doubt that this is going to develop into a war. The Straits are a *casus belli* for us. This will be their end. This will be their grave'.

In the middle of a cabinet meeting, Prime Minister Eshkol passed a note to Eban, his Foreign Minister. It said, 'What are you doing here?' It was time for Eban to leave Israel and embark upon his most important diplomatic mission ever.

## Chapter 8

# Eban's mission

In the early hours of 24 May, Foreign Minister Eban left Israel in an empty Boeing 707. It was the day after Nasser had announced the closure of the Straits of Tiran, and even the most optimistic doubted whether diplomacy could save the day. Eban was on his way to Washington via Paris and London. His mission: to explain to French President Charles de Gaulle, British Prime Minister Harold Wilson and American President Lyndon Johnson that, for political and economical reasons, the closure of the Straits of Tiran to Israeli shipping could not be tolerated by Israel; and to establish what the powers could – and would – do to ensure the safe passage of Israeli shipping through the Straits.

Five hours later, accompanied by Ambassador Walter Eytan, Eban reached the Elysée Palace and was received by President de Gaulle. The meeting was a disaster from the moment it started, for it was based on a misunderstanding. De Gaulle had the impression that Israel was determined to go to war and that Eban had come to recruit his support. He did not realize that Eban had come to Paris in the hope of preventing war by finding ways of opening the Straits to Israeli shipping. Because of this misunderstanding de Gaulle was abrupt, '*Ne faites pas la guerre*,' he yelled at Eban. 'At any rate, don't shoot first,' he warned. 'It would be catastrophic if Israel were to attack.' Eban tried to explain but to no avail. De Gaulle was in no mood to listen.

At No. 10 Downing Street, Prime Minister Harold Wilson invited Eban to join a cabinet meeting. Sitting alongside Wilson, 'Drinking strong tea and receiving assaults of smoke from Wilson's pipe', Eban explained the situation. Wilson responded by saying that his cabinet had agreed that Nasser's policy of blocking the Straits must not be allowed to stand. 'If necessary,' Wilson added, 'Britain will join with others in an effort to open the Straits of Tiran.' Eban's next stop was Washington, the most important leg of his diplomatic mission.

## A change of mission

At National Airport, Washington, Eban, accompanied by Gideon Rafael, Israel's ambassador to the UN, met Avraham (Abe) Harman, Israel's ambassador to the United States. Harman took Eban aside, gave him a closed envelope and said, 'You have to see this before entering into any discussion with any official'. In his suite at the Mayflower Hotel, Eban opened the envelope and took out a telegram addressed to Ambassador Harman, signed by Prime Minister Eshkol, and dated the night before:

URGENT. EYES ONLY.

To: Harman, Washington.

From: The prime minister. Date and hour: 25.5.1967, 2000.

The foreign minister and you should know that, following developments over the last 24 hours, we are anticipating an imminent Egyptian-Syrian attack. Therefore it is necessary to convey to the government of the United States, with all urgency, the following message: A. there is a danger of an all-out imminent offensive on Israel by Egypt-Syria. Against this background there must be an immediate implementation of the American commitment, both in declaration and action., i.e. a declaration of the government of the United States saying that it regards an attack on Israel as an attack on itself. Such a declaration should be accompanied by instructions to American forces in the region to co-ordinate

71

*their activities with the Israeli Defence Forces against any
possible attack.* STOP. *B. whatever they say to you just say
that you will report back to your government.* STOP.
*Because of the urgency of the matter it is necessary to
convey this message immediately to the highest American
level, if possible to the president himself, or in his absence to
Rusk. If the foreign minister is already in the United States
then he should carry out this mission, if not – do it yourself.
Don't, in any circumstances, ring back. Eshkol.*

The telegram shocked Eban 'to the very core'. He had been sent
to warn world leaders that Israel could not tolerate the closure of
the Straits. Now he was being asked to tell the Americans that an
Arab attack was imminent – something he did not believe. For,
while the Arabs *had* concentrated huge forces along their borders
with Israel, Eban knew from his own sources that these forces
were in a *defensive* position and not about to attack. In addition,
the new instructions from Eshkol were for him to demand that
Washington declare that an attack on Israel would be regarded as
an attack on itself. This, thought Eban, was *chutzpah* (impudent
cheek). For why should America, which was fighting in Vietnam,
issue a declaration that would commit it to fight in the Middle
East? Eban, by now very angry, threw the telegram to Gideon
Rafael, saying, 'Look at this!' Having looked, Rafael said, 'The
man who sent this telegram is mad – Prime Minister or not . . .
This telegram is crazy . . . utterly implausible . . .'

What Eban and Rafael did not know was that the message,
signed by Eshkol, had been heavily edited by Rabin who wanted
to know *exactly* how committed the United States was to the
Israeli cause.

When Eban calmed down, he said to Rafael, 'These are orders
with which I must comply'.

A meeting was arranged for Eban to see Secretary of State
Dean Rusk. Eban, accompanied by Rafael, went straight to the
point of the matter in hand: 'I have a most urgent message to
convey to you,' he said, and then told Rusk about the telegram he
had received, and Israel's assessment that the Arabs were about to
launch a massive attack.

Dean Rusk was not expecting such a message. His information

was that the Arabs were *not* in an offensive posture nor any kind of readiness to attack. Eugene Rostow, Undersecretary of State for Political Affairs: 'Rusk was very struck by the telegram and asked Foreign Minister Eban to read it at dictation speed. He and others then took notes of its contents.'

Rusk instructed Rostow to call the intelligence services at the Pentagon to see whether they could confirm Eban's information. When Rostow returned, he said that there was no evidence whatsoever to support what Eban had said and that an Arab offensive was not pending. Rusk, by now annoyed, turned to Eban, and said, 'Did you give me that information to justify a pre-emptive strike by Israel?' Eban, also annoyed, said, 'I gave you the information as I received it'.

The minute Eban left the meeting, Eugene Rostow telephoned the Egyptian ambassador and said, 'We have a report here, which we hope isn't true. We don't think it's true and, from the Egyptian point of view, it had better not be true'.

### 'Israel will not be alone unless it decides to go alone . . . '

A meeting was arranged for Eban to see President Johnson who wanted to make sure that Eban left Washington with the right message. Johnson had enough trouble on his hands with the war in Vietnam. The last thing he needed was a problem in the Middle East. He had to rein in the Israelis. After consulting his National Security advisers, he summed up their views and said, 'Come sundown, I'm the one who's gotta put the bell on this cat'. He then said to Secretary of Defence Robert McNamara, 'Bring Eban in here, into the family quarters of the White House, so we can work him over'. Eban was taken to the Oval Room.

Eban opened the discussion: 'If Israel is denied access to the Gulf of Aquaba, its primary line to East Africa and Asia, half of the world, will be cut off . . . Nasser has committed an act of aggression and his objective is the strangulation of Israel. Israel is confronted with two alternatives: surrender or stand'. Eban then asked the President, 'What can – and will – the US do to carry out its commitment to keep the Straits and the Gulf open?' Turning to the telegram from Eshkol, Eban told the president that the Israeli assessment was that the Arabs were planning to go on the offensive.

73

President Johnson said, 'Your Cabinet should know that our best efforts and best influence will be used to keep the Straits and the Gulf open to Israeli ships . . . ' He then mentioned the idea of sending an international armada to pass through the Straits in defiance of Nasser's closure policy. But he did not volunteer to arrange the armada. On the contrary, Johnson saw it as Israel's task. '*Israel*,' he said to Eban, 'ought promptly to get some judgment as to what other maritime powers are willing to do, what the French and British are willing to do. Any participation of the USA,' he added, 'will need the approval of Congress. I need time. I need the support of the Congress. Without that, I am simply a six-foot-four Texan'. Johnson then added, 'We do not believe that the Arabs are about to attack Israel. And if they do, you'll lick 'em – if not in seven days, in a short war.' Johnson then took out a piece of paper and read it as though it was a sacred text. What he read was: 'Israel will not be alone unless it decides to go it alone'. He finished by saying, 'You are not in danger . . . you are in a very difficult situation . . . '[10]

After Eban had gone, Johnson turned to Rostow and Robert McNamara and said, 'I have failed. They are going to go to war'. 'No, no, Mr President,' said Rostow and McNamara in unison, 'he is certainly going to convey your message, and the Israeli cabinet will take it very seriously.'

Back in Israel, Eban went straight to a cabinet meeting and reported the conversations he had had in Paris, London and Washington, but he did not mention that President Johnson had *not* actually volunteered to arrange for an armada to pass through the Straits, and that the task of organizing such an international force was, effectively, *Israel's*. In the discussion that followed his report, Minister of Labour Yigal Allon suggested that Israel should, 'Act tomorrow'. Minister Haim Givati said, 'If we do not strike first, Nasser will finish us.' General Ezer Weizman, Head of Operations, said, 'The war will be difficult, but we have no other option but to fight . . . We can beat the Arabs simply because we are better.' Even Prime Minister Eshkol, who from the beginning of the crisis had tried to hold back, was now in favour of going to war. There were two reasons for his change of heart: his military advisers were putting him under enormous pressure to take the initiative and act, and he knew that he could not keep the whole nation indefinitely mobilized without damaging the Israeli economy.

But the cabinet was still divided. Several ministers strongly opposed going to war. Eban's reticence about the US stance had clouded the issues and left some with the belief that – across the Atlantic – an American President was trying to arrange an international armada to open the Straits of Tiran and put an end to the crisis. They had no way of knowing this was not so.

The Israeli Cabinet continued to discuss Eban's report until five in the morning, then Eshkol sent his ministers home to get some sleep. A vote was not taken that night, but it was clear that the cabinet was evenly divided. Nine, including Eshkol, were in favour of embarking on war and nine were against.

*Chapter 9*

# Eshkol's black Sunday

On 28 May 1967, the Israeli cabinet gathered at 10 a.m. Eshkol set the tone. Prime Minister Eshkol, who had the night before sided with ministers in favour of going to war, had changed his mind. He said to his puzzled cabinet that he preferred to wait, 'another week or two'. Torn between Israeli pressures to take military action to open the Straits and international pressures not to embark on war, he was, characteristically some might say, finding it difficult to make a decision.

Two events which had taken place since the previous cabinet meeting had prompted Eshkol to change his mind. The first was a letter he had received from President Johnson that morning. In it, Johnson had called on him to show restraint and not strike. Eshkol knew that he should not go to war without American support, for he would need the Americans to neutralize the Soviets and re-fill Israel's arsenal after the war. The letter had significantly added to the pressure that had been mounting on Israel during the last few days not to take military action. Furthermore, in the middle of the night, John Haydon, the CIA representative in Israel, had visited Meir Amit, Head of Mossad. Angry, Haydon had spoken sharply, but it is most unlikely that he had President Johnson's authorization to make the threats he made that night:

> Haydon: 'If you strike, the United States will land forces in Egypt to defend her.'

> Amit: 'I don't believe you.'

> Haydon: 'It is important for you to have the United States on your side, rather than on the other side.'[11]

Amit had probably reported this conversation to Eshkol, and this had reinforced the effect of President Johnson's letter.

Then the Russians began a curious series of interventions. Leonid Chuvyakin, the Soviet ambassador to Israel, woke up Eshkol's aide in the middle of the night and said that he must see Prime Minister Eshkol immediately. Chuvyakin had just received a coded telegram from Moscow and was instructed to deliver it to Eshkol at once.

At 2.10 a.m., Chuvyakin arrived at the Dan Hotel, where Eshkol was staying and gave Eshkol the telegram. It was from Prime Minister Kosygin and it called on Eshkol to calm things down. 'It is easy to ignite a fire,' warned Kosygin, 'but putting out the flames may not be nearly as simple.' Clearly, having lit the fire with false rumours, the Russians were now getting cold feet.

The night meeting between Eshkol and Chuvyakin went on for two hours. Chuvyakin recalls, 'I urged Eshkol to stop the escalation, stop the concentration [of forces] on the Syrian border and to start negotiations with the Arab states'.

The continuous pressure from Washington and Moscow, and especially the letter from President Johnson, had taken their toll on Eshkol. He decided to delay taking action and the cabinet accepted his wish. It was now time for him to convey the cabinet's decision to the nation and to the impatient military commanders.

## A disastrous speech
Eshkol went to the broadcasting studios of *Kol Israel*. The nation was holding its breath in anticipation of his speech. Live on air, Eshkol said that the Israeli Defence Forces were on stand-by. He

then talked about the need to bring about a rapid end to the blockade of the Straits of Tiran, and said that the government had decided on a diplomatic course to spur world powers to take action to assure free passage of international shipping through the Straits. The content of the speech was unremarkable, but the delivery was disastrous. General Sheike Gavish recalls: 'You felt that the man who was speaking either had no self confidence or was afraid. It was very depressing.'

Eshkol's wife, Miriam, heard the broadcast on her car radio. Immediately realizing that something had gone wrong, she ordered her driver to take her straight to the studios. 'The press from all over the world was there,' she said. She found Eshkol. 'He was angry, his advisers all running around like mice.' She asked him, 'What happened?', and then noticed in front of him a piece of paper. It was the speech. Eshkol was sitting there rubbing his eye. 'What happened?' she repeated.

What had happened was that Eshkol had been hardly able to read what was written on the hastily typed pages that his aides had edited and written all over. He had just had a cataract operation – and, having rubbed his eye during the broadcast and displaced a contact lens, he could hardly see. In addition, although fluent in Yiddish, Eshkol was less so in modern Hebrew. One of the words in the speech was *Le'hasig* – meaning to pull back. He just could not pronounce it, nor did he know what it meant. Having seen the speech for the first time when he was about to go on air, he had not had time to study it. 'Have you gone mad?' Miriam Eshkol said to the aides. 'Couldn't you wait? Couldn't it have been written out clearly?'

It was too late. The damage had been done. The speech shocked the nation. Eshkol had failed to reassure his people.

### 'Why are you hesitating? Why are you afraid? Why are you waiting?'

From the radio studio, Eshkol was driven to military headquarters. There, in the 'Pit', were the top army brass.

Minister of Labour Yigal Allon and Chief of Staff Rabin joined Eshkol. Rabin had asked for this meeting because he wanted Eshkol, rather than himself, to explain the cabinet's decision to the commanders. By now, they were impatient. Nasser's closure of the Straits was for them the last straw. They all believed that war was inevitable and they wanted to strike first.

Eshkol was in a black mood because of his speech; Rabin was tired and subdued. Earlier that week, Rabin's prestige had suffered a blow when he had collapsed – from too much pressure, too little sleep and too many cigarettes – and disappeared from public view for twenty-four hours. Now – because Eshkol knew so little about military affairs – all eyes were fixed on him. Those who wanted to strike – obviously the commanders – were criticizing him for not putting enough pressure on Eshkol. Even more difficult for him to bear was the pressure from those who opposed war – notably David Ben-Gurion.

Although a hardliner, Ben-Gurion – the leader of the small opposition party, *Rafi* – had a golden rule that Israel should never go to war unless it had the full support of at least one super-power. Knowing that, in this instance, Israel did not have that support, he strongly opposed Rabin and accused him of bringing Israel to the verge of war. On 22 May, Ben-Gurion had shouted at Rabin, 'You have brought the state to a most dangerous situation. You are to blame for this. We must not go to war. We are isolated'. After this meeting Rabin had paced around the entrance of his home saying to himself, 'And what if he's right? *What if he's right?*' If this were not enough, he had had a meeting with Interior Minister Moshe Haim Shapira, the leader of the religious *Mafdal* Party, who had shouted at him, 'How dare you go to war? *How dare you?* You must dig-in! *Dig-in!*' This had been too much for Rabin. He had telephoned Ezer Weizman, Head of Operations, who recalls: 'I arrived at his home. Rabin was sitting on a sofa. The curtains were drawn. Leah, his wife, was pacing around in circles like a spinning top. Dr Gillon, his GP, was also there. Rabin said to me, "I have made a terrible mistake. I have brought the nation to the verge of war. I should resign". I said to him, "Yitzhak, what are you talking about? You should rest, then come back. You will lead the Israeli army to a great victory". Dr Gillon then gave Rabin a tranquillizer and he went to sleep.'[12] On 25 May, Rabin had put on his uniform and returned to his office.

Now, at the 28 May meeting he had requested with top members of the military, Rabin, Allon and Eshkol went into the room where neon lights emphasized the worry on all the faces. Among the officers present was Uzi Narkiss, the Commander of Central Command. He recalls: 'Everybody but me was chain smoking. The Prime Minister looked pale. He talked for a long time. He told us everything – about LBJ asking Israel not to launch a pre-emptive attack and that the president would deal with the Straits of Tiran; about the visit by the Soviet Ambassador in the middle of the night.'

When Eshkol had finished his monologue, he turned to the officers and said, 'You can talk openly'. They did – and all hammered home the same message, 'Stop holding us back. We must strike now'. The tone was acrimonious. General Matityahu (Matti) Peled, usually a polite soft-spoken officer, raised his voice and yelled at Eshkol, 'Why are you hesitating? Why are you afraid? Why are you waiting? We are ready. We must start – today! We must not wait any more!'

Military (Division) Commander Ariel Sharon rose to his feet, 'Now is the time to move . . . ' And he warned Eshkol of 'a sharp rise in the number of casualties with each day of waiting'. Rabin remained quiet. He also wanted to strike, but did not want to speak against the government in front of the commanders.[13]

Eshkol was visibly moved, but tried to calm things down, saying to the officers, 'We have to exhaust all other possibilities before going to war'. But this just added fuel to the debate until Allon intervened and suggested they bring the meeting to an end. The officers rose and Eshkol went home to his wife. Miriam Eshkol, 'They all attacked him – mercilessly – and were very angry. Like horses, they wanted to go . . . go . . . go. There was not one saint in Sodom and Gomorrah who would stand by him. Eshkol came out of the meeting very depressed . . . something within him was torn.'

## Moshe Dayan

The next morning the liberal newspaper *Ha'aretz* printed a sharply critical editorial on Eshkol:

> *If we could have confidence in Mr. Eshkol's ability to navigate the ship of state at the present time, we would*

*gladly follow him. However, we do not have such confidence. It seems that there are more and more people who lack that confidence; and Mr. Eshkol's performance on Kol Yisrael yesterday evening increased their number. He is not built to be prime minister and defence minister in the present situation . . . he should make way for a new leadership. Time is short.*[14]

Eshkol was isolated. When he returned from one meeting, Miriam Eshkol recalls: 'His face was ashen and I saw his disappointment and deep pain. It was real pain – pain because even his best friends didn't trust him.'

Shimon Peres, of Ben-Gurion's *Rafi* Party, was the prime mover in the efforts to get rid of Eshkol and restore his predecessor, Ben-Gurion, as prime minister. Ben-Gurion, aged eighty-one and leader of the small *Rafi* party – a splinter group that included people, such as Moshe Dayan and Shimon Peres – had been out of office for almost four years and cut off from military affairs. But, even though Ben-Gurion was against going to war without the support of a superpower, he was still considered tough, determined and more charismatic than Eshkol.

Eshkol was asked to stand down for Ben-Gurion, or at the very least accept him in his government as defence minister, but Eshkol refused. 'These two horses,' he said, 'cannot pull the same cart together'. Eshkol's refusal was accepted for, despite the criticism directed against him, his own party was against removing him.

Once Peres understood there was no chance of Eshkol standing down, he went to inform Ben-Gurion. Peres: 'Ben-Gurion was furious. He erupted like a torrent of lava and said, "I thought you were my friend – you are not. I thought you were a statesman – you are not. I thought you could be trusted – you cannot . . . "'

Peres and the *Rafi* group continued to fight for a change of leadership, still insisting that Eshkol should, at the very least, relinquish the defence minister's post and that Moshe Dayan, one of their *Rafi* colleagues, should replace him.

At fifty-two, Moshe Dayan – the former Chief of Staff, with black eye-patch and the hands of a farmer – was one of Israel's most colourful and controversial characters. A brave, charismatic leader, he was admired by men, and especially by women. Dayan was the sort of inspiring leader the Israelis were looking for. Eshkol's energies finally gave out and he agreed that Dayan should become his defence minister.

The *Rafi* party met in Tel Aviv to approve the appointment of Dayan, and Peres was sent to Eshkol: 'Prime Minister,' said Peres, 'I have come to inform you officially of *Rafi*'s decision to serve in your government with Moshe Dayan as defence minister'. After two weeks of calls for him to step down altogether, Eshkol was relieved to have saved his premiership. The compromise of giving up the Defence Ministry was painful but bearable. Then Peres continued, 'I must add Mr Prime Minister that we – the *Rafi* – have not changed our mind regarding your unsuitability for the task of prime minister'. Eshkol merely smiled and said, 'Okay . . . You have made your point'.

On 1 June, a green Saab drove through the gates of the Defence Ministry in Tel Aviv. At the wheel was Moshe Dayan – the new Defence Minister.


*Chapter 10*

# Prelude to war

The day after he said he would close the Straits of Tiran, President Nasser held a meeting at an armed forces headquarters. Turning to his Minister of War Shams el-din Badran, he said, 'I want you to go to Moscow tomorrow to meet the Soviet Minister of Defence and other officials. This will demonstrate that there is co-operation between the Soviet Union and Egypt.' Badran's task was to get Moscow's approval for Egypt to strike at Israel, for Nasser knew that closing the Straits to Israeli shipping meant war was inevitable. He wanted to be the first to strike – because the first to attack always has the advantage. To do so, he needed Soviet support to counteract any intervention by the Americans and re-supply him with arsenals after the war.

Badran left Cairo the next day, 25 May 1967, with a delegation which included representatives of the Foreign Ministry and the army. The same day, they met with a Soviet group headed by Minister of Defence, Marshal Andrei Gretchko.

Gretchko talked at length about the 'Special Egyptian-Soviet friendship'. Then Badran said, 'Since the 14th of May, Egyptian troops have been moving into the Sinai to deter the enemy and, in the event of an attack on Syria, to declare war on Israel'. But the Soviets fearing that they were losing control of the situation still wanted to de-escalate. Marshall Gretchko replied, 'We are sorry to say Minister of War that, as there is no border between the Soviet Union and Egypt, we cannot support you if there is a war between you and Israel.'

Badran, still determined to get permission to attack Israel, asked to meet with the Soviet Prime Minister, Alexei Kosygin. Batzanov Boris Terentievich, the first aide of Kosygin, was there when Badran and Kosygin met: 'Badran began with a long intro-duction about the dangerous situation in the Middle East – Israel threatening the whole world . . . Then he told Kosygin that Egypt wanted to take action against Israel. Kosygin didn't like these plans at all and told Badran that.'

Akopov Pavel Semenovish, a Soviet diplomat and an expert on Egypt, was also in the room when Badran requested Kosygin's approval for a pre-emptive strike: 'Alexei Kosygin in his usual tough style without any diplomatic mannerisms, said, "We, the Soviet Union, cannot give you our consent for your pre-emptive strikes against Israel. This would contradict our policy and our position. Should you be the first to attack, you will be the aggres-sors and we are against aggression. We are against military resolutions . . . We cannot support you."'

Badran brushed aside the Soviet requests to de-escalate and, for three consecutive days, hammered home the same message: let us pre-empt. Kosygin lost his temper and said, 'We support Egypt and the Arab people in their fight for just rights, but we cannot support aggression, cannot support the use of force. This contradicts our policy.'

Behind the scenes, the Soviets were making desperate efforts to rein in Egypt. Vladimir Semenov, Deputy Foreign Minister, asked Ahmad Hassan el-Feki, Egyptian Undersecretary of Foreign Affairs, to join him for dinner. It was a long evening – especially for Salah Bassiouny, Feki's special assistant, who was waiting for him to come back. 'Ahmad Hassan el-Feki returned at three-thirty or four in the morning,' he said. 'He was tired and worried. He said, "I have received a very clear message". I asked him, "What message?" He said, "The message is almost a plea for Egypt not to launch a war and that the Soviet Union is not prepared to be involved in any way."'

The Egyptian delegation had just finally accepted that the Soviets wanted them to de-escalate when a confusing incident changed everything. Badran: 'When I was going to the plane, Gretchko took me on one side and said, "Do not worry. If the Americans interfere, we are with you 100 per cent. If the United States interferes, we will come to help you – will come to your rescue."'

Back in Cairo, Badran reported to President Nasser that the Soviets would not approve a first attack, but then told him what Gretchko had said at the airport. The question, however, remains: Did Badran tell Nasser that Gretchko had said, 'We are with you *if the Americans intervene*'? Or did he just quote Gretchko as saying, 'We are with you'? Whatever the true situation, it seems that Nasser took it that the Soviets would not castigate him if he did not attack first. So, Nasser did *not* de-escalate. He just decided to let the Israelis attack first.

### 'It will be crippling.'

On 2 June, Nasser called a meeting to tell his commanders that Egypt could not strike at Israel because Moscow would not allow it, and that in the coming war they would have to absorb the first Israeli strike. Sidki Mahmoud, the Commander of the Air Force, jumped up and said, 'It will be crippling . . . It will make me a cripple. It will cripple the armed forces'. Shams Badran recalls what happened then: 'Amer said, "Sidki, do you really want to fight the United States? If we are the first to attack, the United States will join in and what will you do then? Do you want to fight the United States or take the first strike?" Sidki said, "Okay, okay, fine," and sat down. Nasser then asked Sidki Mahmoud, "If Israel strikes first, how would you assess our losses?" Mahmoud: "Between fifteen and twenty per cent."'

That same day, Nasser called another crucial meeting. 'Today I can tell you,' he said, 'that it is 100 per cent sure that Israel will attack. An American journalist has just told me that Israel is going to attack in seventy-two hours – the 5th of June.'[15] It is not known how the journalist knew this, but his information was correct. Nasser's comments, however, were not taken seriously – particularly by Amer, his Deputy Commander of the Armed Forces and political rival. Fawzi recalls: 'On the way out of the room, I saw Amer leaving with the Commander in Chief of the Air Force. They went into Amer's office . . . I heard the commander making fun of Nasser. He was being sarcastic, saying he didn't believe that there would be an attack on the 5th of June.'

### 'I read you loud and clear.'

In Israel, there was also confusion. In his report, after his Washington visit, Foreign Minister Eban had said – although he knew to the contrary – that President Johnson had promised, 'To take all measures to open the Straits for international shipping'. Prime Minister Eshkol, in turn, had sent Johnson a letter expressing his gratitude for this promise. But Washington had reacted promptly, saying that, in his meeting with Eban, President Johnson had *not* promised, 'To take *all measures*" to keep the Straits open'.

On 30 May, Meir Amit, Head of Mossad, had left for Washington to find out *exactly* what was going on. In a meeting with CIA Chief Richard Helms, he discovered that nothing had been done to organize an international armada to open the Straits of Tiran for Israeli shipping. He then insisted on seeing American Secretary of Defence McNamara who recalls Amit saying to him: 'I'll make certain statements and tell you certain things and I don't expect you to answer'. Amit then said to McNamara, 'You know our situation. I've come here on an unofficial mission. All we want is three things: one, that you re-fill our arsenal after the war. Two, that you will help us in the UN. Three, that you will isolate the Russians from the arena.' McNamara replied, 'I read you loud and clear,' then asked, 'How long will it take you [to defeat the Egyptians]?' Amit: 'My estimation is that it will take us a week.' Amit then added, 'I am going back home. I am going to recommend that we act. What do you think I should do before I leave?' McNamara: 'You have nothing to do here. Your place is there.'[16]

After this meeting, McNamara went straight to President Johnson, saying, 'The Israelis are intending to act'.

McNamara's way of responding to what Amit had said to him did not surprise anyone in Washington, for it was known that he was in favour of the Israelis striking first.

On his way home, Meir Amit wrote his report, then went straight to Eshkol's home in Jerusalem where the cabinet was meeting. Sitting on a sofa, with all eyes fixed on him, he read the report. When he finished, he said, 'Gentlemen, my impression is that there is not going to be any armada to open the Straits of Tiran'.[17]

Moshe Dayan, the newly-appointed Defence Minister, demanded that the cabinet decide on war. Not everybody agreed with him. Some – even Amit himself – wanted to give the Americans a chance to change their minds. The session continued until the early hours of the morning. At 5 a.m., Eshkol sent his ministers home to sleep. They re-convened at 8.15 a.m. It was Sunday, 4 June, and they decided to strike. There was to be war and Israel would shoot first.

### 'The Rabbi has ordered us to be glad because harder days are coming.'

That same day, Eshkol stayed in Hertzellia, at the Midrasha, a military installation. In the evening, he and his wife took a stroll in the garden. Miriam Eshkol recalls: 'Eshkol started humming. He was completely tuneless, but had this Hasidic song he liked to sing. It went, "The Rabbi has ordered us to be glad because harder days are coming". I knew that when he sang this song he was thinking about something important. I asked him, "Eshkol, what's going on?" He stopped humming and said to me, "You know what, Miriam, tomorrow it will start. There will be widows, orphans, bereaved parents. And all this I will have to take on my conscience." His heart was bleeding.'

*Chapter 11*

# The 1967 War

The general plan was for the Israeli air force to surprise the Egyptian air force and destroy it on the ground. The Israeli ground forces would then move into the Sinai to engage the Egyptian ground forces. The Israelis would reach Sharm el-Sheikh and open the Straits of Tiran to their shipping. If Jordan or Syria joined the war, the Israeli forces would turn against them – first attacking from the air and then engaging their ground forces.

Exactly forty-eight hours before the start of the war, Mordechai (Motti) Hod, Commander in Chief of the Israeli Air Force, assembled his squadron commanders and gave them his instructions. Ran Ronen, a commander, who attended the briefing, said, 'We were told that the time of attack was 07.45 hours. I went back to my squadron, but didn't tell the pilots anything. I wanted them to get a good night's sleep. At four in the morning, I woke up my two deputies and told them that there was going to be a war. We then woke up all the pilots. When they were all sitting in the briefing room, I went up to the blackboard and wrote 07.45.'

While the pilots were making their final preparations to take off, Defence Minister Dayan, Chief of Staff Rabin, and many others, gathered at the air force headquarters in Tel Aviv to follow the attack. This was the most crucial stage of the war. If the air strike succeeded, Israel would control the skies – tantamount to victory in a desert war.

### Meanwhile, in Cairo . . .

Deputy Supreme Commander Marshall Amer, Minister of War Shams Badran, Commander of the Air Force Sidki Mahmoud, and army commanders, were boarding a plane to go on a tour of inspection in Sinai. To ensure their safety, orders had been issued to anti-aircraft batteries to hold their fire. While most of Egypt's senior commanders were on their way to Sinai, General Bahey Edin Noufal was left alone, acting as duty officer at the military headquarters in Cairo.

Back in Israel, the first wave of planes took off at exactly 07.10

hours, for the 07.45 hours attack. Hod: 'The women soldiers who were working in the operations room began to move the formations on the map according to the plan. Two hundred jets took off in complete radio silence and flew to their targets.'

Ran Ronen, a Mirage squadron commander, said, 'I led the attack on Inshas, a large airfield with forty-two Mig-21s, just east of Cairo. We flew at a very low altitude just above the sea, at the height of the waves. Overland – over the sand dunes – we flew at an altitude of less than 100 feet. We flew low over the Delta. Farmers were waving to us, probably thinking we were Egyptian aircraft. We arrived at a point from where we had to climb for our attack. It was exactly 07.45 hours. We pulled up to 6000 feet. I looked down and saw the Egyptian Migs shining – sparkling on the sides of the runways – with the pilots sitting inside the cockpits. I looked to my right and saw fire and smoke coming up from all the other bases near Inshas. It was then that I realized that we had managed to surprise them.'

The Israeli planes had not been detected because they had flown very low and had come from unexpected directions. A warning from a Jordanian radar station, saying that Israeli jets were on the way to Egypt, could not be deciphered. General Noufal explains: 'General Abdel Moneim Riyad [the Egyptian commander sent to Jordan to co-ordinate the two fronts] sent us a warning signal from Ajloun airfield . . . but, as we had changed our code that day, we could not decipher it.'

### In Sinai and Cairo

Military commanders were gathered at Bir Tamada airfield in the Sinai to attend a meeting with Amer who was *en route*. Saad el-Shazly, the commander of a special task force, recalls: 'We were waiting for Amer. Around eight o'clock, we heard a huge explosive burst and went out to find out what was happening. We realized that the Israelis were attacking the Fayed airfield.'

In the air, Amer's plane had already crossed the Suez Canal. Minister of War Shams Badran: 'The pilot took a message from headquarters saying that all airports in Egypt were under attack from Israeli planes. We were astonished, especially Amer . . . '

While Amer was ordering the pilot to make a U-turn and go back, General Noufal was receiving a phonecall from Mahmoud

Barakat, the Chief of Operations of the Air Force. Barakat: 'The airfields are being attacked.' Noufal: 'What airfields?' Barakat: 'Our airfields in Sinai.' Noufal was shocked: 'I was all by myself in the headquarters. I passed on the information that the war had started and ordered all the commanders to get to their posts . . .'

On his return to Cairo, Amer hailed a taxi to take him to his headquarters. Egyptian Colonel Ahmed Fakher was there when Amer arrived: 'Amer looked in a state of collapse . . . He went into the building and tried to assess the situation, but soon realized how hopeless it was. Chief of Staff Fawzi was also there. 'Amer was very upset, angry and confused,' he recalls. 'He told the Commander in Chief of the Air Force [Sidki Mahmoud] to implement *Fahad* – our counter-attack plan. Sidki Mahmoud said: "I can't because we do not have aircrafts". Marshal Amer completely collapsed. I had never seen him like that before.'

### Taking the Sinai

Led by Generals Yisrael Tal, Avraham Yoffe and Ariel Sharon, the Israeli ground forces moved deeper into the desert to engage the Egyptians in the Sinai. On 2 June, at a military meeting, Dayan had said to General Gavish, 'I approve the plans, but I am imposing two limitations. First, you mustn't reach the Suez Canal. You have to stop ten kilometres before it. I don't want to see you on the bank of the canal'. (For Dayan, it was important that *after* the war Nasser could continue to use the Suez Canal. In that event, the Egyptian president would not be tempted to risk another fight which would cost Egypt vital revenues because no ships would be allowed to use the canal.) Dayan's second limitation concerned Gaza. 'You must not take the Gaza Strip,' he told Gavish. 'Let the Arabs stay there. I don't want anything to do with them. We will be outside; they'll be cut off inside. Let them eat each other up. I don't want us to be inside there.' (Dayan believed that, after Gavish's forces had taken Sinai, the Gaza Strip would fall into Israeli hands without a fight; politically, as there were hundreds of thousands of Palestinians in the Gaza Strip, he felt that Israel could do without this burden.)

In the heat of the battle, however, Dayan's instructions to Gavish were ignored. Tal, Yoffe and Sharon just kept moving deeper into the Sinai. Dayan tried to stop them, but when Rabin said that from a military point of view, 'It was impossible to stop,' Dayan accepted the situation and the forces moved to the Suez Canal.[18]

Likewise, on 5 June, when the Egyptian forces shelled Israeli settlements from Gaza, Gavish demanded that they should be allowed to move in. Having received the authorization from Dayan, he took Gaza.

So, although Dayan for long-term reasons had not wanted Israeli forces on the bank of the Suez Canal or in Gaza, he was – in spite of the perception of him as a strong leader – a defence minister who failed to impose his will on his subordinates.

### The tragic retreat

When Amer and Nasser realized that the situation was hopeless and that, with no air cover, their tanks and troops in the Sinai were easy prey for the Israelis, they convened the Revolutionary Command Council members. Amer asked each member present whether they were in favour of retreat from Sinai. He then gave each person's answer to Nasser. The 'vote' was unanimous for a retreat.

Amer phoned Chief of Staff Fawzi and asked him to draw up a plan for the withdrawal of their troops to the West Bank of the canal. Fawzi prepared a three days and four nights retreat operation, which Amer approved. But by the time Fawzi arrived to present his retreat plan to the field commanders, Amer had already telephoned General Salah Mohsen and given him instructions to pull back before daybreak.

It was chaos. Each unit turned and raced for home, its back exposed. None benefited from the phased cover that Fawzi's plan had specified. As the Egyptians pulled back, the Israelis, determined to prevent them from taking their weapons out of the Sinai, gave chase and attacked. Gavish recalls the scene: 'Thousands of Egyptian tanks and other vehicles were attacked from the air and from the ground, and destroyed. They were burning. It was a terrible sight. And the Egyptian army never did manage to get its equipment out of the Sinai. Most of the soldiers got out . . . on foot. They walked across the sands and managed to get all the way to the Suez Canal.'

Egyptian General Abdel Ghani Gamasy also witnessed the

retreat: 'It was an horrendous scene. With so few roads in Sinai, thousands of cars, tanks, artillery units and troops had to use roads that were an easy target for the Israeli air force. This meant a lot of casualties . . . The troops retreated in an unorganized way to the West Bank of the Suez Canal. It was a tragedy'.

Two thousand Egyptian soldiers had died fighting the Israelis. Ten thousand died in the retreat.

## A crushing blow for King Hussein

With his air force in ruins and his ground forces beginning their retreat, Nasser rang King Hussein of Jordan at his army headquarters. As the two leaders spoke, Israeli intelligence was running a tape recorder:

*Nasser: Hallo? Good morning, my brother.*

*Hussein: Yes, I can hear you.*

*Nasser: We are fighting with all our might on all fronts. We had some initial problems, but they are of no importance now. We shall overcome and God shall be with us. Will your Highness publish an announcement concerning the British and American participation? We will make sure the Syrians publish it as well.*

*Hussein: Okay, okay.*

*Nasser: A thousand thanks. Be strong. We are with you with all our heart. Today we have sent all our aeroplanes against Israel. Since early this morning our air force has been bombing the Israeli air force.*

*Hussein: Thousands of congratulations! Be strong![19]*

If Nasser was being economical with the truth to push Hussein to join the war, it was unnecessary. The King's forces were already fighting. Hussein had committed himself to war when he had met Nasser five days earlier and had stuck to his commitment.

Before the war, relations between Nasser and Hussein had been at a low ebb. Jordanian Radio had criticized Nasser for not being tough with the Israelis either on 13 November 1966 when the Israelis attacked the Jordanian village of Samua, or in April 1967 when the Israelis shot down the Syrian Migs. Nasser had reacted to the Jordanian criticism by calling the King, 'The CIA dwarf from Amman'.[20] But after Nasser had mobilized his forces into the Sinai, along with other Arab states, Hussein had decided to join them. On 30 May 1967, he had flown to Cairo for a talk with Nasser, which Amer and Saad Jumaa, the Jordanian Prime Minister, had also attended. Hussein had suggested that they should take the text of the Egyptian-Syrian Defence Agreement, substitute 'Jordan' for 'Syria' and sign a pact. Nasser had gladly agreed. Clause seven of the agreement stated that in the event of war, an Egyptian officer would command Jordanian forces.

The Israelis – through General Odd Bull, the UN truce supervisor – had sent a message to King Hussein: 'This war is between us and the Egyptians. If you don't join in, nothing will happen to you'. But with half his people Palestinians, Hussein felt he had little choice. He would prefer to be a loser than a traitor. When the Israeli message reached him, he had said dryly, 'Jordan is not out. Jordan is already engaged. Jordan is already involved in military activities'.

This was a fateful mistake. The Israelis reacted furiously. King Hussein recalls: 'Our air force was literally destroyed on the ground. We managed to shoot down four Israeli aircraft but, as we had only two bases and those had already been taken out by the Israelis, our remaining aircraft couldn't take off.'

With no air cover, Hussein's forces were forced to retreat. The King was standing on a hill and what he saw shocked him: 'My troops were coming back in small groups, very tired. Many of them were saying, "Please, Your Majesty, find us some air cover and we'll go right back". Of course, everything was over by then and I remember asking all these boys to move on to Zarka, just east of Amman, so we could begin to reorganize whatever remained. There were also air raids on the way there . . . I saw all the years that I had spent since 1953 trying to build up the country and army, all the pride, all the hopes, destroyed. That was a turning point in my life – physically and in every other respect . . . I have never received a more crushing blow than that.'

Within a week of Jordan entering the war, King Hussein had lost the battle.

## Golan Heights–Moscow–Washington

On 8 June at 7 p.m., Prime Minister Eshkol summoned his ministers. Just four days after the war had begun, the fighting had ended on all fronts: the Egyptian Army was defeated, Jordan was crushed, and the West Bank and Jerusalem were in Israeli hands.

The only Arab state, it seemed, that would survive the war intact was Syria. Even the Americans found this ironical. McGeorge Bundy, President Johnson's Security Adviser, said to Foreign Minister Eban who was in America, 'Wouldn't it be strange if the country which had more to do with kindling the war than any other would be the only country to get off free?'[21] This summed up what Eshkol and his ministers were feeling. All the ministers – including Eshkol – wanted to approve what Rabin had just suggested: that they should move on to occupy the Golan Heights. Moshe Dayan, however, disagreed. Known to be suffering from a 'Russio-phobia', he was convinced that if Israel moved against the Syrians, 'The Russians would come' – would fight alongside the Syrians.

Minister of Labour Yigal Allon, himself a former general and a rival of Dayan, thought differently. 'The Syrians,' he stated, 'had been the main cause of the present crisis, and they might be the cause of future troubles.' He suggested attacking them. As for the Russians, said Allon, 'I don't think the USSR will declare war on Israel if we occupy 5 kilometres. I am willing to take the risk'.[22]

Eshkol informed the ministers that he had asked three Israelis who lived in Galilee to come to the meeting and express their opinion. None of the ministers opposed the idea. Even Dayan reluctantly agreed, saying, 'I don't think anything they say will change my mind, but I am willing to hear what they have to say.' The guests were invited into the cabinet room. They talked emotionally about how difficult it was to live in the shadow of the Syrians who, from their positions on the Golan Heights, shelled Israeli settlements. They wanted the ministers to unleash Israeli forces, take the Golan Heights, and push the Syrians back beyond artillery range.

When they left, it was clear that Moshe Dayan, the one minister who was opposing fighting the Syrians, was still unconvinced. 'We started the war with the aim of hitting the Egyptian army and opening the Straits of Tiran,' he said. 'On the way, we also took the West Bank. I don't think we should now open up a new front with Syria. If we are going to fight the Syrians just to make life easier for the settlements then I am against . . . In my opinion, it is easier to remove ten [Israeli] settlements than fight the Syrians . . . [I don't accept the idea that we should] tell the Syrians that *their* border should be moved because *we* have set up settlements close to it.' Dayan also suspected that the people who lived in the settlements were using this as an opportunity to acquire more land in the Golan Heights, and he thought that if they were allowed to do so they would never agree to give the Golan Heights back to the Syrians.[23]

No one – including Eshkol who was in favour of embarking on war against the Syrians – chose to over-rule him. After all, he was Moshe Dayan, the new Israeli war hero. The ministers decided that, for the time being, they would not authorize the military to attack the Syrians. But soon Dayan changed his mind. On 9 June, at 3.30 a.m., Mossad intercepted a cable sent from President Nasser to the Syrian President Nur el Din Attasi. *I think*, wrote Nasser, *that Israel is interested in concentrating its forces against Syria, in order to crush the Syrian Army . . . I would like to advise you to agree to end the hostilities and let U Thant, the Secretary General, know in order to keep the Syrian Army intact. We have lost this battle. God will be with us in the future.*

When Dayan saw the cable, he came to the conclusion that the Syrians would not put up serious resistance and rang David Elazar, who was in charge of forces in the north. Dayan: 'Are you ready for an attack?' Elazar: 'Yes, I am.' Dayan: 'So, go ahead and attack.' As if to explain why he had changed his mind, Dayan added, 'I'll tell you why I have approved the operation: A. Because Egypt accepted the cease-fire, and B. Because I have information that the Syrian front will collapse'. Elazar: 'Collapse or not, I don't know and I don't care. We will attack. Thank you very much. Bye-bye.'[24]

Chief of Staff Rabin was at home while all this was happening. Ezer Weizman, head of the operations branch, rang him. 'Come quickly,' he said to Rabin, 'Dayan has talked with Elazar and has ordered him to take the Golan Heights.'[25] Rabin took a helicopter and rushed to the north.

At the Dan Hotel, Eshkol was in for a shock when his wife called him to the phone. It was 8 a.m., and Dayan was on the line. 'We have gone up to the Golan Heights,' Dayan said. 'It's a farce,' Eshkol raged at him. The night before Eshkol had wanted to take the Golan Heights, and Dayan had said 'No'. Now Dayan had ordered the forces to do so. Was Dayan playing games – wanting to show that he – not the Prime Minister – was in charge? Was he trying to show that he – *not* Eshkol – was the saviour of the Israeli settlers in Galilee?

As General Hod unleashed his pilots to hit Syrian positions, all hell broke loose on the Golan Heights. He recalls: 'We attacked with everything we had . . . We dropped rockets, bombs and Napalm . . .'

Fighting continued throughout Friday night. On Saturday it looked as if the Israeli forces were about to gallop towards Damascus. This was a step too far for the Russians. In Moscow, three men – Premier Alexei Kosygin, Foreign Minister Andrei Gromyko and Head of KGB Yuri Andropov – went down to one of the Kremlin's basements. They passed through to a bulky wooden teleprinter standing in a corner. This was the 'hot line' equipment,[26] the device that enabled American and Soviet leaders direct contact so that they could defuse tension when a nuclear war seemed imminent. Now, the Russians were going to use it to send the following chilling hot-line warning (published for the first time) to President Johnson:

*Saturday, June 10, 1967*
*Sight Translation – 9:00*
*Received by President – 9.05*

*The White House*
*To President Lyndon B. Johnson*

*Dear Mr. President:*
*. . . A very crucial moment has now arrived which forces us, if military actions are not stopped in the next few hours, to adopt an independent decision. We are ready to do this. However, these actions may bring us into a clash, which will lead to a grave catastrophe . . . We propose that you*

*demand from Israel that it unconditionally cease military
action in the next few hours ... We propose to warn Israel
that, if this is not fulfilled, necessary actions will be taken,
including military.*

*Please give me your views.*

*A. Kosygin*[27]

Kosygin's forces in the Middle East had been on high alert since
the beginning of the crisis, and were ready to strike at Israel.
General Reshetnikov Vassily Vassilievich, Commander of Corps
Strategic Aviation, recalls: 'I received an order to prepare a regi-
ment of strategic aviation to fly to Israel to bomb a number of
military targets. We started the preparation, studied the maps,
examined Israeli air defence systems ... It was a real rush ... We
loaded the bombs and were awaiting the signal to go.'

In Washington, President Johnson and his advisers convened in
the White House situation room.[28] Ambassador Llewellyn
Thompson checked the Russian text again to be absolutely sure
that the word 'military' was a part of the message in the phrase
'Necessary actions will be taken, *including military*'.[29] The president left the room and, while he was out, Secretary of Defence
Robert McNamara asked CIA Director Richard Helms whether,
'we should turn the Sixth Fleet around to sail toward the eastern
Mediterranean'. Helms replied, 'If we do so, Soviet submarines
monitoring the Fleet's operations will report immediately to
Moscow that the task force has stopped circling and has begun
heading eastward'.[30]

On President Johnson's return, McNamara mentioned the
possibility of sending the Sixth Fleet to the region. Johnson:
'What distance is the American fleet from the Syrian coast?'
McNamara: 'A hundred miles.' Johnson: 'Move them to within
fifty miles.' McNamara picked up a security telephone and gave
the order.[31]

A serious American-Soviet crisis was developing and tension
in the situation room was high. Helms: 'The conversation was
in the lowest voices I had ever heard in a meeting of that kind.
The atmosphere was tense.'[32] Twenty-five minutes after receiving
the hot-line message from Moscow, President Johnson replied:

*Saturday, June 10, 1967*
*Approved by President – 9:30*
*Transmitted by US Molink – 9:39*

To: *The Chairman of the Council of Ministers of the USSR*
*A. Kosygin*
From: *President Lyndon B. Johnson*

*Dear Mr. Kosygin,*
*I have your message. You should know that late last night*
*our Secretary of State sent a most urgent message to Israel to*
*say that we considered it very important that Israel demon-*
*strate by actions on the ground that its orders for a cease fire*
*are effective . . . Our Ambassador Barbour in Israel has now*
*sent us a message, at 7:45 Washington time, today, saying*
*that Israelis tell him they believe the firing has stopped as of*
*this moment.*

*Lyndon. B. Johnson*[33]

Kosygin instructed Gromyko to check with Barkovsky Anatoly
Aleksandrovich, the Soviet Ambassador in Damascus. He recalls:
'Gromyko asked me what was happening in Damascus. While we
were talking I saw two Israeli planes flying over Damascus. I
described the scene to Gromyko.'

Kosygin dictated the following hot-line message to President
Johnson:

*Saturday, June 10, 1967*
*Sight Translation – 10:00 am*
*Received by President – 10:05 am*

*White House*
*To President Lyndon B. Johnson*

*Dear President Johnson,*
*I have read your reply to our message and I must tell you*
*that your information concerning the cessation of military*
*actions in Syria on the part of Israel is not borne out.*

*We have constant and uninterrupted communications with Damascus. Israel, employing all types of weapons, aviation, artillery, tanks, is conducting an offensive towards Damascus. Obviously your Embassy in Syria can confirm this if you have representatives there. Military actions are intensifying. It is urgently necessary to avoid further bloodshed. The matter cannot be postponed . . .
Respectfully,*

*A. Kosygin*[34]

Meanwhile, extraordinary events were happening on the Golan Heights. On 10 June, the Syrian government, realizing its desperate situation, had issued an announcement on Radio Damascus at 9.30 a.m., that Israeli forces had captured the town of Kuneitra. They were trying to spur the UN Security Council to adopt a cease-fire resolution. In reality, no Israeli soldier was in sight of the town. But when the Syrian troops in Kuneitra heard the news they began to flee, thinking they were encircled by the Israelis. The Syrian general, whom we interviewed but agreed not to name, was on his way to Kuneitra when he realized that troops were leaving the town. 'The pull out [from Kuneitra] was done in total chaos,' he recalls. 'The retreating soldiers had left their weapons behind. Some were running home even before the Israeli soldiers had reached anywhere near their position.'

Moshe Dayan, despite pressure from Washington and the UN to stop the fighting, ordered the Israeli forces to take advantage of the Syrian retreat. 'Move forward,' he instructed. Taking Kuneitra would give Israel better control of the Golan Heights, and turn the battle into a stunning victory over the Syrian army.

Back in Moscow, Kosygin dictated a new message to Johnson. Victor Sukhodrev, an operator in the hot-line room, was there: 'Kosygin was rehearsing what he was going to dictate to President Johnson. He said that one of their [Syria's] towns was about to fall to the Israelis and he wanted to put the name of that town into his message. Gromyko who was also there was having trouble recalling the name of the town. I said, "Kuneitra". Gromyko looked at me with a slight smile on his face and repeated, "Kuneitra."'

The message went on the hot line:

*Saturday, June 10, 1967*
*Sight Translation – 11:40*
*Received by President – 11:43 am*

*White House*
*To President Lyndon B. Johnson*

*Dear Mr. President*
*By my instructions, we have just communicated with*
*Damascus. From Damascus we have been informed that*
*military actions are in progress in the vicinity of the city of*
*Kuneitra . . .*

*Respectfully,*

*A. Kosygin*[35].

Pressure on the Israelis to stop the fighting was mounting from the Russians, the Americans and a dozen others, especially at the United Nations in New York. Foreign Minister Eban tried to telephone Eshkol, but the Prime Minister had gone north to follow the fighting. His wife, Miriam, picked up the phone. Eban: 'Tell Eshkol to stop the war. The United Nations is putting pressure on me.' Miriam Eshkol contacted Eshkol. Shouting, trying to overcome the noises on the line, she said, 'Eban wants you to stop the war because he can't stand the pressure from the United Nations'. Eshkol not wanting to hear that, shouted back, 'I can't hear you'. Miriam, 'What do you mean you can't hear me? I'm telling you explicitly in Eban's words'. 'No,' said Eshkol, 'I can't hear you because the line is not good. I'll come home and then we'll speak.' Apparently, he wanted to give the military more time to finish the job before considering Eban's arguments.

On Saturday, 10 June at 2.40 p.m., Kuneitra fell into Israeli hands.

Gideon Rafael, the Israeli representative to the UN, was telephoned by Moshe Sasson, the director of military liaison in the Foreign Ministry in Jerusalem, and told to agree to a cease-fire. Rafael went to Hans Tabor, the President of the Security Council, and said, 'I have an emergency statement to make'. Fedorenko Nicolai, the Soviet representative, interrupted and said, 'Mr President, you cannot permit a representative to speak out of order in the proceedings. I will not permit that'. But Hans Tabor allowed Rafael to announce that Israel had agreed to accept the cease-fire.

In the White House situation room, President Johnson was keeping an eye on the proceedings in the UN. When he saw Rafael on television, he sent a message to Kosygin. It read: *We have categorical assurances from the Israelis that there is no Israeli advance on Damascus*. At 6.30 p.m., that day, the cease-fire came into effect.


*Chapter 12*

# Land-for-peace offer

Israel was now in possession of large territories – West Bank, Golan Heights, the Sinai, Gaza and Jerusalem – and the government feared that the international community would put pressure on it, as it had done after the 1956 War, to leave *all* the occupied territories. It seemed sensible, therefore, to take the initiative, put forward an offer, and pre-empt international *diktat*.

On 13 June 1967, just three days after the fighting had ended, the ministers met at Prime Minister Eshkol's home to come up with a land-for-peace offer. Israel would withdraw from Arab land it had just occupied during the war if the Arabs, in return, would recognize Israel and sign a lasting peace with it.

In New York, a few days later, Gideon Rafael and Foreign Minister Eban received a long telegram from Jerusalem. It was dated 19 June 1967, and was a summary of the Israeli peace proposal. Rafael and Eban were delighted. Rafael thought that the proposal showed magnanimity; Eban that it was, 'The most dramatic initiative ever taken by an Israeli government'. They met with the Americans. The following is an extract from a report written by Dean Rusk:

*Secretary [of State] and Ambassador Goldberg received Israeli Foreign Minister Eban along with Rafael and Harman 7:15 p.m. June 21. Hour's conversation. Eban stated Israeli inter-ministerial committee had come to some tentative conclusions which he would like to discuss with secretary but not others . . .*

***Egypt-Israel.*** *Israelis wanted peace treaty on basis [of] present international frontiers. From Egypt, Israel wanted only security, no territory . . . Important thing is that there must be treaty which committed Egyptians. Israelis unwilling to accept another understanding on basis of assumptions.*

***Israel-Syria.*** *Israelis would like peace treaty on the basis of the international frontiers with some understanding that Syrian hills overlooking Israeli territory would be demilitarised . . . Eban concluded that Israel was offering both Egypt and Syrian complete withdrawal to international frontiers. These terms not ungenerous.*

***Gaza.*** *Eban noted that Egypt had never claimed Gaza. Israel would make every effort on behalf of Gaza population.*

***West Bank of Jordan.*** *Eban said Israeli thinking 'less crystallised'.*[36]

After Eban had finished his presentation, Goldberg said, 'I've told the President of your proposal and he thinks what you have said is very constructive'.

On 18 July, Goldberg met with Anatoly Dobrynin, the Soviet Ambassador to the US, to come to a formula based on the Israeli peace proposal, which would satisfy both the Israelis and the Arabs. Dobrynin recalls: 'We tried various versions of the resolution text. We went to lunch without our briefcases and were writing the resolutions on napkins. "Let's try it this way or let's do it that way", we kept saying. Finally Goldberg wrote something and said, "Do you think it will fit?" I said, "Yeah, I think it will go right."'

Dobrynin passed on the formula to Moscow so that they could convey it to the Arabs. In the meantime, Goldberg asked to see Eban and Rafael. Eban recalls the meeting: 'Ambassador Goldberg handed us a paper that really made our hair stand on end. It was talking about withdrawal from all the occupied territory [the Sinai, the Golan Heights, West Bank and Gaza] and, when it came to peace, it didn't say, "just and lasting peace". I exploded in indignation.'

Goldberg was taken aback by the Israeli's reaction. 'All right,' he said. 'We'll have to think about this further . . . '

Dobrynin, the Soviet ambassador, was also in for a shock. When he met again with Goldberg to discuss their formula, Goldberg denied having anything to do with it, saying, 'I didn't say this'. Dobrynin searched in his pockets and found the napkin on which Goldberg had written their formula, then rushed to Secretary of State Rusk. 'Dean,' said Dobrynin. 'Do you know the handwriting of Goldberg? Well look at this – who wrote it?' Rusk: 'This is Goldberg's handwriting.'

But none of this really mattered, for the Soviet-American formula had not only made the Israelis' hair stand on end, but the Arabs, too. Salah Bassiouny was on an Egyptian committee which looked into the Goldberg-Dobrynin formula: 'We concluded that this proposal was the best we were likely to get and that we should accept it. We presented our findings to the Foreign Minister. He took the document and went with several of his staff to a meeting with the President. When he got back, we found out that the proposal had been rejected and that he had recommended its rejection'.

Egypt was not yet in a state of mind to make a rational compromise. Soon those in the Israeli cabinet – notably Yisrael Galili and Yigal Allon – who were against the land for peace proposal gained the upper hand, and the 19 June 1967 proposal was withdrawn.

The stalemate would last another decade. The greatest opportunity in the fifty years war to secure peace had been lost.

# 3 SADAT'S HISTORIC QUEST FOR PEACE

## Introduction

On 28 September 1970, President Gamal Abdel Nasser – who had led Egypt since the 1952 coup against King Farouk, and throughout all following wars against Britain, France and Israel – died suddenly from a heart attack. In one of the most astonishing state funerals of modern times, millions of Arabs mourned the man who had championed the Arab cause in the Middle East and throughout the world.

The man chosen to succeed Nasser was his Vice-President, Anwar el-Sadat, who was regarded by colleagues and enemies alike as a 'yes-man' who would continue Nasser's pan-Arabism and pro-Soviet policies. At the time of his appointment, there was nothing to suggest that Sadat – whose autobiography begins with, 'I, Anwar el-Sadat, a peasant born and brought up on the banks of the Nile' – would one day court the US, take the initiative in offering to make peace with Israel, do the unthinkable and expel Soviet military advisers, and go on a visit to Jerusalem that would astonish both the Arab and international world.

In 1971, when Sadat first suggested making peace, nobody, including the USA, took him seriously. When, as a result, he threatened war, his own ministers, military commanders and the Soviets did not at first believe him. His expulsion of Soviet military advisers in 1972, led Israel and the US to conclude that, having lost Soviet support, he would not now attempt to go to war.

In 1973, when he embarked on the October War, Egyptian forces crossed the Suez Canal and won a battle against the

Israelis. Although Egypt, backed up by Syria, lost the war, Sadat – feeling he could now use his military achievements to talk to the Israelis as an equal – re-embarked on his land-for-peace initiative and made his historic visit to Jerusalem.

On 17 September 1978 – following negotiations mediated by President Jimmy Carter at Camp David – a document entitled 'Framework for Peace in the Middle East' was signed by Sadat and Begin (witnessed by Carter). As far as the US and outside world was concerned, peace between Egypt and Israel had been achieved. In reality, it took another six months of haggling over details before President Sadat and Prime Minister Menachem Begin signed the final peace accord – the first ever between Israel and an Arab state.

In 1981, Sadat paid the price for peace with his own life. He was assassinated by Muslim extremist officers in the Egyptian army who had always opposed his pro-Western stance and the peace accord with Israel.

## Chapter 13

# Changing camps?

On Monday, 28 September 1970, at precisely 6 p.m., a telephone call startled Egypt's Vice President Anwar Sadat out of a deep sleep. Along with President Gamal Abdel Nasser and other top Egyptian officials, Sadat had spent a hectic week at an Arab summit attempting to resolve the bloody clash between King Hussein of Jordan and the Palestinian fighters. To everyone's surprise, the summit was a success. But it had taken a heavy toll on President Nasser who was exhausted by the time he accompanied the last of the Arab dignitaries to the airport. At about 3.30 p.m., when Nasser reached his home, he said to his wife, Taheya, that he was too tired to eat lunch, and went to his room. Taheya, realizing he was unwell, called a doctor.

Meanwhile, Sadat – who had given orders not to be disturbed unless it was very urgent – was awakened by the unexpected telephone call. The caller, Mohamed Ahmed, President Nasser's private secretary, told Sadat to come at once to the president's house at Manshiat el-Bakri. Upon arrival, Sadat was taken to Nasser's bedroom. The room was crowded with government ministers and doctors. In their midst, on his bed, lay President Nasser. He was dead.

Nasser's sudden death from a heart attack was a blow to the Arab world. The man who had pioneered the cause of Pan Arabism, defied the colonial powers and supported a plethora of liberation movements, was gone. For Egypt, his death was a catastrophe. Who could replace this charismatic leader?

With the consent of the ministers who had gathered around Nasser's death bed, Vice President Sadat was chosen as acting president. Sadat, a Free Officer who had hardly occupied any ministerial posts, was not a controversial figure. He directed *Al-Gumhuria*, one of Egypt's official newspapers. On 20 December 1969, when Nasser had named Sadat interim Vice President while he attended an Arab summit in Morocco, the news was received with surprise by the cabinet. But none of the powerful ministers was worried about Sadat's sudden rise in the political hierarchy: they thought it was temporary; and regarded Sadat as a Nasser 'yes man' who would not take the initiative. Indeed, Sadat's low profile was so unthreatening that even Nasser, who constantly worried about plots to oust him, did not alter Sadat's status when he returned from Morocco.

Worldwide heads of states and prime ministers flocked to Cairo for Nasser's funeral. It was no surprise that Egypt's Soviet ally sent a top-level delegation headed by Alexei Kosygin, the president of the USSR. But the high level at which the Western powers decided to be represented was a surprise. Nasser was, after all, the symbol of defiance against the West. Egypt had broken off diplomatic relations with the US after the 1967 War and was regarded as a Soviet surrogate in the Middle East. Nevertheless, the US sent Elliot Richardson, Nixon's attorney general, and Britain sent its former prime minister Sir Alec Douglas-Home.

On the day of the funeral, Sadat led the procession along the bank of the Nile. The foreign delegates, left waiting patiently under a canopy of desert-style tents, were meant to follow behind him. However, a soldier suddenly arrived with orders for the delegates to be taken to the nearby Revolutionary Command Council building. The Egyptian leadership had decided that it was too risky for such prominent personalities to march through the crowds. The delegates were crowded into the hall of the building and asked to wait. Elliot Richardson, the head of the American delegation, recalls: 'It was strange, like being at a large cocktail party. All you had to do was make a half-turn and there was the Emperor of Ethiopia, the president of the USSR, the former British prime minister.'

The delegates were not the only ones who were whisked into the Revolutionary Command Council building. Just as the procession started, acting president Sadat collapsed from heat exhaustion and, unknown to the visitors, was now lying in a bed in the basement. As Sadat rested behind the scenes, he committed an almost sacrilegious act by summoning the US delegate to his bedside. Elliot Richardson, whose country did not even have diplomatic relations with Egypt, was astonished when told that Egypt's acting president wanted to speak to him privately. 'I was talking to the prime minister of Ceylon,' he recalls, 'when a soldier weaved his way through the crowd and said would I please follow him, Sadat would like to meet me. We went down the stairs to a dimly lit room. There, propped up in a bed, was Sadat. I could just see his lean face and moustache. He smiled and held out a cold clammy hand. He said he'd been told that he had heat exhaustion and had had to withdraw from the procession.'

Sadat's gesture was a calculated political move that he had undertaken away from the prying eyes of his pro-Soviet colleagues. For Elliot Richardson, the message was clear: 'He began by telling me that he appreciated the United States sending a relatively senior delegation and that he wanted to thank President Nixon for having done so. He conveyed a clear feeling that he wanted to take advantage of this opportunity to turn a new page in the relationship between our countries.'

For Sadat to make such a radical shift in superpower alliance was not a simple matter. Nasser's pro-Soviet policy had become the backbone of Egypt's economic and military development and, with a majority of pro-Soviets within the cabinet, Sadat would need to play his cards carefully. Yet he was obviously keen to reveal his future intentions. Richardson: 'By sending for me, Sadat indicated that, if elected, he was ready to shift the relationship that Nasser had established with the Soviet Union to a new relationship with the United States . . . I was someone with access to the US president, secretary of state, and the national security adviser, and he expected me to convey to them what he had said . . . ' Richardson was thrilled by the encounter. Although he realized that Egypt's old guard would resist Sadat, he was also convinced that, if Sadat were elected president, the US would acquire an unexpected strategic ally and that the US government should seize the opportunity.

After Nasser's funeral, the Supreme Executive Committee of the Arab Socialist Union, convened to recommend the next Egyptian president. In the prolonged late-night meetings, Zakaria Mohiedin – who had held some of the country's most sensitive posts during Nasser's reign – seemed the natural successor. Party members, however, wanted to choose a weaker person who would abide by the will of the party. Thus, Hussein El-Shafei, second vice president, and acting president Anwar Sadat became the front runners. Abdel Majid Farid, who was then Secretary General of Nasser's ASU party, recalls how the decision was reached: 'Sadat was the convenient choice because Sadat said, "I am not Nasser and cannot do the things he was able to do. It will be up to the party to decide on political matters. I will merely implement the party decision". He deceived everyone.' Sadat had cultivated the image of a weak man who would toe the party line. On 15 October 1970, he was elected president. When parliament confirmed his appointment, he bowed to a sculpture of Nasser to reassure the assembly.

## Cloak-and-dagger approaches

On his return to the US, Elliot Richardson went to see President Richard Nixon and National Security Adviser Henry Kissinger. 'I told them,' he recalls, 'that I believed in Sadat's sincerity and that he understood the strategic implications of a shift of alliance and closer relationship with us.' Despite Richardson's assurances, the US administration was unimpressed. Kissinger: 'Our experts believed that Sadat was a transitional figure who would soon be replaced by Ali Sabri, Secretary General of the Arab Socialist Union, a man we knew to be close to Moscow'.[1]

When Sadat realized that his message had gone unheeded, he tried again. Resorting to an old army friend, General Abdel Moniem Amin, who was known to be pro-Western, Sadat asked him to make a discreet attempt to pass on a message to any American who remained based in Cairo. To avoid the attention of Egypt's secret police, General Amin asked a friend's daughter-in-law for assistance. Nadia Rachid, a sophisticated Egyptian, had worked at the American embassy until it was closed after the 1967 War. She knew where to find the few remaining officials, and General Amin assigned her the task of establishing contact. Rachid: 'I had to be very careful and didn't use the phone in case it was bugged. I even used a false name. The message I was asked to deliver was that Sadat wanted to establish direct relations with America, but couldn't do so publicly because the powerful pro-Soviet clique, known as the Ali Sabri Group, wouldn't allow it. What he needed was a secret channel to conduct talks with the US.'

The Americans, although somewhat surprised by this cloak-and-dagger approach, decided to pursue the lead. Nadia Rachid was asked to arrange a meeting between General Amin and Eugene Trone, head of the CIA in Cairo. This took place on 11 January 1971 at Trone's villa in the Cairo suburb of Maadi. General Amin recalls their first meeting: 'We had the radio turned up in case of bugs. I told Trone that Sadat was different from Nasser and was ready to make peace. If Israel would agree to retreat thirty miles from Suez, Egypt would re-open the Suez Canal [which had not been dredged since the 1967 War], normalize relations and move towards a peace agreement. We talked for two hours. It was a very positive meeting.' Two weeks later, the Americans, through Nadia Rachid, delivered a short note to General Amin saying: 'We're interested'.

Sadat's proposal, which followed this message, landed on Assistant Secretary of State Joseph Sisco's desk. 'Sadat,' Sisco explained, 'wanted a small-sized disengagement from the Suez Canal, but the more important thing was that he had taken the initiative and indicated that he wanted to work something out with the Israelis.'

Sadat had struck the right note. Only weeks before, Israeli Defence Minister Moshe Dayan had made a similar suggestion.

As Sisco recalls: 'Dayan also favoured the idea of a partial dis-engagement from the Suez and felt that this was something Israel should seriously consider.' Given that both Egypt and Israel had reached the same conclusion, an agreement now seemed possible. If Israel withdrew from the Suez Canal, then Sadat would dredge and re-open the canal, and peace might prevail.

### Sadat takes the bull by the horns

On 4 February 1971, Sadat took the plunge and bravely, to the surprise of the world and his opponents in Egypt, announced his new initiative in the Egyptian parliament. 'If Israel,' he said, 'withdraws her forces in Sinai to the Passes (see map, page 19) I will be willing to re-open the Suez Canal, have my forces cross to the East Bank . . . make a solemn official declaration of a cease-fire, restore diplomatic relations with the United States, and sign a peace agreement with Israel . . . '[2] In his memoirs, he writes: *None of my opponents had fore-knowledge of my Initiative . . . They were surprised, indeed dumbfounded, to hear me declare it to the world . . .*

In a speech to the Israeli Knesset five days later, Prime Minister Golda Meir responded to Sadat's initiative. Gideon Rafael sums up this occasion: 'After Sadat's February 4th speech, I had strongly urged Golda to respond. In the Knesset on 9 February, she extended a finger to him – not a hand'.

In the US, President Nixon had invited Joseph Sisco to join him in San Clemente. Sisco: 'It was an informal meeting . . . I outlined for him the Dayan conversation [of December], the Sadat initia-tive, and explained that, with such an opening up on both sides, this was a good time for us to pick up the diplomatic ball. I said I wanted to go to the Middle East. Nixon's instructions were very clear: "Press Golda," he said, "but if she reacts negatively, don't press it to a confrontation. We can try again later. Don't cause a major donnybrook between Israel and the United States."'

In August 1971, Sisco went to meet the Israeli cabinet to discuss Sadat's proposal. 'We met in the cabinet room,' Sisco recalls, 'around a huge conference table. Golda Meir, Dayan, Eban, Rabin, Allon – the whole galaxy of Israeli high-level officials – were present. After two days of in-depth discussion, it was clear we weren't making much progress . . . I said, "But, Prime Minister,

Sadat only wants a symbolic 500 riflemen across the canal". But Golda Meir wouldn't budge.'

Before the cabinet meeting, fearing that her ministers would openly contradict her, Golda Meir had given clear instructions about how to 'behave' in the presence of the US envoy. Gideon Rafael remembers: 'Golda instructed them to say nothing and said she'd do all the talking. There they sat, mute, venting their frustration by passing each other notes.'

Foreign Minister Abba Eban had wanted Moshe Dayan to speak up because he knew that Dayan was strongly in favour of the Israeli withdrawal. 'I sent [Dayan] a note,' he recalls, 'saying I think I can get you some support. I mentioned other ministers. He sent back a very abrupt sarcastic reply, saying, "Thank you very much, but if Golda is not for this then I am not for it either."'

The silence of all but Golda Meir did not go unnoticed by Sisco. In a last-minute attempt to sway her refusal to withdraw from the canal, Sisco addressed Moshe Dayan directly, saying, '"Mr Minister, if we don't do anything, what do you think will happen?" Dayan squirmed and expressed his concern that it could lead to war.' The next day, Sisco decided to give the proposal a final try before admitting his mission had failed. 'I paid a courtesy call on Golda just before my departure,' he recalls. 'On the way, I saw some flowers and stopped to buy them for her. When I arrived, she said, "Oh, Joe – now you're saying it with flowers!" Then she added, "But it won't do you any good". "Golda," I replied, "a good diplomat leaves no stone unturned."'

President Sadat's brave initiative had failed.

In Egypt, the pro-Soviet Ali Sabri Group members were infuriated with their president. They had only voted for him as president because he had indicated he would follow the policy they dictated. As they started to plot their revenge, Sadat realized that he would have to move against them. It was, he decided, time to show his real colours.

*Chapter 14*

# Courting the West

Sadat was seated in the presidential car, still driven by Nasser's chauffeur. On the way to the office, Sadat asked, 'Which route did Nasser take to the office?' The driver told him. Sadat said, 'Okay, I will take the same route.' Then, just before the building, Sadat asked, 'Did Nasser turn left or right here?' The driver answered, 'Left.' 'Okay,' Sadat replied, 'indicate left but, when I order you, turn right!' This joke, which was circulated all over Cairo, captures Sadat's behaviour throughout his first year in power. In truth, however, with Nasser's leftist ministers holding all the top posts in government, Sadat realized that, if he were to proceed with his own policies, he would have to go on the offensive. He needed a pretext that would allow him to get rid of Nasser's ministers *en masse*.

In May 1971, Sadat, having managed to obtain proof that pro-Soviet Interior Minister Sharawi Goma'a was tapping his telephone, publicly denounced the outrageous deed. Sharawi Goma'a was immediately dismissed from his post. The Ali Sabri Group was taken by surprise. How dare Sadat fire Goma'a. Did he not fear the repercussions? The group's members met to decide how to retaliate in a way that would force Sadat to resign. A mass resignation of ministers, they agreed, would leave Sadat in a very difficult position. If all his top ministers resigned, Sadat would be obliged to recall them on their terms. But they played straight into Sadat's hands. His wife, Jihan Sadat, recalls: 'On the 15th of May 1971, Ashraf Marwan came to our house to say that the Ali Sabri Group had decided to resign *en masse*, and were announcing their decision on television right then . . . Sadat went to watch television and said: "They have made my life much easier."'

The mass resignation was followed by the arrest of all Nasser's ministers. Having charged them with plotting to overthrow the regime and placed them under house arrest, Sadat was now free to pursue his own policies and, as a bonus, believed the arrests would convince the West that he was moving further away from the Soviet camp. But his action confused the West because, in the same month that he purged the Ali Sabri Group, he also signed a twenty-year friendship treaty with the Soviet Union. Kissinger recalls: 'We, in Washington, were baffled about Sadat's real intentions – the gyrations that lulled Moscow also confused us.'[3]

Throughout 1971, Sadat was fond of saying that it was a 'year of decisions'. The Egyptian masses took this to mean that the president would soon reclaim the land that Nasser had lost in the 1967 War. But, as the year moved on, it became obvious that Sadat was doing nothing to break the stalemate that had existed since then. Sadat, in truth, had never actually specified what the 'year of decision' meant. But, after he failed in his 1971 attempt to seek an agreement with Israel, he prepared himself for war. The problem was that he needed arms and, since Washington would not supply them, his only option was to get them from the Soviet Union.

## A secret trip to the Politburo

In April, 1972, Sadat contacted Soviet Ambassador Vladimir Vinogradov: 'He said that he wanted to make a secret visit to Moscow. We were to leave from a small military airport. To disguise himself, Sadat dressed in an old coat and a velvet hat! In Moscow, without any official ceremony, we went directly to the Politburo.'

General Ahmed Fakher, a member of the military delegation that accompanied Sadat to Moscow, recalls: 'Sadat asked for medium- and long-range bombers, offensive weapons and better tanks. The Soviets didn't think we were serious about going to war. Sadat insisted, "I'm going to war". They still didn't believe him.' The Soviet leadership was sceptical not only because it was aware of Sadat's attempts to seduce the West, but also because Sadat had done nothing to prepare for war throughout 1971.

Soviet Ambassador Vinogradov recalls that the arguments focused on military supplies: 'Sadat wanted such quantities that our Defence Minister Gretchko said, "Comrade President, who gave you these figures? They represent more than our annual production". The Politburo also refused Sadat's request for us to pass to him the command of the Soviet-manned strategic bombers in Egypt. Sadat insisted. Leonid Brezhnev refused again. Suddenly Sadat got angry: "If you refuse, then I don't need your supplies at all. I don't have anything else to discuss. I'm leaving."'

Sadat was persuaded to stay for lunch, but he was furious at the way he was being treated. To add insult to injury, the basic protocol for the lunch was not respected. Egypt's General Fakher remembers, 'They kept us all, including Sadat, waiting in the corridor for twenty minutes. We felt humiliated. They were insulting our president and Egypt. Sadat told us not to worry – it was obvious that he had decided to do something.'

## Expulsion of the Soviet advisers

For Sadat, the visit to Moscow was the last straw. He decided to do the unthinkable – expel the Soviet advisers – and, on 8 July 1972, called in Ambassador Vinogradov to announce his decision. Vinogradov: 'Sadat suddenly announced that our military advisers could return home, as they were "very tired"! I was absolutely furious. "Tired! Mr President," I then challenged, "if you don't need them any more, then say it more directly!"'

In an interview with us and in his memoirs,[4] General Saad el-Shazly, Egypt's Chief of Staff, who was instructed to organize the expulsion in secret, said: 'Sadat told me that the Soviets were to be expelled before August 1st. This was almost impossible because there were so many of them, and they were scattered all over Egypt. They were to hand their equipment to us and we would pay for it. Other equipment, which belonged to Egypt but was manned by Soviet experts, was to be returned to us.'

General Shazly managed to persuade President Sadat to moderate his decision: 'The main problem was the SAM missiles. Egypt didn't have the experts to man these, so we persuaded the Russians to let us keep their experts. We emptied the military academy and asked all the Russian units, which were not going to leave immediately, to move there . . . By the end of 1972, we were able to replace the Soviet military specialists on fifteen SAM missiles. Most of the Soviet advisers didn't leave till October 1972.'

Sadat, in the meantime, was confident that Washington would be impressed by his expulsion of the Soviet advisers and would, in return, help him to recover his land from the Israelis. On 20 July 1972, using a secret channel, he informed the Americans that he was interested in secret talks. On 28 July, National Security Adviser Henry Kissinger responded, saying that he was willing to attend a secret meeting between himself and Hafiz Ismail, Egypt's National Security Adviser.

Seven months later, on 23 February 1973, Ismail went to Washington. The official part of the trip involved a meeting between President Richard Nixon and Ismail – the first high-level meeting between Egypt and the USA since 1967. Ismail's hopes, however, were pinned on the secret part of the trip – the talks with Henry Kissinger. They met for two days, 25–26 February, in a private house hired for the purpose in a New York suburb. Ismail wrote:[5]

> *Henry Kissinger's strategy concentrated on 'step by step' solutions, starting with the same old issue of re-opening the Suez Canal. Sadat, however, refused anything short of a dramatic initiative that would promise the start of a comprehensive settlement, otherwise there would be no alternative to war.*[6]

Kissinger recalls: 'Hafiz Ismail wanted Israel to return to the 1967 borders, in return for which Egypt would be willing to make peace – a big step because no Arab state had ever before flatly said they would make peace.' But Kissinger was not altogether convinced that Sadat's offer was genuine and was still questioning Sadat's motives. Kissinger: 'I thought of Sadat as a character out of *Aida*. I didn't take him seriously. He kept making grandiloquent statements but never acted on them . . . Frankly, I thought he was bluffing.'

Ismail's secret mission in the US had failed and President Sadat was bitterly disappointed. General Shazly recalls: 'After the US visit, Hafez Ismail reported to President Sadat that Kissinger had said, "I cannot deal with your problem unless it becomes a crisis". According to Sadat, this meant that Kissinger was encouraging us to go to war; that there was no way the problem could be resolved politically. War was the only option.'

Sadat had taken some extraordinary steps to break the Israeli-Arab deadlock but, from the US's point of view, he had also created some confusion about his true intentions. His wife, Jihan insists that her husband's war threats throughout this period were only ever a means to an end; that he 'did not want war – did not want to eliminate Israel. The threats were his bargaining chip to generate peace'.

But now, from Sadat's point of view, Kissinger's words to Ismail had scuttled his hopes of resolving the problem through political means and had started the countdown for another major confrontation in the Middle East.


*Chapter 15*

# The road to war

October 24th 1972 was a long day for Egypt's General Saad el-Shazly. He had gathered the army commanders to attend a conference when he received an urgent note from Minister of War General Mohamed Sadeq. The note requested him to cancel the conference, single out the top army chiefs and bring them to the Ministry of Defence at noon sharp. The urgency of the message led Chief of Staff Shazly to expect the worst. But he was mistaken. No immediate crisis was at hand. General Sadeq had been summoned by President Sadat to organize an urgent military council meeting that night at 21.00 hours, and he needed to co-ordinate with his staff.

The meeting took place at Sadat's villa in Giza. Since everyone was tired after *Iftar* – breaking the fast after sunset – the tone was subdued. Sadat started by outlining his view of the general situation. General Abdel Ghani Gamasy, Chief of Operations at the time, recalls: 'Sadat said we had no hope of going further along the political path and that he was not ready to surrender to Israel. The Soviet Union was not giving us equipment to go to war. So, he had decided to go to war with what we already had.'

Sadat was not suggesting a full-scale war against Israel, but a limited war. The main aim of this was to break the stalemate. As Shazly recalls, Sadat said to his commanders, 'If you get back ten centimetres of Sinai, I can solve the problem.' The idea of a limited war was both new and controversial. It meant, in effect, that Sadat was prepared to compromise and to accept that a limited war would only liberate *part* of the land occupied by the Israelis during the 1967 War. By the same token, it implied that Sadat would consider negotiating the remaining portions of Egypt's occupied land – this was an unthinkable proposition for most Egyptians who had been swayed by a decade of rhetoric that had focused on revenge and the destruction Israel.

Sadat opened the discussion. The following is an extract of what followed:

> General Khabir: *'If we consider normal consumption and wear and tear, it is possible to argue that our capabilities are actually decreasing rather than increasing . . . Isn't that an important factor to weigh up before we decide on war?'*
>
> Sadat: *'The mobilization of the country is my responsibility not yours . . . We must accept the calculated risk.'*
>
> General Hassan: *'The uncertainties of battle are such that whatever we wished, it might develop into total full-scale war . . . The upshot could be that the Israelis would be in a stronger position than they are now . . . '*
>
> Sadat angrily (using Hassan's given name): *'Abdel Kader, you don't have to tell me what to do. I know what my duties are . . . Keep to your limits. You are a soldier not a politician . . . '*[7]

Most of the participants spoke strongly against going to war. But Sadat was adamant. He summarized the meeting: 'We will simply have to use our talents and our planning to compensate for our lack of some kinds of equipment. God bless you.'[8]

On 26 October 1972, just two days after the meeting, Sadat dismissed Generals Khabir and Hassan who had spoken against going to war. He also dismissed Minister of War General Sadeq, appointing in his place Ahmed Ismail. Sadat's next step was to approach President Assad of Syria – who was determined to recapture the Golan Heights – about the possibility of a co-ordinated Egyptian-Syrian attack against Israel. But, knowing that Syria would reject a 'limited war', Sadat did not stress this aspect of his plan. The Syrians agreed.

## Deceiving the enemy

Chief of Staff Saad Shazly remembers: 'We couldn't hide, but we could make the Israelis misinterpret our actions. The two main deceptions were: One, disguising the five infantry divisions gathered to cross the canal. In order to avoid any mass gathering being detected before the attack, we made the breakthrough start simultaneously from five different points. Two, the system of mobilization. Between 1972–73, we mobilized our forces twenty-two times for four-to-five days, then sent them home. This got Israel used to our repetitive call-ups. The Egyptian-Syrian attack actually happened on the twenty-third mobilization call!'

This deception proved effective. Between April and May 1973, the mobilizations provoked a major debate about whether or not Israel should mobilize its forces. Director of Military Intelligence Eli Zeira said that the probability of war was low; Chief of Staff David Elazar, however, convinced that the situation was dangerous, requested permission to implement a counter-concentration plan called 'Blue White'. His request was granted. Israel's reserve forces were mobilized, the fortifications strengthened, and several million dollars spent in the process.

When Israel realized that the Egyptians were not attacking, and ordered its forces to disperse, the cost of this false alarm made the Israeli military cautious about ordering further mobilizations. In October 1973, when the Egyptians mobilized in order to launch the attack – the Israelis misread the action as just one more of the repetitive build-ups on their border. The Egyptians' deception plan had worked.

General Bahey Edin Noufal, Egypt's Chief of Operations for the Federal Command, was especially proud of the minor deceptions that had helped to keep the Israelis off guard: 'The army published an advert in the papers offering pilgrimage trips for officers. The pilgrimage season was right after Ramadan, when the war was going to take place. Also, a week before the war was due, the Egyptian army gave a holiday to 25,000 soldiers who were later discreetly called back.'

The total secrecy that shrouded the preparation period lasted a year. Up until four days before the war, only fifteen men in Egypt and Syria knew the details of the plan.

With such secrecy paramount, it was often difficult for the

Egyptians and Syrians to plan joint meetings between their top military staff. Noufal recalls that the most important joint meeting, held to finalize the details of the war, was a logistical nightmare. The meeting was scheduled to be held in Alexandria between 20–23 August 1973. The problem was how to camouflage the arrival of the top six Syrian military ranks – including the Defence Minister – in Egypt. Syrian Minister of Defence Mustapha Tlas remembers this escapade with amusement: 'We travelled aboard a Russian ship wearing civilian clothes. The Soviet ambassador accompanied us and told the captain: "This person in civilian clothes is the Syrian Minister of Defence. Protect him during the journey and don't tell anyone who he is". Of course, the ship also carried civilian passengers, and among them was Dr Badi'e Kasm – a university professor – who recognized me. I said, "Forget you ever saw me here. Pretend you don't know me. Don't even say hallo!"'

Noufal recalls how a mini-deception plan was devised to pass them off as holiday-makers: 'In the morning the Egyptians were seen swimming and having fun; in the afternoon we met at the Ras al-Tin Palace to discuss the war. At night, we went to parties and fashion shows. We made a point of ensuring that the top army brass was seen in nightclubs clapping the belly-dancers. The idea was for Israel to say: "Look at the Arab commanders. They're sitting around watching belly-dancers. They can't be serious about war"'.

The war plan proposed a surprise air force attack launched simultaneously from Egypt and Syria at 14.00 hours on 6 October. For the land battle, the Egyptians would use water-pumps to pierce a hole in the Bar-Lev sand barrier – built by Israel on the edge of the Suez Canal to prevent Egypt's troops crossing over and entering the Sinai. A simultaneous attack by the Syrians on the Golan Heights would force the Israelis to split their forces and thus weaken them.

It was agreed that the Egyptian troops would fight their way to the Mitla and Gidi passes, about 48 kilometres into the Sinai. The Egyptian commanders did not tell the Syrians that their intention was to halt well before then – 10 to 15 kilometres into the Sinai – so that their troops could stay under the cover of the Egyptian missiles. General Shazly recalls: 'We made another military plan extending our advancement all the way to the passes, so that we could show this to the Syrians.' The Egyptians convinced the Syrians that they were together engaged on a full-scale war. This difference in strategy would subsequently become the basis of major discord between Egypt and Syria.

President Sadat called a 13 September Arab summit in Cairo for talks with Syria and Jordan, and used this occasion for behind-the-scenes' deliberations with President Hafez Assad of Syria. King Hussein of Jordan, despite asking specific questions about the Israeli-Arab conflict, was not told about the war plans. Prime Minister Zeid Rifai accompanied King Hussein to the Cairo Summit: 'Discussions touched on the Arab-Israeli conflict, but neither Sadat nor Assad mentioned the possibility of war. We Jordanians, however, were suspicious because we had already found out there was a joint Egyptian-Syrian war plan.'

### Hussein's warnings go unheeded

King Hussein, who was against another war, resented being kept in the dark. His country, which had the longest border with Israel, was the most vulnerable. If war broke out, he risked losing what remained of his kingdom. Since the defeat of the 1967 War, King Hussein had avoided confrontation with Israel. Although he had not become an Israeli ally, he had established secret channels that enabled him to avert crises through 'diplomatic means'. It was not uncommon for him to pilot his own helicopter to the Israeli border for secret talks with Israeli leaders to resolve urgent matters.[9]

When, on 25 September 1973, King Hussein asked for an urgent meeting with Prime Minister Golda Meir, the request did not come as a surprise. A top Israeli intelligence officer who knew about the meeting told us that the discussion – held in a house near Tel Aviv – was in English and that every word was recorded. The following extract from the secret meeting is published for the first time:

*King Hussein: ' . . . from a very very sensitive source in Syria that we have received information from in the past and passed it on . . . all the [Syrian] units that are meant to be in training are now, as of the last two days or so, in position for a pre-attack . . . That includes their aircraft, missiles,*

*everything else ... in pre-jump positions [to attack Israel]
... Whether it means anything or not, nobody knows.
However, one cannot be sure. One must take this as
fact.'*

*Golda Meir: 'Is it conceivable that the Syrians would start
something without the full co-operation of the Egyptians?'*

*Hussein: 'I don't think so. I think they are co-operating.'*[10]

As far as Golda Meir was concerned, there was no sign that Egypt
was preparing for war; and she did not consider the Syrian war
preparations sufficient reason to sound the alarm. She did not
heed King Hussein's warning and did not even cancel a scheduled
trip to Vienna. Her private secretary, recalls: 'The King was livid,
but Golda was not impressed by his information ... ' Referring
to his warning that only rapid talks could avert war, Hussein
recalls, 'I made it very clear that we were concerned. I was asking
for everything to be done to bring about a peace process ... '

King Hussein failed to avert war. The clue that finally convinced
the Israeli military establishment that war might not be too far off
was given by President Sadat himself. Despite the utmost secrecy
of the operation, Sadat had decided to warn the Soviet leadership to evacuate their nationals – several hundred advisers and
their families who had remained after the mass expulsion in 1972.
Syria followed suit. The simultaneous evacuation of thousands
of Soviet nationals from Egypt and Syria inevitably aroused Israeli
suspicion. Director of Military Intelligence Eli Zeira was the first
to be informed: 'At 2 a.m., on Friday [5 October], just one day
before war started, I got a telephone call saying that all Russian
families in Syria and Egypt were leaving. Nobody knew why. At
9 a.m., there was a meeting at Dayan's office. He asked, "What's
going on?" I said, "Either the Russians think we are going to
attack or the Russians think the Arabs are going to attack us."
Dayan said, "I'm going to send a message to Kissinger to give to
the Arabs."'

The Israeli leadership still did not appreciate how close they were
to war. The 9 a.m. meeting at Moshe Dayan's office, in Tel Aviv,
was spent debating whether the situation warranted mobilization.
Military intelligence once again evaluated that the Syrian-Egyptian

attack was 'certainly not probable', and that calling up the reserves was not a priority.

At 11.30 a.m., Prime Minister Golda Meir called a meeting in Tel Aviv, which included some ministers and military commanders. Peres recalls: 'Our military intelligence persisted in their view that there was no likelihood of war and this was accepted.'

At the beginning of the meeting Golda Meir, obviously living on her nerves, was chain-smoking. As the meeting progressed, however, she was reassured. It was the eve of Yom Kippur – the most sacred Jewish holiday when the whole country comes to a standstill – and it would have been a logistical nightmare to embark on full mobilization. In her memoirs, Golda Meir recalls: *In the face of such total certainty on the part of our Military Intelligence – and almost equally total acceptance of its evaluation on the part of our foremost military men – it would have been unreasonable of me to have insisted on a call up.*[11]

She did not mention King Hussein's 25 September warning that the Syrians were in pre-attack positions and that, in his view, the Egyptian and Syrian forces were co-operating.

Meanwhile, in Egypt, Bahey Edin Noufal, Chief of Operations of the Federal Command of the Egyptian and Syrian armies, had just flown back from Damascus after giving the go-ahead to the two Arab armies. The time for attack was 14.00 hours the next day. On arrival at Cairo Airport, Noufal was suddenly confronted with a situation that could have compromised the whole operation only hours from its beginning. 'As I landed at Cairo Airport,' he recalls, 'I suddenly panicked because the airfield was totally abandoned – not a single plane was on the tarmac. This was a real give-away that could have ruined the whole deception plan. I went straight to the Minister of War's office [Ahmed Ismail] and told him what I had seen. He, too, was surprised. He called the Minister of Aviation who said that President Sadat had told him that there was a possibility of an air strike against Egypt, and that he would hold him personally responsible if any damage happened to the Egyptian planes. The Minister of Aviation had, therefore, ordered the airport to be cleared of planes. Ismail was furious. He called Sadat and told him that this would jeopardize the whole plan, so Sadat ordered a return to normal.'

This final give-away was missed by the Israelis.

*Chapter 16*

# The 1973 War

On the morning of 6 October 1973, the tenth day of Ramadan, President Sadat carefully put on his newly-tailored Supreme Commander's uniform and all his medals. He had not told his wife, Jihan, when the war would start; simply that she should pack her bags and send the children to school like any other day. These instructions were sufficient for her to understand that war was imminent.

In Israel, Eli Zeira, the Director of Military Intelligence, was still asleep. It was Saturday morning, Yom Kippur. 'At 4 a.m.,' he recalls, 'the phone rang and I was given information from a reliable source that a high-ranking agent was saying that war would break out today at around six o'clock in the evening.'[12]

Still, the Israelis could not agree on the next step. Eli Zeira recalls: 'A terrible argument began between [Defence Minister] Dayan and [Chief of Staff] Dado [David Elazar]. Dayan wanted to mobilize only three divisions and Dado wanted to mobilize the entire army. In the meantime, nobody was mobilized!' The argument ended only after the matter was brought to Prime Minister Golda Meir to decide. She decided on full mobilization.

In Egypt, Sadat – accompanied by his Minister of War Ahmed Ismail – made his way to the secret concrete bunker known as Centre N° 10, which housed the army's main operations' centre. When Sadat arrived in the underground bunker at 13.00 hours, the hand-picked military commanders were still running around on last-minute errands. As the hands of the white enamel clock moved towards 14.00 hours, a deadly silence settled in the bunker. General Abdel Ghani Gamasy, Chief of Operations of the Egyptian Army, recalls: 'When the time came, more than 200 planes flew from seven different airfields and 100 planes took off from Syria – each, one minute apart. They all flew very low until they crossed the Suez Canal Zone. At exactly 14.05 hours the aircraft were on target. We were all silent, focused on the radar. Then the first brigade crossed the canal and put up the Egyptian flag on the other side. We all cheered.'

121

## Israel wakes up to war

In Israel, the surprise was almost total. Golda Meir's secretary recalls the prime minister's initial reaction: 'When Golda heard the news of the invasion, she was shocked. General 'Gandhi' [Rehavham Ze'evi who was assistant to the Israeli Chief-of-Staff] came and told her we'd been "caught with our trousers down". She didn't understand this expression. Several hours later she asked me what it meant.'

Even the military, already at the front, hadn't a clue that war had broken out. General Amram Mitzna recalls: 'It was one o'clock in the afternoon, and I was driving my jeep to meet my commander. Suddenly I saw planes. I was very surprised. The Israeli air force flying on Yom Kippur! And then I saw black things coming out of the planes. It was only when these reached the ground and blew up that I understood we were in a war.'

If the cabinet and the army were surprised, the civilian population was dumbfounded by the attack. The majority were at the synagogue praying and celebrating Yom Kippur. Suddenly the sirens sounded and panic broke out. All the radio stations were broadcasting orders, in code, for Israelis to join their military units. The reserve soldiers – practically everyone between the ages of eighteen to fifty-five – had to report to their units.

By the time the Israeli army had started to engage, the Egyptians, as planned, had broken through the Bar-Lev line. Having brought the sand barrier down with water-pumps, the Egyptian forces crossed in commando boats to the eastern side and erected bridges across the canal. The crossing was a success. The real battle could now start. For the first time since the 1948 War, the Arab soldiers had the advantage of a surprise attack against the previously invincible Israeli army.

## An ill-fated decision

The first few days of the war were successful for the Egyptian-Syrian coalition forces. The initial mission of penetrating 10 kilometres into the Sinai was achieved and the positions consolidated. On 8 October, the Israeli forces in the Sinai counter-attacked, but failed disastrously. The Egyptian army commanders then started to differ about how to proceed. Abdel Ghani Gamasy, recalls: 'Having fulfilled the initial mission, Commander Ahmed Ismail came to the conclusion that we should halt. He argued that, during the halt, we would be able to inflict more losses on the enemy from a defensive position than from an offensive. I said that there was no need to stop. The Israeli counter-attack had already failed.'

It was now up to President Sadat to decide whether to stick to his limited war plan or ride the wave of victory and move further into the Sinai. The euphoria of success was making it difficult for him to curb his enthusiasm. Chief of Staff General Saad Shazly, who did not want to move too deep into the Sinai, feared that Sadat would make the wrong decision. 'On 11 October,' he said, 'Sadat's morale was very high and he kept repeating, "All my Arab brothers are encouraging me to push on". The following day, Ismail [Minister of War] called me and said, "We want to move on to the passes". I repeated all the reasons why we shouldn't over-extend ourselves and leave the cover of our missiles. But he wouldn't hear of it.'

Shazly strongly believed that if the Egyptian troops remained where they were, Israel would be psychologically and economically devastated by the need to keep its troops on a lengthy mobilization. On 14 October, the signal was given for the Egyptian forces to move on.

On the same day, Prime Minister Golda Meir called a critical meeting of her cabinet and military commanders. Deputy Chief of Staff Yisrael Tal recalls: 'We considered whether to switch immediately to an offensive on the Egyptian front or to wait until the Egyptian divisions moved [deeper into Sinai] and then conduct tank battles to exhaust them . . . The majority thought we should switch to the offensive. I thought the opposite and argued for a tank battle. I spoke harshly to Golda Meir, and said, "Madam, you have the best tanks and soldiers in the world. We will destroy the Egyptian divisions". It was, however, the Egyptians who solved the differences of opinion in our cabinet. While we were arguing . . . one of our intelligence people came into the room and announced that the Egyptian armoured divisions were moving deeper into the Sinai.'

The Egyptians had handed the Israelis exactly what they were waiting for. As they moved in the direction of the Passes, the Israeli tanks retaliated and hit them.

General Ariel Sharon watched the start of the Egyptian offensive. 'At 6.20 a.m., the Egyptian tank forces moved out of the bridgeheads towards our lines . . . By early afternoon, between 100 and 120 Egyptian tanks were either flaming like torches or lying dead on the sand. Those that survived retreated.[13] That night, approval came for my division to cross the canal, break through the Egyptian lines, secure a corridor, and establish a crossing point at Deversoir on the East Bank. Intelligence had told us that the seam between the Egyptian second and third armies was wide open and apparently unnoticed.' In his memoirs Sharon writes: *My plan was to attack at dusk and fight the main battle during the night . . . It wasn't till 1 a.m., that the [Israeli] paratroopers crossed the canal in their rubber assault boats. We had taken the Egyptians utterly by surprise. The paratroopers radioed back the code word Acapulco – success!*[14]

The news of the successful Israeli counter-attack was received by General Abdel Ghani Gamasy, Egypt's Chief of Operations. 'Taysir Al-Akad, the commander of the second army,' he recalls, 'called saying that seven Israeli tanks were in the Deversoir area. He told us he would destroy them before the end of the day.'

The Egyptian Command was not too concerned. The destruction of seven Israeli tanks seemed an easy task. But, with their resources already stretched to maximum because of the advance towards the Mitla and Gidi Passes, the Israeli force was able to be reinforced rapidly and became impossible to contain.

In Cairo, President Sadat was reluctant to make an issue of a handful of tanks that had crossed the canal. He did not want what he regarded as a minor event to interfere with his scheduled Parliamentary speech. On the morning of 16 October, he had decided to commence political bargaining with Israel. In his speech, he proposed that Egypt would stop the war in return for negotiations with Israel about the return of the occupied territories. This initiative, however, had come a day too late. He no longer held the trump card that would give him effective bargaining power.

Sharon recalls the moment when the situation turned to Israel's advantage: 'On the 16th of October we eliminated five ground-to-air missile sites, tearing a gaping hole in the Egyptian anti-aircraft umbrella that had, until then, effectively closed the area to Israeli jets.

Nothing now stood in our way. Then I heard a field commander's voice come over the radio saying: "We can get to Cairo!"'

The Israeli bridgehead had paralysed the Egyptian army and, within days, Israeli troops had encircled the whole of Egypt's third army. The United Nations called for an immediate cease-fire. US Assistant Secretary of State Joseph Sisco participated in the drafting of the UN Resolution, which paved the way to ending the war. Sisco recalls: 'We were invited to Moscow to talk about a cease-fire . . . I drafted the agreement which became UN Resolution 338.' [The opponents sent out joint instructions to their ambassadors at the UN and the resolution was adopted.] 'Then we flew to Israel. We had a very difficult conversation with Golda Meir. She was under tremendous pressure not to stop. We told her that if she didn't, there was a great risk of Russian intervention.'

## The disengagement talks

On 23 October, US Secretary of State Henry Kissinger called President Sadat, proposing that the disengagement talks be conducted directly between Egyptian and Israeli military representatives. (These talks would be the first public talks between Egypt and Israel.) UN representatives would also be in attendance. Sadat nominated his recently appointed Chief of Staff General Abdel Ghani Gamasy to conduct the disengagement talks with Israeli Director of Military Intelligence General Aharon Yariv. The talks were to be held in a tent, in the middle of the desert, near a signpost for Kilometre 101, which is why the disengagement negotiations became known as the KM 101 talks.

General Gamasy accepted his mission with a heavy heart, but he had no time to brood. He was told to be at the site of the talks within a few hours.

Getting the talks going was not an easy task. General Gamasy recalls the first awkward moments: 'When we arrived, we found six officers standing in front of this makeshift tent. They were lined up in a straight line and all saluted at the same time. So we saluted back. Then we sat at the table with the UN representative at the head. They started first, asking, "Do you want tea?" We said, "No." "Coffee?" We said, "No." They said, "It's cold, do you want a coat?" We said, "No." Everything they offered, we replied, "No". Then my counterpart started talking about peace, but I wanted to get down to military matters. We stayed around two hours and got nowhere.'

General Gamasy and General Yariv subsequently held several meetings without getting any closer to an acceptable compromise. General Yariv, a close aide of Prime Minister Golda Meir, was then summoned to go on a trip to the US, and Deputy Chief of Staff General Yisrael Tal was chosen to replace him at the next KM 101 session. The talks took a sudden turn for the better. Tal: 'Gamasy and I came to a quick agreement on the supply of food and medicine to the third army. Then, as both of us felt we had not taken full advantage of the meeting, I suggested that we should talk privately without the presence of the UN representative. We left the tent, spread a map, sat on one of the sand dunes and talked.'

For the first time, two top-ranking military men had the chance to speak informally, and it was during this meeting that the basis of the disengagement agreement was agreed.

Tal recalls that he was, however, shocked by one of Gamasy's proposals: 'General Gamasy said, "Look, this is the first time that a war has ended between us in equality [As a result of this war, the Egyptians had regained land that it had lost in the 1967 War and, having occupied the Bar-Lev sand barrier, held a substantial portion of the Suez Canal front]. We can say we won and you can say it's a tie. From this position, we can negotiate. This time we want to end the conflict. But there is one principle involved: We will never hand over one inch of Egyptian land conquered in this or the 1967 War." I replied, "First we have to establish a friendship between us. The best way to do this is for you to withdraw from the East bank and for us to go back to our previous lines. Then we can continue the negotiations."'

Gamasy agreed on the spot. Tal recalls: 'Gamasy said, "Bring us a map, showing in colours where you propose to retreat to, and where we will gradually retreat to. In the framework of a cease-fire, I promise you we will sign the map without further bargaining." I said, "You're talking about talks that will lead to a final peace agreement . . . Are you speaking on behalf of Sadat, the president of Egypt? Is this a message from him?" He said, "The president does not give messages to his generals, but everything I'm telling you is known by – and approved by – the president."'

Sadat had lost the war, but, by giving the Israelis a beating and crossing the Suez Canal, he had won an important battle. He could now negotiate with them as an equal. True to character, he was already planning another bold initiative.

*Chapter 17*

# Sadat astonishes the world

Fawzy Abdel Hafez had been President Sadat's private secretary for over twenty years and had learned to recognize his moods. On the morning of 7 November 1977, Sadat had been cheerful and relaxed when he told Hafez to pass on a personal invitation to PLO Chairman Yasser Arafat to attend the opening session of the Egyptian parliament. The request was unusual. Normally, such messages were passed through the Ministry of Foreign Affairs. From long experience, Hafez knew that his boss had something up his sleeve. He called Said Kamal, the PLO representative in Cairo. Despite the short notice – the opening session was on 9 November – Kamal recalls that he was delighted to receive such an invitation. He had worked hard to establish a closer relationship between President Sadat and Yasser Arafat. 'It was,' he said, 'a great achievement for me to get Yasser Arafat invited as a guest of honour. I immediately called Arafat in Beirut and told him the good news. He was flattered, but there was a problem. He had an appointment with Colonel Gaddafi in Libya that day, and the Egyptian parliamentary session was due to begin at 6 p.m. He said, "Can you ask if they can make it 7 p.m?" It was a difficult and delicate request, but I said I would try.'

President Sadat's secretary responded by emphasizing that Arafat would need to be in Cairo on Wednesday at 5.45 p.m. sharp. The Egyptian's insistence did not arouse Kamal's suspicion, but Arafat was uneasy about the sudden haste of the invitation. Kamal: 'Arafat asked, "What's all this about?" I said, "I don't know, but this is a great occasion. It's the first time you've been invited to attend a parliamentary session of an Arab country. You can't miss it." He said, "I know, but are you sure there isn't more to it?" I must admit I was not suspicious.'

### Surprise, shock and disbelief

Arafat didn't get to the Egyptian parliament until 7.30 p.m., and was surprised to find that Sadat had held up the session for his arrival. It was only then – too late to ask any questions – that Kamal started to wonder what this was all about. As guest of honour, the PLO chairman was seated in the front row flanked by Egypt's highest ranking officials. Kamal was led to the diplomats' balcony. He recalls the scene: 'Just as I started to relax from the stress of the past few hours, I heard President Sadat saying, "I am ready to go to the end of the world, to their own homes, even to the Knesset in search for peace". Everyone started clapping, and I suddenly realized why Sadat had invited Yasser Arafat. I leaned over the balcony to see Yasser Arafat's reaction, but could only see his *keffiyeh*, then he slowly started clapping.'

Yasser Arafat was not the only one to be taken by surprise – the whole world was stunned by Sadat's words. But was he serious? Was he really prepared to go to Israel or were his words a figure of speech? No one was sure. Arafat suspected that Sadat had carefully planned his move and had asked him to attend the session in order to lend some legitimacy to the initiative he was about to announce.

Boutros Boutros Ghali, who had that very day been appointed Minister of State for Foreign Affairs, recalls: 'When I heard the speech, I was under the impression that it was just rhetoric . . . Sadat was expressing that he was in favour of peace, wanting a dialogue, but nothing more.'

All doubts about Sadat's intentions were dispelled when he assembled the Egyptian newspaper editors and told them to make his offer the main headline. Sadat had thrown the ball in Israel's court. It was now up to Prime Minister Menachem Begin – the leader of the Israeli Likud Party who had come to power on 21 June 1977 – to take up the offer and extend a formal invitation. Sadat blatantly tried to hasten the process by giving an exclusive television interview to CBS's Walter Cronkite. Dan Pattir, Begin's

*Above: Tel Aviv, Museum Hall, 14 May 1948. The official ceremony to declare the new Jewish State. David Ben-Gurion, leader of the Jewish community in Palestine, reads out from the Scroll of Independence: 'We hereby proclaim the establishment of the Jewish State in Palestine, to be called* Medinath Yisrael *[The State of Israel].'*

*Above: Gamal Abdel Nasser, President of Egypt (right), with Abdel Rahman Sadeq, a press attaché at the Egyptian embassy in Paris, who conducted top-level secret talks with Ziamah Divon, an Israeli diplomat, between 1953 and 1954.*

*Right: Nasser (left) and Field Marshall Abdel Hakim Amer (right) enjoy a joke with Egyptian pilots during a visit on 22 May 1967 to the airbase at Bir Gafgafa in the Sinai desert.*

*Above: Nasser embraces
King Hussein of Jordan
on his arrival in Cairo on
30 May 1967. Having
resolved their feud,
Hussein and Nasser
signed a mutual defence
pact placing Jordanian
forces under Egyptian
command in case of war.
Five days later the King's
forces joined the 1967
War and were defeated.*

*Right: Israeli Prime
Minister Levi Eshkol and
his wife Miriam. Eshkol
was Prime Minister
during the 1967 War.*

*Above: An Israeli column advancing on the Syrian Golan Heights on 12 June 1967.*

*Above: Egyptian government leaders raise their hands in a final tribute of prayer at the funeral of Gamal Abdel Nasser, President of Egypt, on 1 October 1970. He died on 28 September 1970, just one day after the Arab summit held to resolve the bloody clash between King Hussein of Jordan and the Palestinian fighters was brought to a successful conclusion. Worldwide leaders flocked to Cairo for his funeral.*

*Above: General Abdel Ghani Gamasy, Chief of Operations of the Egyptian army, and Israeli Deputy Chief of Staff General Yisrael Tal, Sinai desert, 1973. Gamasy and Tal were the chief negotiators in the disengagement talks after the 1973 War. These were the first public talks between Israel and Egypt, and it was the first time that two top-ranking military men had the chance to speak informally.*

*Above: Golda Meir (right), Prime Minister of Israel between 1969 and 1974, with Defence Minister Moshe Dayan. Meir and Dayan, who led Israel through the October 1973 War, were forced to leave office after the war.*

*Above: Egyptian President Anwar Sadat on his arrival at Ben-Gurion Airport, near Tel Aviv, on 19 November 1977. His historic visit to Israel paved the way for the Camp David peace treaty which was signed on 26 March 1979.*

*Above: Israeli Prime Minister Menachem Begin (left), American President Jimmy Carter (centre) and Egyptian President Anwar Sadat (right) at Camp David, Maryland, USA, September 1978. Sadat's signing of the peace treaty so angered other Arab states that Egypt was subsequently expelled from the Arab League. On 6 October 1981 Sadat paid the price for peace when he was assassinated by Egyptian Muslim extremists.*

*Above: Israeli defence minister Ariel Sharon (left) talks to Israeli troops on his visit to East Beirut, during the 1982 Lebanon War.*

*Above: PLO leader Yasser Arafat in Beirut, bidding farewell to a young Palestinian fighter. After years of conflict in Lebanon, Arafat and his troops were finally expelled. Arafat was the last to leave, on 30 August 1982, for exile in Tunis.*

*Left: Israeli Prime Minister Yitzhak Rabin (front) and Foreign Minister Shimon Peres, at the Knesset, Jerusalem, 18 April 1994. Their relationship was always a difficult one, but they managed to overcome their differences and lead Israel to signing the first ever agreement with the PLO on 13 September 1993.*

*Above: Madrid, 30 October 1991. The heads of delegations participating in the Middle East peace conference pose on the stairway of the Palacio Real just before the opening session. In front are the two sponsors, President George Bush (right) and Mikhail Gorbachev (left) with host Felipe González.*

*Above: Uri Savir (right), the Israeli Director of the Foreign Ministry, and Abu Ala'a (left), the chief PLO negotiator in the secret Oslo peace talks with Israel.*

*Left: President Clinton draws Israeli Prime Minister Yitzhak Rabin (left) and PLO Chairman Yasser Arafat to shake hands after the signing of the Declaration of Principles between Israel and the PLO in Washington on 13 September 1993.*

*Above: Yasser Arafat and Hanan Ashrawi, in jubilant mood following the signing of the historic Declaration of Principles between Israel and the PLO.*

*Right: The incoming Israeli Prime Minister Benjamin Netanyahu (right) with his predecessor Shimon Peres, 19 June 1996.*

*Above: Gaza City, 4 September 1996. Israeli Prime Minister Benjamin Netanyahu (right) shakes hands with Yasser Arafat, President of the Palestine National Authority, as they meet for the first time.*

media adviser, recalls: 'Cronkite phoned me on the 15th, a Monday, and said he had an interview with Sadat in the can. Sadat had told him that if he received an invitation in writing, he would go to Israel the following week. Cronkite wanted to fix up a parallel interview with Begin to get his reaction.'

Pattir located Begin at the Hilton Hotel: 'I told him what Cronkite had said, what Sadat had said, and that they wanted his reply. He said he would do an interview then and there. We did a link-up from the hotel manager's office!'

## President Carter's pursuit of peace

In Cairo, US Ambassador Herman Eilts was thrilled by the sudden progress in a peace process that had been in deadlock since the disengagement talks that followed the October War. Three weeks after becoming president, Jimmy Carter had announced that he would pursue a comprehensive peace in the Middle East. He had sent a handwritten letter to Sadat asking for a 'bold move' to break the deadlock. The US had expected a token gesture from the Egyptian president, but Sadat had offered the unthinkable: a visit by an Arab president to Israel. Sadat, in return, had stated that he would require a total US commitment to the peace process that would follow. Ambassador Eilts: 'I met President Sadat after he had done his interview with Cronkite. I told him that he would probably be getting an invitation from Begin within the next few days. He said, "I cannot accept an invitation from Begin. [Only contacts through intermediaries were acceptable; direct contact with Israelis would have been frowned upon by other Arab heads of state.] It has to come through President Carter". I sent this message to Washington and Tel Aviv.'

In Israel, American Ambassador Samuel Lewis told Prime Minister Begin that President Sadat was expecting a formal invitation. When Begin's invitation arrived in Cairo, it came with a short covering message from President Carter. Ambassador Eilts: 'I took the letters to President Sadat who read them and said, 'It's a nice invitation'. Then he called in Hosní Mubarak, his deputy, and read it to him.'

Sadat had received the invitation on the morning of 17 November, just hours before he was leaving for a visit to President Assad of Syria to rally support for his visit to Jerusalem. Sadat had decided to propose that the Syrians refrain from condemning his move and, that if it reaped fruit, Assad could then jump on the bandwagon and they could start a comprehensive peace process in earnest. Syrian Minister of Defence Mustapha Tlas remembers the encounter between Sadat and Assad: 'The two presidents had a seven-hour meeting. President Assad was not convinced by Sadat's arguments and tried to persuade him not to travel to Jerusalem.'

After the meeting, Assad met with his cabinet to decide how to proceed. Tlas described how the cabinet reached the conclusion that if Sadat insisted on the trip he would be betraying the Arab cause: 'To prevent such a betrayal, the cabinet proposed that President Assad should imprison Sadat to stop him from travelling. But Assad refused, saying that Arab tradition did not permit the detaining of a guest.'

Sadat had failed to get Assad on board, but this did not affect his determination to go ahead with the visit to Israel. Back in Egypt, he held a press conference and publicly announced that he had accepted Prime Minister Begin's invitation. US Ambassador Herman Eilts recalls: 'I asked Vice President Mubarak when Sadat wanted to go. He said, "This coming Saturday". I said, "You had better liaise immediately with the Israelis". He said, "We don't want the Israelis to know". I said, "They've got to know! There are security considerations and formal arrangements to be made. This is an important event, and, besides, Friday is the Jewish Sabbath". Finally he agreed that I could send a message to our Ambassador in Tel Aviv asking, "If a certain President wants to visit a certain country on a Saturday, what time should he arrive?"'

In this way, Eilts forewarned the Israelis that the visit awaited by the whole world was to take place only two days later, on 19 November 1977. The haste, imposed by the Egyptians, however, increased the suspicion of some Israeli officials. Dan Pattir recalls: 'There was worry, mistrust and great scepticism about the intention behind Sadat's visit. Chief of Staff Mordechai Gur said he was afraid that it could be a trap. When Sadat's plane was late, the heads of security were saying that, perhaps, the plane would land and, instead of Sadat, a group of suicide commandos would come out and kill the whole Israeli leadership waiting on the runway.'

Although only a forty-minute flight separated the two countries, they had remained worlds apart for three decades. The speed of events had not allowed either side to make a mental adjustment or break with ingrained taboos. Boutros Ghali recalls his own arrival in Tel Aviv: 'It was completely new – like coming to outer space. I found myself in a small car with Moshe Dayan and had to find a way to begin a conversation. I had read that he was interested in archaeology, so I mentioned that I was, too. We started to talk archaeology, then moved from that to the Middle East problem.'

## Friends and foes

Dayan and Boutros Ghali were cautious not to antagonize each other at such an early stage, but it was obvious they didn't see eye to eye on how to proceed. Boutros Ghali insisted that only a comprehensive peace settlement could be considered. Dayan was keen to start with a separate peace agreement with Egypt. The difference in their approach led Dayan to give Boutros Ghali a hint, hoping that he would pass it on to Sadat. Boutros Ghali: 'Dayan mentioned the importance of Sadat's speech at the Knesset. He said, "The best thing would be for Sadat to avoid mentioning the PLO [Palestine Liberation Organization, led by Yasser Arafat], because, if he does, this will provoke a negative reaction from the Israeli side and Prime Minister Begin will be compelled to have a negative attitude, too."'

The following extracts are from Anwar Sadat's speech to the packed Knesset on 20 November 1977:

'I come to you today on solid ground to shape a new life and to establish peace. Any life that is lost in war is a human life, be it that of an Arab or an Israeli . . . There was a huge wall between us, which you tried to build up . . . but it was destroyed in 1973 . . . Conceive with me a peace agreement in Geneva that we can herald to a world thirsting for peace. A peace agreement based on the following points: Ending the occupation of the Arab territories occupied in 1967 . . . Achievement of the fundamental rights of the Palestinian people and their right to self-determination, including their right to establish their own state. The right of all states in the area to live in peace . . . commitment of all states in the region to administer the relations among them in accordance with the

131

objectives and principles of the United Nations charter. Particularly the principles concerning the non-use of force and a solution of differences among them by peaceful means . . . You, sorrowing mother, you, widowed wife, you, the son who lost a brother or a father, all the victims of wars, fill the air and space with recitals of peace, fill bosoms and hearts with aspirations of peace.'

The speech was considered tough by the Israelis. Begin's response was considered tough by the Arabs.[15]

Later that day, Sadat's dinner-engagement encounter with Begin, at the King David Hotel in Jerusalem, almost turned into a disaster. Although Sadat had brought his cook from Cairo, he hardly touched his food. Sadat's adviser, Mustapha Khalil, recalls: 'We were very disappointed by Begin's speech. He put the prepared text into his pocket and spoke using lots of biblical references. At the dinner afterwards, Sadat was seated next to Begin, but they sat with their backs to each other and didn't exchange a word.'

It was obvious that Sadat and Begin were not getting on with each other. It was also obvious that Sadat disliked Foreign Minister Moshe Dayan. He preferred Defence Minister Ezer Weizman. As the tension became obvious throughout the dinner, Mustapha Khalil and Boutros Ghali exchanged worried glances. Boutros Ghali recalls: 'The dinner went so badly that Mustafa Khalil and myself decided that something had to be done, otherwise the trip would be without any follow-up. Khalil suggested we have an informal drink and we decided to invite Ezer Weizman and Yigael Yadin [Deputy Prime Minister], but not Moshe Dayan. They accepted. We went to Khalil's room and I asked for a bottle of Scotch whisky. We began, all four, to drink and have a relaxed conversation. Weizman talked about his memories of the Royal Air Force in Cairo, Khalil asked questions. I was trying to convince the Israelis that this was a sincere quest for peace, that it was not a gimmick, not just a spectacular visit. After two or three hours everybody was talking to each other like friends.'

But, outside the door, Israelis were worried. Khalil recalls: 'During the meeting I noticed that every now and again an Israeli bodyguard would open the door, peek in, and close it again. I wondered what was going on. Later, Mrs Weizman told me she had been so worried for her husband's safety that she had asked the guards to keep an eye on us!'

President Sadat returned to Cairo thinking that his trip had transformed the nature of the conflict and paved the way for the peace process. He was wrong. His spectacular move was not, in itself, sufficient to bridge the gap between the former enemies. Many reverses lay ahead before formal peace negotiations could begin.

## Chapter 18

# Negotiating peace at Camp David

Ezer Weizman's heart-to-heart talk with Mustapha Khalil and Boutros Ghali in Jerusalem had endeared him to the entire Egyptian delegation. He was soon seen by President Sadat as the man he could talk to. Whenever there was a point that needed clarification, Sadat would say: 'Bring me my friend Ezer'. Weizman was invited to Cairo on several occasions, but much more was needed to get the peace process moving.

The Egyptians wanted Egyptian units deployed in the Sinai; Israel wanted the Sinai to be demilitarized east of the Gidi and Mitla Passes (see map, page 19). Egypt wanted Israel to dismantle Israeli settlements in the Sinai; Israel wanted these to remain. Egypt was strongly against Begin's four principles that: 1) IDF units be deployed on the West Bank and Gaza; 2) Israel should be allowed to continue building settlements in these areas; 3) the PLO should not be involved in the negotiations; and 4) that there should be no Palestinian state.

On 25 December 1977, Prime Minister Begin, Moshe Dayan, Ezer Weizman and other top Israeli negotiators met President Sadat and his top ministers at Ismailia. Sadat had long protested that there could be no separate peace between Egypt and Israel without resolving the whole Palestinian problem. Now, within minutes, Sadat revealed what the Israelis had hoped for and suspected – he was willing to compromise. Dan Pattir, a member of the Israeli delegation recalls: 'It was clear that Sadat was willing to move further forward in the bilateral Israeli-Egyptian context than his Foreign Ministry which maintained the Pan Arab position. When Begin mentioned that a large number of Palestinian organizations in the West Bank and Gaza were pro-communist, Sadat interrupted and said, "Mr Prime Minister, *all* of them are Communists". We realized then that he didn't want to get sidetracked into the Palestinian issue.'

Boutros Ghali remembers: 'Begin spoke for more than an hour, making it clear that there would be a kind of autonomy for the West Bank and the Gaza Strip; and that he had no intention of withdrawing the Israeli settlements built on Egyptian territory. We realized we were still at square one.'

As Sadat sat listening to the Israeli proposal, the growing tension could be felt. Ezer Weizman recalls: 'We were all confined in a small room and things were not going well. Sadat took out a handkerchief and wiped the sweat from his brow. Then he clapped his hands and said in Arabic, "Open the window". I bent over Begin, and said, "He's very very tense". Begin looked at me and said, "So am I."'

The Ismailia meeting was a bitter disappointment for both Sadat and Begin. Sadat had expected the Israelis to be tough on the Palestinian issue, but more open-minded where Egypt was concerned. Begin's proposal, revealing his plan for permanent settlements in the Israeli-occupied territories, was totally unacceptable. Sadat's insistence that Israel declare its readiness both to withdraw from the territories it had occupied in 1967, and solve the Palestinian problem, was more than Begin could deliver at this stage.[16]

On his return from Ismailia, Sadat asked US Ambassador Herman Eilts to come and see him. Eilts: 'Sadat was furious. He threw two Israeli negotiating documents on to the table. One offered to give back only part of the Sinai; the other offered some autonomy on the West Bank. "Look!" he said, "Begin does not appreciate the tremendous steps I have taken". That was a charge he would make many times in the coming months.'

The Ismailia meeting had done nothing to ameliorate the antipathy between Sadat and Begin. Both sides felt it was useless to continue a dialogue when the gulf between them seemed so insurmountable. The next US attempt to get the two sides together between 17–19 July – this time in England, at Leeds Castle, failed miserably. Neither side could agree on a framework for direct talks. Sadat's historic initiative had reached an impasse.

## Rosalyn Carter's magic formula

On the other side of the Atlantic, President Carter, frustrated by the deadlock, had publicly stated that peace in the Middle East was one of his administration's priorities. Against the recommendations of his advisers, he decided to stake his reputation on it. National Security Adviser Zbigniew Brzezinski: 'The president and I discussed the stalemate and the need to do something unconventional, assertive and, perhaps, even dramatic to cut the Gordian knot. We talked about the possibility of promoting a summit at which the president would exercise his personal leadership and leverage.'

President Carter's wife, Rosalyn, came up with the magic formula. 'We were walking around the beautiful secluded area of Camp David,' President Carter recalls, 'when Rosalyn said, "This would be a great place to get the Egyptians and Israelis together. Maybe, then, they would put aside their animosities". That's where I got the idea from.'

On 30 July 1978, Carter decided to invite Begin and Sadat to Camp David. On 5 September, the Egyptian and Israeli delegations arrived there. President Carter and his handful of advisers were not simply present to be mediators – they were there to propose ideas and seek ways to surmount misunderstandings. The informality of the occasion took their guests by surprise. Boutros Ghali recalls: 'We arrived by helicopters and saw the president of the United States in casual clothes, peering out of his house, saying, "Hallo. Welcome to Camp David". People were very relaxed – walking in the forest, riding bicycles, swimming. It was quite strange for us. We were used to negotiations taking place around a table with everyone wearing suits. What was also new, was the complete isolation. At Camp David, we were far from the outside world, confronted by each other.'

Ezer Weizman remembers his reaction: 'We were surprised to see that Camp David looked like a kibbutz, with lots of trees. Then we discovered that this "kibbutz" also had a billiard table, cinema, swimming pool and tennis court. There was also a dining room which – as in a kibbutz – was a mess hall. When we went to eat, we found ourselves sitting next to the Egyptian delegation.'

Although Weizman approached the Egyptian team in the dinning hall, they did not eat together. A year of failed attempts at direct talks had created bad blood between them. President Sadat had come prepared for a confrontation with Begin who he felt had thwarted his initiative. Ambassador Eilts recalls: 'We advised President Carter to keep Sadat and Begin apart . . . But, to our surprise, on day one Carter brought them together and said to Sadat, "Mr President, why don't you run through your position paper for us". Sadat did so in stumbling English. Begin listened tetchily. Seeing this, Carter said, "Let's leave our responses until the morning". When he came out of the meeting, he said to me, "You told me there'd be fireworks if I got them together. Well, they're getting on fine."'

Begin, in fact, had hardly been able to restrain himself during this meeting and, by the time he returned to his cabin, he was fuming. Dan Pattir: 'Begin came back, saying that Sadat had read out eleven pages of extreme and rigid demands. If the Egyptians persisted in such demands, they would blow the Camp David summit out of the water.'

### Personal animosities

The next day, Begin presented his analysis of Sadat's position paper. Begin read out Article 5 which stated that the Palestinians would 'execute their natural right to self-determination.' 'Would they,' asked Begin, 'be allowed to vote for an independent Palestine state?' Sadat nodded and said, 'Yes'. Carter intervened, saying that he was against a Palestinian state. Begin turned to Article 6, in which Sadat was proposing that Israel withdraw from East Jerusalem which it had occupied in 1967, annexed and unified with West Jerusalem, and which it declared was its eternal capital. 'So you propose to divide Jerusalem?', said Begin, adding, '*Never*'. Begin then exploded with fury as he read Sadat's 'compensation article'. In this, Sadat was demanding that Israel should pay compensation for the damage it had caused in its wars with Egypt. 'Only defeated nations are asked to pay compensation', said Begin, clearly remembering that Germany and Japan were asked to pay compensation after the Second World War. Sadat misunderstood, clearly thinking that Begin was saying Egypt was a 'defeated nation'. 'Mr Begin,' he said angrily, 'after the October War, Egypt is not any longer a defeated country!'[17]

President Carter could hardly control the fury of Sadat and Begin. Carter: 'We were in a very small room. I was keeping meticulous notes on a yellow pad, but I couldn't get them to look forward. They kept resurrecting all the betrayals that they felt had caused the four wars during the previous twenty-five years. There was a personal animosity between the two men.'

Begin rose from his chair and blurted out, 'Mr President, if he [pointing towards Sadat] is presenting yesterday's document as the basis for discussion, it is unacceptable'. Sadat riposted by blaming Begin for not appreciating all he had done to try and achieve peace. Carter, caught in the middle, couldn't let the summit fail on its second day. Carter: 'They wanted to storm out. I jumped up from the desk where I was sitting writing, and stood in front of the door. I wasn't going to let them out of the room until they both agreed to let me try to continue. After that, the two men did not see each other for the next ten days.'

Carter had believed that the summit could be limited to five days. The clash between Sadat and Begin, however, made it obvious that progress would take longer. By the tenth day of their seclusion, nothing had been agreed by the two leaders – everything was conditional on something else. Then it was time to address the main stumbling block: Israeli settlements. Defence Minister Weizman had led Sadat to believe that Israel would be flexible on the dismantling of settlements; he then made the problem worse by coaxing Sadat into a one-to-one meeting with Dayan. Sadat, who had taken a dislike to Dayan since his first trip to Jerusalem, insisted that any problem dealt with by Dayan became more complicated and insoluble. Weizman: 'I went to Sadat and said: "You can't leave here and go home without talking to Moshe Dayan. You can't just talk to me because you like me and I like you. You must talk to him."'

President Carter also urged Sadat to meet Dayan, hoping that together they could, at least, discuss the means to bridge the gap. In the event, the opposite happened. Dayan enraged Sadat by saying forthrightly, 'Mr President, if anybody has told you that

Israel can leave the Sinai settlements they are deluding you.' The meeting between the two men was short.

The previous day Begin had rebuked National Security Adviser Brzezinski on the Sinai settlements' topic. Brzezinski: 'Begin and I went for a walk in the Camp David woods. Suddenly, he said dramatically, "Dr Brzezinski you insulted me and the people of Israel this morning". I was alarmed and asked how? He replied, "This morning you said that the settlements are a form of colonialism". I replied, "Mr Prime Minister, what I said was that the Arabs regard the settlements as a form of colonialism". Begin took a deep breath and said, "I want you to understand that my right eye will fall out, my right hand will fall off, before I sign a single scrap of paper permitting the dismantling of a single Jewish settlement."'

### 'A betrayal of friendship'

The moment Dayan left him, Sadat called his delegation to his cabin. Sadat had mostly excluded them from the negotiations and was making all the decisions himself. Foreign Minister Mohamed Ibrahim Kamel was constantly complaining that Sadat was too willing to make concessions and was pursuing a bilateral solution, rather than a comprehensive one which should include the Palestinians. Boutros Ghali recalls Kamel's delight at the decision Sadat now announced: 'Sadat told them that he had decided to leave Camp David. Foreign Minister Ibrahim Kamel rushed off to begin packing his luggage. Then we saw Carter going into Sadat's cabin.'

Carter recalls: 'Dayan had, in effect, told Sadat that the Israelis were adamant. Then, without consulting me, Sadat told Dr Brzezinski to call a helicopter to carry him and his people back to Washington for the return trip to Egypt. I was horrified. I walked over to Sadat's cabin. All his bags were on the front porch, with a car waiting. I asked Sadat if he would go back in his living-room and talk to me.'

President Carter saw the summit to which he had committed so much about to collapse. He tried a personal-blame approach. Carter: 'I told Sadat, in effect, that he had betrayed me, had betrayed our friendship, and had violated the commitment he had made that he would give me every opportunity to resolve any differences that arose. I told him that his pre-emptive action in leaving, without giving me another chance, would seriously and adversely affect the relationships between our two countries. I made my statement as strongly as I could. Sadat was taken aback, then told me that he would stay and give me another chance.'

Carter found a pretext to visit Begin. Carter: 'Begin had asked me to sign some photographs of me, him and Sadat for his grand-children. I got the names of his grandchildren and personalized every photograph. I asked if I could bring the photographs over to his cabin. Begin was still very angry with me and, when I walked into his cabin, there was a frigid atmosphere. I said, "I've brought you the photographs". He said, "Thank you". I handed him the photographs and, as he looked down, he began calling out the names of his grandchildren. His voice trembled and there were tears running down his cheeks. Then he said, "We can't leave a war for these little children to fight!" I went back to my cabin.'

President Carter tried to make use of the tears he had witnessed. 'The only way I could think of was to let the Knesset, instead of Begin, make the decision [about whether or not to dismantle Israeli settlements in Sinai]. The next step was for me to get him to agree not to be a negative influence on the Knesset. He agreed . . . '

## A bilateral treaty

Within two days, practically all the other obstacles were untangled. The United States agreed that it would build airfields to replace any that Israel left behind in the Sinai. The Egyptians agreed to accept vague commitments from Israel regarding the West Bank and Gaza. Israel agreed to provide full autonomy to the inhabitants of these areas, but not to discuss territorial issues with the Palestinians – meaning that it would retain control of the land.

To avoid any last-minute arguments, the delicate issue of the status of Jerusalem – which had been avoided until then – was shelved. The US simply reiterated the position it had maintained since 1967. The Camp David final text stated that the US 'has not changed its position', rather than spelling out its rejection of the Israeli annexation of Jerusalem. This, of course, aroused the fury of the Egyptian delegation, but by now it was obvious that, despite the lip-service paid to Palestinian autonomy and a comprehensive peace, the Camp David summit would lead to a bilateral Egyptian-Israeli peace treaty. Only Egyptian Foreign Minister Kamel remained adamant in expressing his protest. On the plane back to Washington, where the signing ceremony was to take place, he resigned.

At the 'family lunch' held by President Carter and his wife in honour of the Sadats and the Begins, there was a last-minute panic. President Sadat's wife, Jihan, recalls: 'The six of us at the White House were all full of hope and happiness that we were going to sign the peace treaty. All of a sudden Mrs Begin, who had been laughing a moment before, had an asthma attack and her face turned blue. I started praying: "God, not now. I know we all have to die, but if she dies now the ceremony will be cancelled". I was not only the one who felt this – all of us did.'

Mrs Begin recovered, the ceremony went ahead, and the document entitled 'Framework for Peace in the Middle East' was signed on 17 September 1978. As far as the outside world was concerned, peace between Egypt and Israel had been achieved. In reality, it would take another six months of haggling over details before the two former enemies signed the final peace accord on 26 March 1979.

On 6 October 1981, Sadat paid for this peace accord with his life. While he was reviewing a military parade celebrating Egypt's achievements in the 1973 War – the war that had paved the way for his historic visit to Jerusalem and the subsequent signing of the Peace Accord between Egypt and Israel – Egyptian Muslim extremists gunned him down.

Sadat's peacemaking had dramatically reduced the probability of war between Israel and the Arabs. Those who plotted to end Sadat's life knew that the only chance the Arabs had of beating Israel was by attacking it simultaneously from more than one direction. Militarily, Egypt was the strongest Arab country, but Sadat had taken it out of the fight.

In August 1981, a few weeks before Sadat's assassination, Israel appointed a new Defence Minister. Soon after his appointment, Ariel Sharon would send Israeli forces into Lebanon where Arabs were fighting Arabs in a civil war. The world looked on in amazement as Israel invaded an Arab state and Sadat's peace held.

# Introduction

In 1947, the UN vote to partition Palestine, which all the Arab states rejected, sparked off a civil war in Palestine. When neighbouring Arab countries[1] – Egypt, Syria, Lebanon, Jordan and Iraq – intervened, this expanded into an all-out war in the Middle East that resulted in hundreds of thousands of Arabs fleeing the country – most of them to Gaza, others to the West Bank, Lebanon and Syria where they lived in tents and refugee camps.

On 16 June 1948, even before the war had ended, the Israeli leadership decided not to allow the Palestinians to return their homeland. This decision meant that those who had fled had become permanent stateless refugees.[2]

On 11 December 1948, the United Nations addressed the refugee problem and passed Resolution 194, which stated that 'the refugees wishing to return to their homes and live at peace with the neighbours should be permitted to do so at the earliest practicable date'. But the Israeli leadership refused to comply.

Between 1948 and 1967, the Palestinians hoped that a coalition of Arab armies would liberate Palestine. But, following the defeat of the Egyptian, Jordanian and Syrian forces in the Six-Day War, the Palestinian refugees – now joined by another 200 to 300,000 refugees from this war – lost hope. This despair gave momentum to Yasser Arafat's Fatah – and the other eight factions of the umbrella organization, Palestine Liberation Organization (PLO) – to take direct action to liberate Palestine. In the 1968 *al-mithaq al-watani al-filastini* (the Palestinian National Covenant), Article 9 stated, 'Armed struggle is the only way to liberate Palestine'.

The hinterland that the Palestinians chose to launch their 'armed struggle' attacks on Israel was Jordan. In 1970, however, when the armed struggle caused chaos in Jordan, King Hussein drove Arafat and the PLO out of his kingdom. They then moved to Lebanon where, in 1982, during the Lebanon War, the Israelis drove them into exile in Tunis.

Throughout these years, the Palestinian problem began to attract world attention – especially during the 1970s when George Habash's Popular Front for the Liberation of Palestine (PFLP) resorted to international terrorism to attract attention to their plight – and the PLO became recognized as the body representing the Palestinian people. On 13 November 1974, Yasser Arafat, by then the Chairman of the PLO, was invited to address the UN General Assembly.

The following chapters follow Arafat and his resistance fighters from the first crossing of the Jordan River into the occupied West Bank in 1967, through the years spent in Jordan during the 1970s, the Lebanon War and his expulsion to Tunis in 1982.

*Chapter 19*

# The young Yasser Arafat

On 31 July 1967, just a few weeks after the end of the war, a group of young Palestinians left Hama, near Damascus, on the way to the newly-occupied territories on the West Bank of the River Jordan. One of the group was Yasser Arafat whose *nom de guerre* was Abu Ammar. By the time they reached the River Jordan it was evening. From the bush where they were hiding, they watched the opposite bank, waiting for the Israeli patrol vehicle to pass by. Then they started crossing. Abu Ali Shaheen, one of the group, recalls: 'We had to take off our clothes and shoes to keep them dry for the long distance we had to walk.'

Yasser Arafat, he added, was the first to cross. As he is only 5ft 4in, the water came up to his shoulders, and he had to hold his clothes and weapon above his head. Reaching the other side, he fell to his knees, kissed the ground and waited for the rest of the group, twenty-eight in all, to join him. Then, with compasses to guide them, they began walking westwards through the mountains. At 7.30 a.m. the next day, they stopped near Jenin – a West Bank town – and made camp. They were risking their lives, but Arafat's mission was to recruit young Palestinians in cafés and allocate them to small secret cells.

In the following weeks, Arafat spent most of his time in the West Bank town of Nablus. Then, on the run from the Israeli security forces, the new masters on the West Bank, he moved to Ramalla, a West Bank village, and set up his headquarters in a local restaurant called Naum. His life, in the summer heat of 1967, was totally dedicated to the Palestinian cause, and ramming home the simple message to the Israelis that, although the Arab armies had just failed to liberate Palestine, the Palestinians themselves were still fighting for the liberation of their land upon which they would build their own nation.

From the end of August 1967 onwards, the young Palestinians whom Arafat had organized blew up irrigation pipes in kibbutzim, placed bombs in Jerusalem, and generally set about making life difficult and hazardous. The Israelis fought back and, towards the end of the summer, forced Arafat and 300 of his activists out of the West Bank and back on to the eastern side of the River Jordan where, since the war, thousands of refugees were camping.

In Jordan, on the land of the young King Hussein, Arafat and his guerrillas settled in Karameh, a small market village. Hussein, whose relationship with the PLO had been tense even before the 1967 War, was now – following his terrible defeat in that war – too weak to prevent Arafat and his activists from settling on his land.

In Karameh – where the summer heat is intolerable and strong winds blow in winter – Arafat organized an office for himself. Despite the weather, Karameh was an ideal location. Just 4 kilometres from the River Jordan, it provided easy access to the occupied territories. Nearby was a large supportive Palestinian community, most of whom had arrived after the 1948 War when many of the 750,000 Palestinian refugees fled from Israel. Now, after the latest war, they were joined by more than 200,000 new refugees who had fled from the advancing Israeli army. Immediately after the war, many of the refugees had tried to cross back to the West Bank, but when they did so the Israeli soldiers shot them.[3]

From Karameh, Arafat and his Fedayeen (Arabic word for a person who sacrifices his life for a cause) would sneak across the River Jordan to the West Bank to activate their secret cells, and carry out attacks on the Israelis. The Israelis tried to stop them, but this was not easy – the border was long, the river zig-zagged, and the thick bush offered good hiding places. Arafat and his people considered themselves 'Freedom Fighters' whose cause was the 'Armed Struggle' – the use of force to liberate Palestine. The Israelis considered them 'terrorists' and their cause 'indiscriminate terrorism'.

The following year, on 18 March 1968, a Fedayeen group crossed the River Jordan and scattered mines on a road near Be'er Ora, some twenty-five miles north of Eilat. A bus carrying Israeli children from Hertzellia Secondary School in Tel Aviv hit one of the mines. Two children were killed and twenty-seven adults and children injured.

General Uzi Narkiss, the Israeli in charge of the region, Chief of Staff Haim Bar-Lev, who had recently succeeded Yitzhak Rabin, and Defence Minister Moshe Dayan were determined to retaliate.

### 'All hell broke loose'

On 20 March 1968, Jordanian Commander Zaid Bin Shakir, a relative of King Hussein, stood on a hill on the East side of the border, and looked across at the Israelis. 'They were massing their forces,' he said, 'and not even bothering to hide their preparations for the attack.'

On a tour of inspection, Bin Shakir stopped at Karameh and watched the Palestinians – who now knew that an Israeli attack was imminent – preparing their positions. Although he was one of the fiercest opponents of Palestinian activities against Israel – because they often led to Israel retaliating and inflicting damage on Jordan – he could not tolerate the thought of an Israeli attack on Jordanian soil, and asked the Palestinians if they needed any help. No, he was told, they were in good shape, ready to fight. He wished them luck and hurried back to Amman to attend a birthday party in honour of Crown Prince Hassan Bin Talal – the King's brother.

During the party, King Hussein took Bin Shakir aside, and said: 'You should leave early and try to get some sleep. The attack will probably happen tomorrow'.

Fully aware that the Israelis were making preparations to attack the Palestinians in Karameh, Hussein instructed his commanders to 'muster the troops in the best possible way to deal with this threat'. He could not stand by and watch the Israelis launching an attack on his land.

At around 5 a.m., the next morning, the telephone rang and Hussein was told that the Israelis were crossing the river into his territory. He immediately telephoned his officers. 'The fun has started,' he said.

Also, around this time, the telephone rang for Jordanian Commander of the Front Mashour Haditha el-Jazy. On the line was Major Samih Hanoun, the duty officer. 'Sayyidi,' [Sir] shouted Hanoun in excitement, 'the first Israeli tanks are crossing the bridge.' Commander Haditha was instantly awake, and recalls: 'I jumped from my bed. "Shoot", I ordered. I was excited. I wanted to face the Israelis, wanted to teach them a lesson. Yes, by God, I did . . . '

King Hussein recalls: 'The heavens had intervened. Low clouds made it very difficult for the Israelis to engage their air force.'

The Israeli forces crossed over three bridges and advanced in a three-pronged column towards the Jordanian defenders. Then, as they moved deeper into the valley, they encountered intense resistance from the Palestinians. The Palestinians were well prepared. They held their ground against the onslaught of shells, tanks and aircraft. Salah Tamari, a Palestinian, was there: 'It was hell . . . like a volcano. The sound of fighting everywhere – planes, guns, explosions . . . ' Despite the low cloud, the Israeli air force, managed to drop 180 tons of bombs in 360 sorties, and penetrate into Karameh.

It was a bloody battle. From start to finish, it lasted for just over ten hours. The Israelis were defeated. In the middle of the operation, Israeli Chief of Staff Bar-Lev ordered General Yisrael Tal to rescue the forces. Tal took a helicopter, rushed to the scene and took charge of the Israeli retreat.

The Israelis had lost twenty-nine soldiers; the Jordanians twenty-five; the Palestinians 128. It was a victory for the Arab nations.

When the battle was over, Yasser Arafat played down the role of the Jordanians, and presented the day's events as a Palestinian triumph. He described how the Palestinians had 'faced huge up-to-date military Israeli forces', and how, after five hours of fighting alone, they were joined by 'some small battalions, sent by the Jordanian government, who fought with us without any central instructions from their headquarters'.

This exaggeration proved to be a successful propaganda coup for Arafat who succeeded in convincing the Palestinians and many other Arabs that the battle was a Palestinian rather than a Jordanian victory. King Hussein, though, was unconvinced: 'The Palestinians claimed it as a victory for them . . . It was not!'

During the following weeks, one of Arafat's men could be seen writing down the names and addresses of the 5,000 volunteers from many Arab countries who, inspired by the story of the Palestinian triumph in Karameh, flocked to join the Fatah organization, one of eight movements that constituted the PLO.[4]

Yasser Arafat, aged thirty-nine, had found fame. Practically unknown until Karameh, he was suddenly projected on to the world stage. In December 1968, a sketch, showing him wearing sunglasses and a *keffiyeh*, appeared on the cover of *Time* Magazine, sold worldwide.

*Chapter 20*

# Black days

After the victory at Karameh, the Palestinians' confidence soared. They had succeeded where other Arab armies had failed and launched a successful counter attack on the Israelis. They now left the Jordanian valleys and moved into the cities – choosing Amman as their prime seat. King Hussein was not happy, but could do little to stop them. After the fighting at Karameh, they were just too popular.

Arafat, who was made Chairman of the Palestinian Liberation Organization (PLO) in February 1969, declared that his quarrel was *only* with the Jewish state, *only* with Israel. But not all his fellow Palestinians agreed.

George Habash, a Palestinian Christian and paediatrician by profession, was the founder and leader of the leftist group, Popular Front for the Liberation of Palestine (PFLP) which was also based in Amman. A Marxist-Leninist, Habash had adopted the Socialist slogan 'Defeat the Forces of Reaction' and wanted to bring about a revolution to topple his host in Jordan – King Hussein. 'Our political ideology,' he said, 'had always been against Arab reactionary regimes, and King Hussein was the symbol of these.' Habash believed that Hussein was responsible for a conservative regime which was against the revolutionary reforms that he hoped to bring about.

There was also a practical reason why some Palestinians wanted to get rid of King Hussein. As Yasser Abd Rabbo, of the Democratic Front for the Liberation of Palestine (DFLP), explains: 'We needed a strong base – a hinterland from where we could launch guerrilla actions against Israeli occupation. A base from where we could support the revolution we were dreaming of inside the occupied territories. We thought that Jordan should be that base. From there, we could liberate our occupied homeland. We felt that King Hussein was an obstacle and that, in order to make our revolution succeed, we would need to remove this obstacle. We were determined to show we were the bosses in Jordan. We were naive in those days; we thought we were leading an international revolutionary movement and wanted to copy Lenin. We decided to celebrate Lenin's birthday throughout Jordan. This really annoyed the Jordanians, who were so conservative . . . We adopted Lenin's slogan, "All Power to the Soviets", and then changed it to, "All power to the workers, peasants and soldiers". This was a significant moment. For the first time, it challenged the authority of the King.'

Hussein was furious. 'It was a nightmarish scenario,' he recalls. 'A breakdown of law and order; a situation where people were not able to go around without being stopped and searched by Palestinians, where vehicles were confiscated, people shot, people disappeared.'

The Palestinian organizations in Amman then picked on the Jordanian army upon which the King's survival depended. They teased and humiliated his soldiers to such an extent that, soon, when they returned on leave from duties on the front with Israel, they did not dare to wear their uniforms. Under this stress, army discipline began to disintegrate. When Hussein – trying to avoid sparking off a confrontation with his Palestinian population – failed to take tough enough measures against the Fedayeen, his soldiers took the law into their hands. They descended on Amman to seek revenge on the Palestinian districts.

King Hussein recalls: 'I saw a very ugly situation developing, leading, at one point, to the possibility that I could totally lose control, and any junior could lead them into something that would mean the destruction of the country.'

### 'Shame on them. How dare they.'

On 9 June 1970, some shooting broke out in Amman. Hussein, with his close aide Zaid el-Rifai and some members of his staff, drove off to investigate. Reaching a crossroad outside the city where a barrier and an army lorry were blocking the road, they suddenly found themselves in danger.

Hussein: 'We stopped and found ourselves under intense machine-gun fire. We lost a sergeant of my guard in the car in front, and had about four wounded. Everyone jumped out of my car and yelled at me to do the same, but I was very angry. My first reaction was to swear, then to say, "Shame on them. How dare they!"'

Bullets were coming towards them, hitting the asphalt. Hussein and his men scrambled into a ditch.

Zaid Rifai: 'On the spur of the moment, I tried to protect His Majesty physically, and the Commander of the Guard had the same idea at the same time.'

Hussein: 'They converged from both sides to give me body cover, and nearly broke my back in the process.'

Their driver was asked to turn the car around.

Hussein: 'We got into the car, shooting still going on all around us, and suddenly I realized I had left my beret in the ditch.'

Zaid el-Rifai: 'The King said "I'm not leaving without it", and walked back to the ditch and put his beret on his head.'

Hussein: 'When I got back into the car, the engine was revving like mad, but we remained stationary. I had to tell the driver to engage the gear, which, in his anxiety, he had forgotten to do! Then we shot off.'

King Hussein had survived, but he was very angry. He – and his staff – had been shot at in his own kingdom.[5] Another humiliation was to come three months later, on 6 September 1970.

### Dawson's Field – 'Revolution Airport'

King Hussein recalls the day when, at his palace, west of the city in the suburb, 'an aircraft passed over almost knocking the roof off my palace. We knew there had been an incident in which some aircraft had been hijacked, but we didn't know their destination. Suddenly, it turned out that all these aircraft were heading for Jordan.'

The plane was one of four that had been hijacked by George Habash's PFLP. Inside were hundreds of captive passengers from Germany, America and Switzerland. The hijackers forced the pilots to land on an abandoned military airport, called Dawson's Field. They instantly re-named it 'Revolution Airport', hoping that the hijack would attract international attention to the plight of the Palestinians, and would achieve the release of Palestinian prisoners from Israeli jails.

The hijacking was the last straw for King Hussein. Humiliated and embarrassed, he sent General Haditha who had good contacts with the Palestinians, to Dawson's Field to resolve the situation. The next day, 7 September at 10.30 a.m., Haditha arrived at the airport, escorted by two Ferret scout cars and a military police Land Rover. He began to negotiate with Abu Ali, one of the hijackers. Haditha recalls: 'I said, "What's going on?" He said, "Those are the planes we hijacked." I said, "What about the passengers?" He said, "We need them". After lengthy discussions – it was very hot and I was keeping in the shade of the plane – I recommended that we should take the passengers to Amman, and they should hang on to the aeroplanes.'

In the end, the planes were emptied of the hostages and crew. Then the hijackers activated their explosives and the planes, valued at over £12,000,000, became a cloud of dust, black smoke and debris. No one was hurt but, as the PFLP had hoped, the action attracted international attention and forced King Hussein's hand. He recalls: 'The humiliation of having aircraft flown into Jordan and innocent passengers being whisked away to various parts of the country, and being unable to do anything about it, and having the aircraft blown up, was something that questioned whether Jordan really existed. Well, that was the limit. As far as I was concerned, something had to be done – and done quickly.'

Hussein assembled a crisis military team, declared a state of emergency, and said, 'This is a moment of truth as far as this country and its future is concerned, and I feel responsible. I think we are losing control. We have a responsibility towards the people of Jordan. It is a matter of law and order, and saving this country.'

At first light on 17 September, Hussein's army attacked the Palestinians. The shelling was heavy. Amman was in flames.

### Palestinian or Syrian tanks?

On the third day of the fighting, Hussein was in for a shock. Reports were coming in that Syrian and Iraqi forces were crossing into his kingdom. The T-54 and T-55 tanks had PLO markings. Behind the tanks were heavy 152 millimetre guns. It was a substantial invasion force.

The Syrians had dispatched the tanks into Jordan after Arafat, who had established his command headquarters in Jabel el Hussein, near the centre of Amman, asked the Syrians to intervene.

The request had led to a fierce debate within the Syrian leadership. A top general, who cannot be named, said in an interview for this book: 'We had a political leadership meeting to discuss how to react – whether to stay out of the clash or help the Fedayeen. There were two opinions. Hafiz Assad [Commander of the Syrian Air Force and Minister of Defence] was against intervening. A few others, such as Hikmat Shihabi [Syrian Military Intelligence Chief] and myself, were also against. But the leadership at the time, mainly Dr Atassi and Yousef Zuayen, insisted that Syria should intervene. Assad was not happy with the decision.'

Mustapha Tlas, Assad's Deputy and Chief of Staff, confirmed: 'Assad did not want to commit the Syrian air force' to the battle. He then explained that the compromise they came up with was not to involve the air force and that, when Syria went into action, the Syrian invasion of Jordan was not against the Jordanians but *for the Palestinians*: 'We were just protecting the Palestinians from the Jordanian forces . . . We participated, but it was a restrained kind of participation. We didn't want any conflict between us and the Jordanian forces . . . Jordan, of course, is our ally . . . Jordanians are Arabs.'

This was what the Jordanians had thought, too. Zaid Bin Shakir: 'Some of us, including myself, did not really think the Syrians would attack. We didn't believe that an *Arab* country would attack another *Arab* country . . . but we were proved wrong. The Syrians entered Jordan on the 19th of September . . . '

King Hussein turned to the Soviets – the patrons of Damascus. 'Stop the Syrians,' he urged the Soviet ambassador. The ambassador replied: 'But these are Palestinian army units and tanks. They are not Syrians.' Despite this assertion, he must have known that the Palestinians did not own any tanks.

The Syrians moved deeper into north Jordan. The King's units took them on, fighting hard and stopping many in their tracks, but they were outnumbered and things were getting desperate. 'What's the situation?' Hussein enquired, walking into his headquarters. 'The situation, Sir, is that the army is still not in control of Amman,' he was told, 'and there is very heavy fighting. The Iraqi troops are making aggressive moves and the Syrians are still in full attack.'

The pressure on King Hussein mounted hour by hour. Army headquarters told him that Jordan needed outside help. They pressed him to ask the Americans for help, and to ask any other quarter that would be willing to help. In panic, Hussein called American Ambassador Dean Brown: 'What can you Americans do? You must come in. You physically must come to Jordan and help.'

Ambassador Brown passed the message to American Undersecretary of State Joseph Sisco, who, after consulting with National Security Adviser Henry Kissinger, summoned Soviet attaché Yuli Vorontsov to the State Department. Sisco: 'We hold you responsible and accountable . . . it's up to you to get the Syrians to withdraw.' Vorontsov: 'What if they just stop where they are now?' Sisco: 'Absolutely not. They have got to withdraw behind the line.'

With the approval of President Nixon, the Sixth Fleet was sent to the area and airborne units were placed on standby. But this did not stop the Syrian tanks. Hussein continued to plead for help.

In Washington, Henry Kissinger and Joseph Sisco went to see President Nixon. 'Mr President,' they said. 'We think the Israelis are in the best position to help the King. They're close to the scene, and their resources can be employed rapidly.' President Nixon agreed.

Asking the Israelis to help King Hussein was one thing; selling it to him was another. He was afraid that if the Israelis moved into Jordan with their ground forces to stop the Syrians, they would stay for good and that he would be denounced by Arabs as a traitor. But he was in dire straits and, after much negotiation with Ambassador Brown, he agreed to turn a blind eye when the Israelis sent in planes to frighten the Syrians.

The Israeli government, led by Prime Minister Golda Meir, and Defence Minister Moshe Dayan were keen to oblige. They reasoned that if they helped the Americans to help the King, they would be rewarded – the Americans would put less pressure on them to pull out of occupied territories.

Mordechai Hod, Commander of the Israeli air force, personally briefed the leader of the quartet of planes they were sending: 'Fly over them,' he instructed. 'Make absolutely sure they see and hear you, and make mock attacks so that they understand what we want them to do – that we want them to turn around and go back.'

Israeli ground forces were also sent to the Beit Shean area. Tank transporters and military vehicles were moved in broad daylight within full view of anyone who was watching from the Syrian side of the border. They were meant to be seen.[6] The Israeli cabinet convened for an emergency session and issued a statement: 'If Jordan's neighbours, Syria and Iraq, started carving up the kingdom between them, then Israel would probably have to take action'. With American forces on alert, the Soviets denouncing outside intervention in Jordan for 'whatever pretext', and Israeli planes flying over the Syrian tanks and ground forces, the Syrians got cold feet.

In Damascus, Minister of Defence Assad, who was against the invasion into Jordan, called a top Syrian general. '"The decision,"

Assad said, "to withdraw our forces from Jordan has been made", and he instructed us to draw up a plan for retreat.' General Awad Bagh, the Commander of the Syrian invading force, was at the front, and transmitted the withdrawal order. By lunchtime, Wednesday, 23 September, the Syrians withdrew. They had lost 100 tanks and 170 vehicles; the Jordanians had lost nineteen. The number of dead and wounded is not known.

With the Syrians gone, King Hussein could finish the job of getting rid of the Palestinian organizations that had brought his kingdom to the verge of collapse. The battle between his and Arafat's fighters intensified. Many Palestinians fled, but not all gave up. Many dug their heels in and continued to fight – one of them was Yasser Arafat.

## President Numeiry of Sudan

Hiding somewhere in Amman, Arafat sent out grim reports of battles and thousands of casualties, and Arab leaders felt they had to do something to sort out the mess. In Cairo, President Nasser called an emergency summit.

While Arab presidents and princes convened in the Nile Hilton Hotel, two leaders – Colonel Mu'amer Gaddafi of Libya and President Jafaar Numeiry of Sudan – got talking. It was a private conversation. Nasser came in and joined them. 'What are you saying?' he asked. Colonel Gaddafi replied, 'Numeiry is saying that to solve a problem, you have to see what the problem is. But we are far away from the problem, and cannot solve it.' Gadaffi then suggested that they should act on President Numeiry's idea and go to Amman to see the problem at first hand. Nasser agreed that a delegation should go to talk to King Hussein.

Numeiry boarded the private jet of the Kuwaiti Defence Minister and, leading an eight-man delegation, flew into the thick of the Amman fighting. King Hussein – who was busy fighting to save his throne – reluctantly arranged for Numeiry and his team to meet him at his Hummar palace. Numeiry recalls: 'We had dinner with the King and kept on talking until daybreak.'

Numeiry's message to Hussein was simple: 'You have to stop the fighting'. King Hussein replied: 'We can't stop! We are in the middle of a life-and-death struggle!'

Numeiry and his delegation left and went to the shell-torn

Egyptian embassy, in Jebel Webda, where they were staying. The delegation was determined to find Arafat. Numeiry managed to get the frequency of Arafat's walkie-talkie and tuned in. He could hear Arafat pleading for help: 'My people are dying . . . ', and outlining what he needed from the Arabs.

Through Palestinian contacts, Numeiry's delegation learned where Arafat was hiding and set off to find him, first driving, then on foot. 'It was a beautiful night with a full moon,' recalls Numeiry, 'though the sound of bullets was very loud and frightening.' Eventually, they reached a house, went down to the cellar and waited. Five or ten minutes later, Arafat showed up. He was dirty, unshaved and tired. Numeiry recalls: 'He hugged me and we cried as we greeted each other . . . I told him, "Okay, you will be saved. We will go, and you will come with us". We went to the Egyptian embassy where we were going to spend the night. Arafat shaved, bathed and rested for a while, and when morning came he was okay.'

Next day, Numeiry and his delegation went to see King Hussein and informed him they were returning home.

Reaching Cairo Airport, Numeiry climbed out of the aircraft. The plane remained on the runway, but it was not empty. Inside was Yasser Arafat. He climbed out in the dark and was taken to the Nile Hilton Hotel where the Arab leaders were staying. Arriving there only minutes behind Numeiry, he went up to a suite on the fourth floor, just next door to King Feisal of Saudi Arabia. After his cellar in Amman, the suite was a joy, and it was now renamed 'The Palestine Suite'.[7]

On 26 September, at 10 p.m., the leaders, including Arafat, went into the Hall of 1001 Nights and sat with President Nasser. Numeiry told Nasser what he had witnessed in Amman. At 2 a.m., Nasser drafted an angry cable to King Hussein and, before going to sleep, instructed Numeiry to convene a press conference and tell what he had witnessed in Jordan.

Numeiry did as he was told. 'We left Amman,' he explained to the journalists who had gathered, 'with the impression that there was an overall plot for the annihilation of the brave Palestinian resistance. The Jordanian authorities have a pre-arranged conspiracy to crush the Palestinian people.[8]

In Amman, King Hussein was shocked: 'Suddenly I heard with

utter disbelief that they had arrived in Cairo, and had Arafat with them.' He was also upset by what Numeiry told the press conference: 'His statement was very harsh and bore no relationship to the truth. He accused us of atrocities and inhuman behaviour.'

Hussein felt that he had to defend himself. At the controls of a Royal Jordanian Airlines' Caravelle, he left Amman on Sunday, 27 September, at 9 a.m., and flew to Cairo. President Nasser was waiting to welcome him and take him to the conference. Arab Heads of states were waiting.[9] The first to come and shake Hussein's hand was President Numeiry. 'What have you done?' said the King, referring to the 'abduction' of Arafat from Amman. Others, especially Gaddafi, were in aggressive mood. Just before Hussein had come in, Gaddafi had suggested that the King should be shot. Now, Gaddafi was saying that the King should 'go and have his head examined'. Nasser replied: 'There are others present who are more qualified for that', and suggested that Gaddafi 'might need some care himself'. Arafat was also present, wearing his *keffiyeh*, army shirt and dark glasses.

The meeting went on for six hours. At 9.30 p.m, a fourteen-point agreement to stop the fighting in Amman was ready to be signed. Under pressure from Arab leaders, King Hussein signed first, followed by Nasser and Arafat. The agreement was sealed with a reluctant handshake between the King and Arafat.

The next morning at 11 a.m., Arafat flew to Amman in an Egyptian military aircraft. King Hussein also returned, flying himself home.

From September 1970 to the beginning of April 1971, all was quiet in Amman. But King Hussein – who was clearly unhappy with the Cairo Agreement and regretting his signature – repudiated it, and decided to continue the battle to rid himself of Arafat and his people. On 6 April, he entrusted Prime Minister Wasfi al-Tal with this task. Fighting resumed. This time, the King's army succeeded in evicting Arafat and his PLO from the cities.

Some of the Palestinians went to Mafrak, in Jordan, and were then led from there in convoy to Syria. Most went to Lebanon.

## Chapter 21

# 'A big explosion will happen in Lebanon'

The Lebanon in which Arafat and the PLO arrived – with its high mountains, turquoise sea, fancy French restaurants, casinos and fashion houses – was widely regarded as the most attractive country in the Middle East. But it lacked a strong central government. Lebanese politics represented a fragile balance between Christian and Muslim interests, with Maronite Christians in the dominant position. The arrival of large numbers of Palestinian refugees, the majority of whom came into Lebanon after the 1948 and 1967 Wars in Palestine-Israel, plus the growth of Islamic militancy, destabilized Lebanese politics. As Arafat and his fighters entered the country, political power lay in the hands of factional group warlords who, backed by their militias, concentrated on looking after their own people.[10]

The strongest of the Christian militias was the Phalange, established by Pierre Gemayel and led by his son, Bashir. American-educated Bashir Gemayel had a brusque manner, impulsive character and a penchant for violence, but he was a charismatic leader.

Another Christian militia, established by former President Camille Chamoun, and led by his youngest son, Dany, was the 'Tigers militia' (Al Noumour).

The two young Christian leaders, Bashir Gemayel and Dany Chamoun, were vying for control of the Christian community in Lebanon and their militias often clashed. But more important than their hatred for each other, was their opposition to Palestinians who were allowed, according to an agreement they had signed in Cairo with the Lebanese government in 1969, to carry arms. The arrival of Arafat and his fighters exacerbated the already tense situation.

### 'A big explosion will happen in Lebanon'

Just after midnight on 10 April 1973, an Israeli commando unit landed in Beirut. The Israeli government, which was targeting the PLO in Lebanon, had authorized them to revenge the killing of eleven Israeli athletes at the Olympic Games in Munich in

September 1972. The commandos reached Verdan Street, and broke into the flats of three senior PLO officials – Kamal Nasser, Yusif Najar and Kamal Edwan. Riddling them with bullets, the Israelis killed them all and left. The Lebanese army, located in the same neighbourhood, did not stop the Israelis. This inaction erroneously reinforced Palestinian suspicions that the Christian leadership had tacitly approved the Israeli raid. Tension between the Lebanese Christians and the Palestinians, already intense, increased.

Karim Pakradouni, a member of Phalange, arranged a meeting between Pierre Gemayel and Yasser Arafat in Ashrafiya, a Christian quarter in East Beirut. Jumping into Pakradouni's car, Arafat said to his bodyguards: 'I'm going alone with Karim to Ashrafiya. You stay here'. The bodyguards protested. It was dangerous for Arafat, the PLO leader, to go unaccompanied to Ashrafiya. Pakradouni wanted to take Arafat straight to Gemayel's heavily guarded house, but Arafat protested. Taking off his *keffiyeh* and putting on a green army cap, he said, 'I've never visited Ashrafiya. I want to see it'. So, Pakradouni drove him through the streets of Ashrafiya. At one point Arafat saw a slogan on a wall, saying 'No to the PLO'. Turning to Pakradouni, he said, 'A big explosion will happen in Lebanon'.

Two years later, Arafat's prophecy came true. His talks with Gemayel had led nowhere and tension between Arafat's guerrillas and the Christian-Lebanese remained as acute as ever. Lebanon, after the killing of the three PLO officials, was a powder keg. The spark that ignited it came on 13 April 1975.

A gunman, riding in a speeding car, fired on a church in the Christian East Beirut suburb of Ein Romaneh, killing four Christians. That same day, in the afternoon, a bus returning Palestinians to the Tel Zatar refugee camp, was attacked by Christian Phalangists. Twenty-seven Palestinians were killed. Civil war had started in Lebanon.

### 'Helping the Christians to help themselves'
In the early spring of 1976, Bashir Gemayel was standing at the window of his office with his colleague Josef Abu Khalil. It was evening and fighting was going on in the commercial centre of Beirut. Gemayel's Christian militia was fighting a coalition of

157

Palestinians-Muslims-Druze. Down the street, Gemayel and Abu Khalil could see about 200 of their fighters standing idle. 'We cannot send them to the front,' said Bashir to Abu Khalil. 'We don't have any weapons to provide them with.'

Abu Khalil decided to go in secret to the enemy – the Israelis – and ask for weapons. Israel was, after all, the enemy of Arafat's PLO, and he had reason to believe that the Israelis would help. Contact had already been made some time before between a Christian colleague, Mugagbag, and a Mossad agent.[11] The Christian and the Israeli agent arranged to meet on the steps of the Magdalene Church, Paris, and the Mossad agent promised, albeit unofficially, that, if asked, Israel would support the Christians in their fight against the Palestinians.

Abu Khalil then decided to approach the Israelis in secret himself. Asking Mugagbag to join him, he recruited a sailor and took a yacht – a pleasure craft – from Kaslik, and set sail. The destination was Haifa, the northern Israeli port. The aim: to ask Israel for weapons to fight Arafat's guerrillas. Abu Khalil recalls: 'We left Beirut at about 2 a.m., on 12 March 1976. The sea was very rough. I saw another boat and was afraid . . . But then they called us, using a loud-hailer. They were using a language we didn't understand [it was Hebrew]. We replied in Arabic and one of them understood.'

Ordered by the Israeli patrol to keep his hands held high above his head, Abu Khalil climbed into the Israeli frigate. It was his first ever meeting with Israelis. He had expected to see 'supermen', but, 'they were just like us, afraid just like us'. He was taken to Haifa, then to Tel Aviv.

The unexpected arrival of a Lebanese leader prompted a late-night meeting of Israeli defence staff. It was headed by Defence Minister Shimon Peres. 'Why have you come and what do you want?" Peres asked in French. 'I have come to ask you for weapons,' said Abu Khalil. 'We need ammunition. I've come on a gamble. If you help us, we'll thank you. If not, I'll just go back to where I came from.' Peres: 'I'll put the question to my government and give you the answer tomorrow. Now go and have a good night's rest.'

Peres discussed the matter with Prime Minister Yitzhak Rabin. They decided that it was in Israel's interest to help the Christians.

First, because the Christians were fighting the enemy – the PLO. Second, if the Christians were defeated by the Palestinians-Muslim-Druze alliance, then Lebanon might fall into the lap of Syria. Mossad people were also keen to support the Christian Militia. They saw Lebanon as a window to the Arab world that would help them gather intelligence. It was also a novel experience for the Israelis to be asked for help by the Arabs – albeit Christians – of a neighbouring country.

The next day Peres met with Abu Khalil in a Tel Aviv restaurant. 'Yes,' he said. 'We are willing to help you.'

### Benjamin Ben Eliezer's secret mission

Two weeks after Abu Khalil's secret visit to Israel, Shimon Peres approved the sending of Benjamin Ben Eliezer, an Arabic-speaking Israeli army commander, to Beirut. The mission of this commander, of Iraqi origin, was: to visit the Christian Arabs who were asking for weapons and assess their military organization and fighting capabilities.

After training with Mossad in the techniques of covert rendez-vous at sea, Ben Eliezer, known as 'Fuad', set off with a small team aboard an Israeli missile boat. Dressed in civilian clothes and armed with pistols, their destination was Junieh, the Christian-held seaport near Beirut.

The day after his arrival, Ben Eliezer was taken on a trip by Dany Chamoun. He was in for a shock – the outing exposed the harsh realities of the situation in Lebanon: 'I saw thousands of people standing on both sides of the road, clapping their hands. "What's going on here?" I asked. Dany Chamoun replied: "Come and see." And then I saw two trucks approaching. In one, people were shooting in the air; the other had a rope tied to it. Tied to this rope were other ropes, and at the end of each rope was the body of a terrorist [a Palestinian]. The trucks were dragging the bodies along the ground, while men sitting on the trucks were shooting at the long-dead corpses. I was shocked. I said again: "What's going on?", and Dany Chamoun replied: "We're killing the terrorists."'

Ben Eliezer, having been instructed to give equal treatment to the rival Christian militias, also met Bashir Gemayel on his trip.

Back in Israel, he reported what he had seen and heard, and listed the Christians' demands for weapons. Israel was willing to supply them. A Mossad agent, involved in the supply of arms, described for us how Israeli boats began sailing back and forth delivering arms to both Chamoun's and Gemayel's Christian militias. A boat would sail to the Lebanese water, towing craft heaped with weapons and ammunition. Off the Lebanese coast, the craft would be released for the Christians to tow away. The ammunition, left by Arab armies on the battlefield in past wars, was given to the Christians.

But the Christians wanted still more weapons. As their links with Israel became closer, Dany Chamoun and Bashir Gemayel, were allowed to visit Israel to speak to Defence Minister Peres. Peres recalls: 'In came the two men, very impressive, handsome, athletic, dressed in the best French fashion, as was the custom in Lebanon. They brought me a gold watch as a gift, and we sat down to dinner at my house. I said: "The question is whether you two can work together, because if you can't it's a waste for us to invest in you." They answered one after the other – Bashir began, Dany continued. They said that everything was agreed between them. Bashir would be politically responsible, Dany militarily responsible. They gave the impression of a perfect couple.'

Gemayel and Chamoun asked for canons, mortars and tanks. Israel supplied them. They asked for communication instruments, mines, explosives. Israel gave them. But the rules of the game were made clear: Israel would help the Christians to help themselves – that is, to fight Arafat's guerrillas and their allies in Lebanon. Israel would never intervene directly in the fighting.

For the next five years, the civil war raged in Lebanon. Israel continued to help the Christian Arabs, but maintained its policy of non-intervention. However, when Ariel Sharon was made Defence Minister in 1981, all this changed.

*Chapter 22*

# Sharon and Gemayel

Few Israelis wanted to see Agriculture Minister Ariel Sharon enter the gates of the Defence Ministry in 1981. No one disputed that Sharon – a charismatic man, and formerly one of Israel's brightest military commanders whose forces had been the first to cross the Suez Canal in the 1973 War – could efficiently control the Defence Ministry's operations. But some considered him too dangerous a person to head the sensitive Ministry.

Sharon's critics felt that if he were made Defence Minister, he would surround the Knesset with tanks and carry out a *putsch* – the removal of one government by force and the replacement of it by another. Menachem Begin, who, since the resignation of Ezer Weizman in May 1980, was holding the posts of both Premier and Defence Minister, was well aware of Sharon's weaknesses. Once, sitting in the restaurant of the Knesset, he pointed at Sharon, and whispered to his guests, 'He's a brilliant general, but a vicious man'.[12] This was echoed in what Prime Minister David Ben-Gurion had once said of Sharon: 'He's a brilliant soldier, but very economical with the truth'.

Inspite of these apprehensions, Sharon was made Defence Minister. According to the Peace Agreement with Egypt, 1981 was the year when Israel had to evacuate its settlements in the Sinai, and Prime Minister Begin wanted Sharon alongside him for this task. Sharon, who had been responsible for the building of many of the settlements in Sinai, knew the settlers and was the best person to persuade them to leave. Begin could not bear the idea of confronting the settlers himself.

But other issues were uppermost in Sharon's mind. His presence – and first priority – were felt immediately. 'I want,' he said, 'to solve the problem of Lebanon once and for all.' First, he wanted Arafat and his 'terrorists' out of Lebanon – not only out of the south, from where they were shelling Israeli settlements, but also out of Beirut, where Arafat had established his head-quarters. Second, he wanted the Syrians out of Lebanon. They had been invited into Lebanon in 1976, with the tacit agreement

161

of Israel, to stop the civil war between the Palestinians and the Christians. Sharon thought this was a grave error of judgement, for it had allowed the Syrians to take over Lebanon and could, if the need arose, block Israel's option of passing through Lebanon in a hook manoeuvre to strike at Damascus from the west. Third, he wanted a peace treaty between Israel and Lebanon.

## A crucial meeting between Sharon and Gemayel

'To understand fully what's going on in Lebanon,' said Sharon to Prime Minister Begin, 'I should visit the place myself.' Begin approved and arrangements were made for him to go there in January 1982. It was a complicated and risky operation. Sharon was Defence Minister and would be visiting an Arab country with which Israel was officially in a state of war.

A helicopter was prepared to fly him into Lebanon, and to rescue him in an emergency. A rescue squad was trained in case Sharon's helicopter was forced down at sea.

Sharon's helicopter left Tel Aviv under cover of darkness and, flying along the coast to Haifa, headed north. On its right were the lights of Tyre, then those of Sidon. Half an hour later, Beirut came into sight. Turning back out to sea, away from Beirut which was lit by canon and artillery fire, his helicopter reached Junieh and landed on the beach. There, waiting for him, was Bashir Gemayel.

By now Gemayel was the dominant Christian leader in Lebanon. The promise to co-operate with each other that Gemayel and Chamoun had made to Peres in 1976, had not been fulfilled.

Murdering his way to the top, Gemayel had ruthlessly eliminated his rivals. In June 1978, his gunmen had assassinated Tony Franjihe, the leader of a pro-Syrian Maronite faction. Then on 7 July 1980, while Dany Chamoun was with his mistress, Gemayel's forces had stormed Chamoun's Tigers' headquarters, killed eighty of his people and effectively liquidated his militia. Dany Chamoun had escaped to Europe, and Gemayel had proclaimed a merger of all the Christian factions. Two leaders of small Christian groups, Georges Adwan and Etienne Saqre, had agreed to integrate their forces into Gemayel's.

The minute Sharon's helicopter landed, Gemayel rushed towards him, hugging him and kissing him on both cheeks. 'I knew you would be the one to visit us,' he said, excited. 'Even though they didn't tell me, I was sure it would be you.' They stood for a moment on the beach. Sharon noticed many lights out at sea. 'What are all those lights?' he asked. 'Those are merchant vessels,' answered Gemayel. 'But,' said Sharon, surprised, 'there's a war going on here.' 'War is war,' said Gemayel, 'and business is business.'

With Gemayel at the wheel, and two security cars at their front and back, Sharon and Gemayel entered Beirut. Sharon recalls: 'We went through the city streets. There were metal shutters torn by shells, but the place was full of life. There were expensive cars, pretty young ladies walking around, and the night clubs were open. It seemed so strange for a country in a state of war.'

The next day Sharon went to the Gemayel family house in Bikfaiya, where two elderly Maronites, Pierre Gemayel and Camille Chamoun (Dany Chamoun's father), were waiting for him. They lunched and talked. Sharon was frank. 'You should know,' he said to his hosts, 'that we, in Israel, have taken a decision to invade Lebanon. We are simply waiting for the opportunity to accomplish this.' And he added: 'We are studying two possibilities. One, a limited invasion of forty to forty-five kilometres into Lebanese territory, aimed at striking the Palestinians in southern Lebanon. The other, a wider operation that would take into consideration not only the interests of Israel, but of the Christians, too. In this instance, we would invade up to Beirut and strike at the resistance within Beirut.' Then Sharon added: 'When we arrive at the gates of Beirut, we will ask you for two things: One to participate militarily in the Beirut battle; two, to sign a peace treaty with Israel.'[13]

Pierre Gemayel rebuffed the idea of signing a peace treaty: 'We are part of the Arab world,' he said sternly. 'We must remain on good terms with the Arab world.' He also rejected the idea of fighting shoulder-to-shoulder with the Israelis. Bashir Gemayel turned to his father: 'Papa, why are you talking to them like that? Are we going to sit around singing lullabies while they do all the work?'[14]

## Gemayel plays safe

If, after what Bashir had said to his father, Sharon thought that the young Gemayel was in his pocket, he was wrong. Bashir Gemayel was in fact hesitating. His dream was to become president of *all* of Lebanon. Could he fight – as Sharon wanted him to – against the Shi'ites, Palestinians and Druze, and then ask them to accept him as their president?

The moment Sharon returned to Israel, Bashir Gemayel called in his adviser, Karim Pakradouni. They discussed the visit and Sharon's demands for the Christians to fight alongside the Israelis and clear Beirut of Arafat's PLO. According to Pakradouni, Gemayel said, 'I have to participate because only Israel is capable of saving Lebanon from the Palestinians and the Syrians'. Pakradouni: 'If Israel has an interest in coming into Beirut, it will do so anyway, with or without you. But it is *not* in your interests to participate militarily with the Israeli army. If you do, you will lose your chance to be a presidential candidate.' Gemayel accepted Pakradouni's advice. He also remembered what his father, Pierre, had once said to him: 'You can use Israel to threaten the Arabs, but don't collaborate with Israel'.

Through the services of Colonel Jonny Abdou, the Lebanese Chief of Military Intelligence, Gemayel contacted the Syrians. At Abdou's house, overlooking the presidential palace of Ba'abda, he held secret talks with the Syrian Intelligence Chief Mohammed Ghanim. 'I have information,' he said, 'that the Israelis are preparing to invade Lebanon.' Then he gave Ghanim the full details of his talks with Defence Minister Sharon. Ghanim listened, but didn't discuss details.[15] He was wondering if Gemayel was trying to frighten him with talk of the Israelis, so that the Syrians would leave Lebanon.

Gemayel also tried to strike a deal with Arafat, the man Sharon wanted him to fight. At Jonny Abdou's house, he met with Hani Hassan, a leading Palestinian and one of Arafat's closest colleagues. Gemayel: 'I have information about a possible Israeli invasion that could reach as far as Beirut.' Hassan was shocked. 'Our information,' he said, 'is that the invasion will stop at Sidon.' Gemayel: 'Don't bet on a limited invasion – expect a bigger one. The aim is to get you out of Lebanon.' Puzzled, Hassan rose to leave, to pass on this important information to Arafat, but Gemayel stopped him. 'Just before you go,' he said, 'I have a suggestion. Tell Yasser Arafat that if we agree together on the withdrawal of the Palestinians from Lebanon, and the Palestinian weapons are handed over to me, then I can stop Israel from invading Lebanon.' He added, 'If Israel then invades, I'm prepared to help the PLO fight them.'[16]

Hassan left to pass on the information to Arafat. He never returned with a response. Did he also suspect that Gemayel was trying to frighten him with talk of the Israelis, so that the PLO would leave Beirut?

*Chapter 23*

# The 1982 War

Sharon would not go to war in Lebanon without alerting the Americans. They were Israel's allies and must *not* be taken by surprise. In December 1981, he invited Morris Draper, US Special Ambassador, and Philip Habib, President Reagan's Envoy, to a meeting. Sitting in a conference room, with an enlarged map of Lebanon in the background, Sharon told the Americans that the PLO shelling of Israeli settlements in Galilee from South Lebanon could not be tolerated. 'If the terrorists continue to attack us,' he said, 'we will wipe them out *completely* in Lebanon.' 'This is madness,' Philip Habib replied. 'The PLO isn't carrying out many raids. There is no need for such an Israeli reaction. We are living in the twentieth century . . . You can't just invade a country like that.'

After the meeting, Habib and Draper went back to Washington to report on Sharon's plan. Habib met with President Reagan and Secretary of State Alexander Haig: 'The Israelis,' he said, 'are planning to knock out Lebanon once and for all . . . They are going to do it using US missiles. That's gonna look bad throughout the Middle East, and everyone will assume they have our acquiescence.' On 25 May 1982, Sharon flew to Washington to meet Secretary of State Haig and the upper echelons of the State Department. Once again, Sharon spread out an enlarged map of Lebanon. 'We, in Israel,' he said, 'have reached an impossible situation in which we have no choice but to destroy the PLO infrastructure in Lebanon.' Arafat's people, he explained, were shelling Israeli settlements in Galilee, turning life there into hell. Pushing the 'terrorists' from the Israeli border would free the Israeli settlements from the 'terrorist' threat.

After the formal meeting, Haig took Sharon to his office for a private chat. 'Ariel,' he said, 'I am telling you that this is unsatisfactory . . . Nothing should be done in Lebanon without an *internationally recognized provocation*, and the Israeli reaction should be *proportionate* to that provocation.' Sharon replied: 'What is a clear provocation? When one Jew is murdered? Two? Five? What, for you, is a "clear provocation"? And, let's say for example, that Jews are only wounded, and don't die of their wounds . . . What exactly is a "clear provocation?"' Then he added, 'This is unacceptable.'

Sharon, however, had already achieved the purpose of his visit. He had not come to America to get the 'green light' to strike in Lebanon. He had come to let them know what his intentions were. Haig's response that nothing should be done in Lebanon without a 'clear provocation' was good enough for Sharon.

## A clear provocation
On 3 June 1982, some men were waiting for Israeli Ambassador Shlomo Argov outside the Dorchester Hotel, London. When he left – it was close to midnight – the men approached him, one took out a pistol and shot him in the head. Argov was badly wounded, but not killed.

In Beirut, at 3 a.m., on 4 June 1982, Arafat was still working in his office. A messenger – Abu el-Feda – came in. 'I have just received this from London,' he said, handing Arafat a cable, telling of the attempt on the life of the Israeli ambassador in London. When Arafat had finished reading the cable, he knew that, although the PLO was not involved in the assassination attempt, Sharon would use this as a pretext to justify striking at the PLO infrastructure in Lebanon.

On his way to the airport – he was going to Jeddah on a mediating mission to end the Iran-Iraq war – Arafat took out a pad and wrote a cable, warning all the Palestinian forces to be on high alert.

In Jerusalem, several hours later, ministers hurried to an emergency cabinet meeting. At 9.30 a.m., Prime Minister Begin entered the cabinet room. The ministers were already seated around the table. Ariel Sharon, the Defence Minister, was absent on an official visit to Romania. Begin took his seat at the middle of the table. All eyes were fixed on him. 'Ambassadors represent the state,' he said, 'and an assault on an Israeli ambassador is tantamount to an attack on the state of Israel.' Turning to Avraham Shalom, head of Shin Beit, responsible for the security of Israeli ambassadors abroad, Begin asked him to report.

Shalom's report was sketchy. The attempted assassination had happened only a few hours before. What he could say was that the assassin had used a small Polish WZ63 pistol, indicating that the attack had been carried out by the Abu Nidal organization, the only organization using this kind of weapon.

A Palestinian, Abu Nidal (real name Sabri al-Banna) was born in Jaffa, Palestine, in May 1937. Driven from there during the 1948 War, he became, some years later, the world's most notorious Arab terrorist responsible for countless deaths. Abu Ali Shaheen, who knew him, said, 'The gun was his ideology and his ideology was the gun. The gun – only the gun'.[17]

Security chief Shalom suggested that Gideon Machanaimi, Begin's adviser on the War Against Terrorism, should tell the ministers about Abu Nidal's organization. He wanted the ministers to know that Abu Nidal was *not* close to Arafat and the PLO; that Abu Nidal and Arafat were vicious enemies; that Arafat could not control Abu Nidal. But Begin cut Shalom short, saying, 'They're all PLO'.

For Begin, it made no difference which Palestinian organization had carried out the assassination. Arafat was the leader of the umbrella organization – the PLO – and, as such, was responsible, in his view, for all Palestinian activities.

Rafael Eitan, Begin's Chief of Staff, suggested that they should send Israeli planes to attack the PLO positions in and around Beirut. The ministers approved and the meeting ended. 'Gentlemen,' said Begin, just before the ministers dispersed, 'after the air force attack, we should be prepared for the maximum. We will strike and see what happens. Let us convene again on Saturday night at my home.'

Just before 3 p.m., on 4 June 1982, the Israeli planes took off. At 15.15 hours, they struck at PLO positions in Beirut. In the absence of Arafat, who was still in Jeddah, Abu Jeddah convened a meeting of leading Palestinians. They decided to hit back. Two hours later, their canon shells and Katyusha rockets rained down on Israeli settlements at Galilee.

For those Israelis who were looking for an 'internationally recognized provocation', the maiming of Argov and the shelling of Galilee provided reasons to go to war.

### Peace for Galilee?

The Israeli ministers gathered again at Begin's residence. It was a quiet Saturday evening in the Jerusalem suburb, Rehavia. Sharon, back from Romania, took his place among them. Begin opened the meeting: 'Mr Defence Minister,' he said, turning to Sharon, 'would you be kind enough to explain the military plan to the cabinet.' Sharon took the floor. He recalls: 'I presented the operation. I explained what the targets were, and that the aim was to hit the PLO in Lebanon. Then Minister Simcah Ehrlich asked: "What about Beirut?" I said, "Beirut is out of the picture. This operation is not designed to capture Beirut, but to create a forty to forty-five kilometre area in which there will no longer be any terrorists.'

The ministers approved the operation. It would be called 'Operation Peace for Galilee'. It would be short – between twenty-four and forty-eight hours. It would be limited – just pushing the PLO artillery back out of range so they could not strike at settlements in Galilee. The Syrians who were in Lebanon would not be attacked unless they took action against the Israeli forces.

Sharon left Jerusalem and hurried back to his farm at Havat Ha'shikmim in the Negev. At 3 a.m., a helicopter was waiting in a nearby field to take him to the northern command. On arrival, he met with the military commanders and gave his final instructions. He was still talking in terms of a limited operation in Lebanon. At 11 a.m., Sharon was standing alongside a road, just by the Israeli-Lebanese border, waving to his Israeli troops crossing into Lebanon.

*Chapter 24*

# Homelands

Within hours of arriving in Lebanon, the Israeli forces took the Beaufort Castle, the Tyre area and most of the PLO-controlled areas between the Litani and Zaharani Rivers. Sharon had managed to pressurize the Israeli cabinet into allowing the forces to move even deeper into Lebanon than was originally planned.[18] While the forces were doing this, Prime Minister Begin, standing on the podium of the Knesset, was reassuring the Israelis: 'If we achieve the forty-kilometre line from our northern border, the job is done. All fighting will stop'. But, even while he was talking, the tanks and troops were continuing to roll on, with the forty kilometres limit already far behind them. Soon after an Israeli soldier could see a city which seemed to him 'as dull as Haifa'.[19] It was Beirut.

The city, that Sharon had promised was 'out of the picture' was now very much *in* the picture.

On 13 June 1982, the eighth day of war, wearing a helmet and bullet-proof-vest, and riding on top of an armoured personnel carrier, Sharon drove with Israeli forces into the Ba'abda neighbourhood. By now, West Beirut – occupied by the PLO, 500,000 Palestinians, Muslim Lebanese civilians, and the 85th Syrian Brigade – was encircled by the Israelis. The siege would last seventy days.

During that time, anybody who approached Beirut would see hundreds of canons and mortars all aimed at the heart of the city. From what was once a school building in Ba'abda, with a full view of Beirut, Israeli artillery officers were directing the bombardment that subjected the Palestinian districts to saturation bombing. The artillery fire would occasionally stop to allow Israeli planes to unload their bombs on Beirut, and then start all over again. Electricity and water would occasionally be cut and supply of food stopped. All these things were done to put pressure on the Lebanese government, and, through it, on Arafat and his PLO to leave Beirut.

With Bashir Gemayel refusing to enter the city and clear it of

169

Arafat and the PLO, Sharon was forced to ask the Americans for a go-between. Sending his own troops into Beirut to drive out the PLO was out of the question – he knew that the Israeli government and Israeli public would oppose entering the capital; and that, in addition, his forces would suffer many casualties in house-to-house fighting with the PLO. He hated asking the Americans, who had not given the green light for the Israeli invasion of Lebanon during his Washington visit, and who had not subsequently regarded the invasion as a 'proportionate' retaliation for the attempt on the life of Ambassador Argov, but he had no other option. The US sent Philip Habib, an American diplomat of Lebanese ancestry, to act as a go-between for the Israelis, the Lebanese government and – through the auspices of the Lebanese government – the PLO. Habib then commenced his mediating efforts to stop the fighting and ensure that Arafat and his guerrillas left Lebanon. Sharon's terms were simple: Arafat and his guerrillas, as well as the Syrians, had to get out of Beirut, leaving behind their heavy arms.

In Yarzah, at the house of Jonny Abdou, Sharon and Habib discussed the departure of Arafat and his PLO. Habib: 'Who has to leave Beirut? All the 10,000 or just their leaders?' Sharon: 'All the terrorists. They must all leave. If they refuse, they will be destroyed . . . Tell them to leave.' Habib: 'I think it will be impossible to do what you ask.'[20]

Sharon was adamant. He had brought all his forces to Beirut and was determined to see Arafat out. Unleashing his artillery and air force, he hit Beirut hard. The Lebanese government could not stand it any more. Now they, too, wanted Arafat to leave. Only in this way would Sharon stop destroying their city. But no government minister wanted to be the first to tell Arafat he had to go. President Sarkis turned to Jonny Abdou: 'We have nobody but you to tell Arafat he has to go'.

Abdou went to Arafat: 'You have to leave Beirut,' he said. Arafat was shocked. No Lebanese, he explained, had so far told him that he had to leave. 'Well,' said Abdou, 'I am informing you now.' Arafat was distraught. 'Do they want us to be or not to be?' he asked a colleague standing beside him. But, by now, he understood that he had to leave Beirut. Later, he would say, 'It was only my allies, the Lebanese, who pushed me into leaving Beirut. Only when they told me, "Please, Arafat, this is enough . . . what are you waiting for, Abu Ammar? Look, we are facing death from shelling and bombing from the sea, the land, the air . . . " that I began to feel responsible for killing their children. If I insisted on carrying on the fighting, I would kill more of their children. I felt guilty.'[21]

Arafat called a meeting. The PLO leaders faced a stark choice. With pressure coming at them from all directions, they decided to leave. 'I will be the last one to leave,' Arafat said to the other Palestinian leaders. 'That is the condition I have made with Philip Habib.' He was determined that nobody would say that he had been the first to run away from Beirut.

Arafat informed Lebanese Prime Minister Chafiq al Wazzan, that he was willing to leave Beirut. The Prime Minister rang Habib: 'They are willing to leave,' he said. Habib, knowing that Sharon would not accept vague promises, replied, 'Do you have written confirmation to prove this?' Wazzan: 'Of course not.'

Arafat then had to provide a signed guarantee and deposit it with Prime Minister Wazzan. Taking a small delegation, Arafat went through the dark abandoned streets of Beirut to Wazzan's house to hand him the guarantee. There was no electricity in town, the lift was out of order, and Arafat had to climb to the sixth floor. At midnight, the delegation knocked on the Prime Minister's door. They went in. 'Mr Prime Minister,' said Arafat, 'we have come to present you with this letter.' Wazzan was moved: 'I didn't open the envelope,' he recalls. 'I took it, and my hand was shaking because I found it humiliating.' He went into his bedroom, and, when he came back, handed Arafat a Koran. 'While you are leaving us, to go to another exile, and Jerusalem is still occupied,' he said, 'I don't have anything to offer you, but this Koran.' If this were just a show – for, in reality, Prime Minister Wazzan did want to see the back of the Palestinians – then it was a good one.

With Arafat agreeing to leave, Philip Habib had to find Arab states that would accept the Palestinians. Not many would do so, for Arafat and his PLO were considered troublemakers. King Hussein told the Americans that if armed guerrillas went to Syria, they must be placed far from his border. Hussein, although reluctant, agreed to allow some Palestinians with Jordanian passports to enter his Kingdom. The Tunisians, South and North Yemen,

Sudan, Iraq and Algeria, also agreed to take some. Egypt and Syria refused.

On Saturday, 21 August, the first contingent of PLO evacuees left Beirut by ship. Over the course of twelve days, 14,398 Palestinians left. The Americans, who had negotiated this departure on behalf of the Israelis, contacted the Tunisian President and arranged for Arafat to go to Tunis.

### Lebanon, Beirut

Arafat was the last leader to leave. On 30 August 1982, through the gun sights of a rifle, the Israelis followed him embarking on the Greek cruise liner *Atlantis*. They could have killed him – just one pull of the trigger would have finished him once and for all. But it was forbidden. Sharon had reluctantly promised the Americans that he would guarantee Arafat's safe exit and passage to Tunis.

From the deck of the *Atlantis*, Arafat looked back at the ruined city of Beirut where he had spent so many years. He had been forced out, just as he had been driven out of Jordan twelve years before – and for exactly the same reasons. Now, he was about to set sail to a new exile – 1500 miles away – in Tunis.

## Chapter 25

# All falls apart

On 1 September 1982, just two days after Arafat left Beirut, Bashir Gemayel was invited to meet Prime Minister Begin in Naharia, a town in northern Israel. By now, he was President-elect of Lebanon. With Israeli bayonets to keep law and order and protect the delegates with the power to choose, and a special helicopter to bring them from isolated areas to vote in Beirut, Gemayel had won the general elections. He would become President of Lebanon on 23 September.

From beginning to end, the meeting in northern Israel was a disaster. Just before it started, Samuel Lewis, the American ambassador in Israel, went to see Begin, to present to him the 'Reagan Plan'. This was a new American peace initiative, calling for the creation of 'self-government by the Palestinians of the West Bank and Gaza in association with Jordan'. For Begin, this was a stab in the back: with the PLO in disarray, and Arafat on his way to a far-off exile, he had thought that Israel's grip on the occupied territories could be tightened.

While Begin was meeting with Samuel Lewis, President Elect Gemayel, who had been kept waiting for two hours, was on tenterhooks. As Begin had arrived for the meeting, Gemayel had made to embrace him, but Begin, who was in a black mood, had just given him a cold handshake. As, at last, they sat around a table – Israelis and Christians, politicians, security people and aides – Begin rose and, turning to Gemayel, said in English: 'Sir, the President Elect, I congratulate you'. He then gave a speech and Gemayel responded. When this stage of the meeting was over, Gemayel, Begin and others went into an adjacent room to talk business. For Begin, there was one important item on the agenda: a peace treaty between Lebanon and Israel.

The following is an extract from this meeting:

*Begin: 'I want from you a peace treaty before the 15th of September.'*

*Gemayel: 'First, I can't sign on the 15th of September because I will not be president by then. I become president on the 23rd. Second, I can't sign such a treaty if I don't agree with the prime minister and my government in Lebanon. I need to prepare the Lebanese for such a treaty. I cannot make peace with you, and have the whole Arab world against me.'*

*Begin: 'You are manoeuvring.'*

Begin continued to press Gemayel: 'We think you should visit Jerusalem, or at least Tel Aviv. Such a visit is important in terms of assuring the people of Israel of your sincerity and desire for normal relations.' Then, interfering in internal Lebanese affairs, Begin said: 'Mr President . . . we have reports that indicate that some of your associates in the Phalange party are openly hostile to Israel and are maintaining unacceptable relations with the Syrians'. Begin thought he was being generous in offering Gemayel the Israeli reports, so that Gemayel could: 'use them to deal with whoever should be kept far from Ba'abda, and so that you won't be surprised one day if there is a deficiency in loyalty'.[22] Begin asked Gemayel to move into the camps of Sabra and Shatilla and clear them of the remaining 'terrorists'. (Sharon believed that Arafat had bluffed him and had left behind about 2000 of his fighters.) Gemayel flatly refused, saying, 'How can I do such a divisive thing? I am President elect'.[23]

At one point, during the meeting, Gemayel held out his arms and said to Begin, 'Put the handcuffs on'. He then added, 'I am not your vassal.' David Kimche, the Director General of the Foreign Ministry, who had excellent relations with the Christians from his Mossad days, turned to Joseph Abu Khalil, a close colleague of Gemayel: 'Joseph,' he said in French, 'please accept what we are asking from you and let us get it over with. If you agree, Jordan will make peace with Israel. Please help us in this process'. In truth, Abu Khalil was as angry as Gemayel, and humiliated by the way Begin had treated the President elect. He recalls: 'Begin spoke to Bashir in a condescending tone, as if to say you owe us something, and the price we're asking is that you make a statement tomorrow that you want a peace agreement with Israel.'

The meeting ended in chaos. Begin and others went to Jerusalem, worried. Gemayel went to Beirut, called in his adviser, Pakradouni, and complained, 'Begin treated me like a child. I'm going to President Sarkis [of Lebanon] to tell him what has happened, and I will ask him to open up a contact between me and President Assad [of Syria]'.

The Syrians were furious with Gemayel for flirting with the Israelis. But Gemayel did not realize it was much too late to do anything about this situation.

## A well-planned assassination

'Does Bashir see himself as a candidate for the presidency of Lebanon?' Syrian Foreign Minister Abdul Halim Khaddam had asked, when Karim Pakradouni, Gemayel's aide, came to see him before the elections in Lebanon. Pakradouni: 'Yes he does.'

Khaddam: 'What are the chances of Bashir winning the presidential elections?' Pakradouni: 'The chances are good.' Khaddam: 'Come on, he doesn't stand a chance.'

At 4.10 p.m., on 14 September 1982, a massive bomb went off in Beirut. It brought down the three-storey building housing the headquarters of the Phalanges's Ashrafiya Branch, turning the building into a pile of debris. The bomb exploded while President elect Bashir Gemayel, was inside giving a speech to young women activists. When Karim Pakradouni heard about the blast he rushed to the scene. Bashir Gemayel was already dead. He recalls: 'We took the remains of the body, which was in two halves, to the Hotel-Dieu Hospital. There, we identified Bashir Gemayel from a ring that he wore. When I saw the ring I was able to say: "This is the ring of Bashir Gemayel."'

It was a well-planned assassination. Three days before Gemayel went to the meeting, Habib Tanious Shartouni, a twenty-six-year-old Syrian intelligence agent, moved a large bomb into the flat of his sister who lived just above the place where the speaker's podium stood on the floor below. On 14 September 1982, when Gemayel entered the building, Shartouni pressed his remote control and detonated the bomb.[24]

No one suspected him. After all, his sister lived in the building, and one of his cousins was Pierre Gemayel's aide-de-camp. Nobody knew that, back in 1979, when Shartouni was a student in Paris, he had been recruited by a Syrian group called the People's Party (SPP).

## The revenge of the Phalangists
The remains of Bashir Gemayel were put in a coffin, which was wrapped in a Lebanese flag, and paraded through the streets of Beirut. At 6 p.m., on the same day – Thursday 16 September – 150 Christian Phalangists, led by Eli Hubbeika, entered the Palestinian camps of Sabra and Shatilla. They had been allowed into the camps by the Israelis to pursue PLO fighters the Israelis thought were hiding there. When Hubbeika led his Phalangists into the camps, the last thought he had in mind was the fourth clause of the agreement between Arafat and the Americans which guaranteed the safety of 'Law-abiding and non-combatant Palestinians who remained in Beirut'.

When, thirty-six hours later, the Phalangists evacuated the camps, they left behind them between 700–800 dead Palestinians – men, women and children. This massacre was their revenge for the assassination of their leader Bashir Gemayel, who, in fact, had been assassinated by Syrians.[25]

On February 1983, Defence Minister Sharon, the architect of the war in Lebanon, was forced out of office. Seven months later, Prime Minister Begin, who had allowed Sharon to plunge Israel into this disastrous war, summoned his ministers: 'I can't carry on any more,' he said – and resigned. Bashir Gemayel was long dead by then. Yasser Arafat, however – the master of survival who had been projected on to the world stage after the battle of Karameh and then expelled from Jordan to Lebanon and from there into Tunis – survived.

# 5 THE LONG ROAD TO MADRID

## Introduction

The run up to the November 1991 Madrid peace conference was dotted with secret talks, failed initiatives, bitter disappointments and bloody events. Peace seemed a long way off. But then the politics of the Arab-Israeli-Palestinian conflict were transformed by two unrelated events. The first was the *intifada*, Palestinian uprising, which erupted in Israeli-occupied territories in December 1987 and proved to the Israeli leadership that only a political solution could resolve the Palestinian-Israeli problem.

The second was Iraq's invasion of Kuwait in August 1990. When pressed by the international community to withdraw from Kuwait, Saddam Hussein, the President of Iraq, cunningly tried to broaden the Gulf War into an Arab-Israeli conflict by offering to get out of Kuwait if the Israelis got out of the occupied territories. The United States, the superpower leading the anti-Saddam Hussein coalition forces, refused to acknowledge any linkage between the two issues. Nevertheless, President Bush did promise President Assad of Syria that, 'Once we are done dealing with Saddam, once we are done with liberating Kuwait, the United States will turn to the peace process, and will turn to it in a determined fair way'.

After Saddam Hussein was defeated and the Gulf War ended, President Bush honoured this promise by sending Secretary of State James Baker to the Middle East to persuade the political leaders involved in the conflict to take part in an international peace conference in Madrid. This was to be followed by substantive discussions in Washington.

For the first time, Israel and its Arab neighbours agreed to face each other across a negotiating table.

The following chapters tell the story of the failed attempts to open the peace talks between 1987 and 1991 and how, after the Gulf War ended, the American-sponsored peace process got under way with the Madrid conference.

*Chapter 26*

# Searching for partners

On 10 April 1987, Shimon Peres, Israel's Foreign Minister, arrived in London aboard a small executive jet. Looking around the arrivals hall, he was reassured that none of the passengers coming in on the commercial flights had recognized him. His disguise, a stylish brown wig, had worked. When he reached the customs counter, the duty officer asked, 'Have you come to London for business or pleasure?' After a moment's hesitation, Peres replied, 'Business'.

Peres's 'business' trip was top secret. He had come to meet King Hussein of Jordan, bringing with him Yossi Beilin, the political Director General of the Foreign Ministry, and Efraim Halevi from Mossad. Only these two people and Prime Minister Yitzhak Shamir, who had given his consent for the meeting, knew of his trip to London.

The meeting between Peres and Hussein had been arranged through a mutual friend, the London solicitor, Lord Victor Mishcon, and was to take place at his London home. To maintain absolute secrecy, Lady Mishcon sent all the servants on leave and she, personally, cooked lunch and attended to her guests. Shimon Peres: 'Lady Mishcon served the meal. Afterwards, King Hussein said, "Come, let's wash up the dishes". I agreed immediately, but Lady Mishcon absolutely refused. She could not imagine a king washing up dishes at her house!'

The two sides settled down to political discussions. Peres recalls: 'The meeting went on for about eight hours. In the first four hours, I presented our ideas to King Hussein. When the answer was "no", the Prime Minister (Zaid el-Rifai) said it; when it was "yes" the King said it. That was the tactic they used.'

Peres proposed that there should be an international conference to launch a peace process – something that Israel had repeatedly rejected in the past because the government favoured bilateral talks with the Arabs; and something that, for years, the Arabs had insisted was necessary for reaching a peaceful solution with all the parties involved in the conflict. Now, Peres had come up with the idea of an international conference that he hoped would satisfy both Arab and Israeli demands, while still excluding the PLO which Israel considered a terrorist organization. Peres: 'I suggested that representation should be through a Jordanian-Palestinian delegation, but that *only* Palestinians who accepted [UN resolutions] 242 and 338 should participate.'

Resolutions 242 and 338 were passed by the UN on 22 November 1967 and 22 October 1973 (the first after the 1967 War, the second after the 1973 War). The two most important points of these resolutions were: 1) Withdrawal of Israeli armed forces from territories it had occupied; 2) Termination of all claims or states of belligerency, and respect for and acknowledgement of the sovereignty, territorial integrity and political independence of every state in the area and their right to live in peace within secure and recognized boundaries, free from threats or acts of force.[1]

While neighbouring Arab states accepted these resolutions, the PLO had rejected them because 242 referred to the Palestinians simply as refugees and did not recognize their right to national self-determination. Israel had always refused to talk to the PLO – even at an international peace conference level – because it had rejected its right to exist, and because, in its covenant, the PLO called for Israel's destruction.

The details of Peres's proposal were hammered out by Zaid Rifai and Yossi Beilin who haggled over the different points. King Hussein, who saw that the talks were progressing rapidly, asked to be excused briefly for a social engagement. 'I wanted time to think about it,' he recalls, 'to see if I had any last-minute thoughts before such a monumental decision was taken. Then I decided, all right fine, we'll go with it, and returned to Lord Mishcon's house.'

They then agreed that an international conference should be convened to launch the peace process, but that this should not impose any solutions and should not have any decision-making powers. The conference would assemble once. Then the parties to the conflict would negotiate face to face in bilateral committees. These subsequent sessions would require the consent of all the parties. There would be a Syrian delegation, a Lebanese delegation and a unified Jordanian-Palestinian delegation which would include only those who accepted resolutions 242 and 338.[2]

With the details agreed, the problem now was how to present the agreement. Peres: 'We decided that all our suggestions should be presented as American initiatives, so that it would not seem as though the Jordanians were accepting our offer, or we were accepting theirs.'

The two teams decided to put their agreement in writing. Yossi Beilin was the scribe: '[The King] went over the paper line by line, and we exchanged copies. It was hand-written – in my handwriting – and when the King looked at it, he said, "Since we're not signing this, let's at least add London, 11th of April 1987, so that we remember when we did this."' Dating it added an air of formality to the occasion. They called it the London Agreement.

Delighted with his achievement, Peres returned to Israel. But now he had to sell it to Prime Minister Yitzhak Shamir. The relationship between the two men was strained and their co-existence within a Labour-Likud National Unity Government had not run smoothly. However, if the London Agreement was to lead anywhere, the incumbent prime minister would have to ratify it. Peres requested a meeting with Shamir: 'I read him the paper we had agreed in London, and he said, "Read it to me again". I did. He said, "Okay, leave it with me". I said, "No, I can't, because if it is leaked – not from you but from your office – the matter will explode. This paper must appear as an American paper". Shamir was uneasy. He didn't like the fact that I didn't want to leave the paper with him.'

To get the support of US Secretary of State George Shultz for the US to sponsor and present the agreement as its initiative, Peres sent Yossi Beilin to show the text to US Ambassador Thomas Pickering.

Beilin: 'When I went to Tom Pickering with the paper, he said, "Listen, don't waste any time. Shultz is on his way to a meeting with Mikhail Gorbachev and is in Finland making preparations for his departure. It's very important for him to know what you have achieved – perhaps he'd like to raise it with Gorbachev."'

Beilin booked the first flight out, and a commercial aircraft on its way to Denmark was held up at Tel Aviv airport until he arrived. Beilin: 'I went without a ticket, a passport, anything. When I arrived, Shultz was busy preparing for his meeting with Gorbachev, so I presented the story to Charlie Hill [his political aide]. He said: "Okay, wait for me in the hotel. I'll tell you what Shultz's reaction is". A few hours later he phoned me and said, "This paper is a wonderful surprise for him. He's willing to intervene in order to help carry it out."'

Beilin and Peres were delighted, but they were soon in for a setback. Prime Minister Shamir had decided to block the London Agreement. Peres's refusal to leave him a copy of the text had been a bad start, but that was not the only reason for his reluctance. Shamir: 'It was always Peres's position that we must make an agreement with King Hussein . . . and give up a large piece of Judea and Samaria [the West Bank] to make peace. I was against this . . . I was also against the idea of an international conference. That, for me, was like a pig in our temple. I believed we would come out of it completely broken. Of the five Security Council members, everybody was against us except for the United States of America. What could we have hoped to achieve? At best, we would have had to withdraw to the '67 lines, and therefore I objected . . . I saw a danger in the mere arrival of Shultz.'

Shamir sent Moshe Arens, a Minister Without Portfolio, who had served as the Israeli Ambassador to Washington from 1981–82, to dissuade Shultz from coming to Israel to announce the initiative. Arens: 'I went in secret. It's not hard to see why this was more advantageous [to Prime Minister Shamir] than advertising the fact that I was being sent to undo something that his Foreign Minister had done . . . Shamir suggested that I should convince George Shultz that the agreement had not been authorized by the Prime Minister of Israel or its government.'

Arens recalls his talk with Shultz: 'I said, "This is a matter that is in dispute in Israel and if you endorse the agreement you'll be getting directly involved in Israeli politics. You ought to consider whether this is something you want to do". He said to me, "I don't want to do that and I'm not going to do it."'

Shultz immediately cancelled his plans to visit Israel. Peres, having come so close to an agreement with Jordan – an Arab country – could do nothing but accept that all his efforts had been in vain. Peres was furious and recalls: 'Arens went to Shultz without my knowledge. I considered resigning, but it was difficult to do this because the whole matter had been top secret. What could I say? I couldn't say I had come to an agreement with Hussein and that the Israeli cabinet did not agree with it!'

King Hussein was also disappointed. 'We had accomplished almost the impossible,' he recalls, 'something that had been eluding us for so many years . . . But, within a very short lapse of time, it was obvious that nothing was going to come of it.'

The Jordanian option, as agreed between Peres and Hussein, was the policy of territorial compromise over the West Bank, which the Labour party had adopted back in 1967. Under this option, most of the West Bank would come under Jordanian control. The Palestinian option would have involved finding a solution to the West Bank problem to be agreed between the Israelis and the Palestinians. This lost opportunity would be the last of its kind.

Ironically, although Prime Minister Shamir had been so intransigent, it was a member of his own Party – Moshe Amirav – who took the first step and talked to the very people that Shamir regarded as their worst enemies.

## Talking to the Palestinians

Moshe Amirav was a right-wing Israeli whose beliefs were anchored in the principles of Zionism. An activist in Likud's student group at an early age, he had fought in most of Israel's major wars. Wounded as a young paratrooper during the 1967 War, he had jumped out of the hospital window to attend the Israelis' capture of the sacred Jewish Western Wall. For him, taking Jerusalem, was a first step towards the re-creation of Greater Israel – the backbone of his Zionist belief. Thus, the thought of relinquishing an inch of '*Eretz Yisrael*' to the Palestinian inhabitants was out of the question. 'Peace with the Palestinians,' he states, 'has always been a much more sensitive matter for the Israelis than, say, peace with Egypt. It touches the very nerves of Zionism because it's an us-or-them situation. If they have the right to the land, then who are we?'

However, during the Lebanon War in 1982, seeds of doubt were sown in his mind. A simple incident led him to question the basis of his Zionist ideology. 'I was a reserve soldier in Lebanon,' he recalls. 'I was with a friend, both of us in uniform, when suddenly a young man, also in uniform, came up to him, and they hugged. It was his son. I watched them standing there, in the middle of a war in Lebanon, in the Shuf mountains, and I thought to myself: This is like a Greek tragedy . . . these wars will never end. It will be his son's son, his grandson . . . For me, this was the moment when I decided that we must find a way, and that even if we had to compromise, okay, so we would compromise.'

Amirav returned from the Lebanon War a changed man, but it wasn't until 1987 that he plucked up the courage to publish his ideas in a pamphlet which he distributed among Likud Party members. He was advocating the unthinkable: to obtain real peace, Israel would have to deal with the source of the problem – the Palestinians. Soon afterwards he was approached by David Ish-Shalom, a journalist who had read his pamphlet, and who offered to arrange a meeting between him and a Palestinian leader. Since it was illegal for an Israeli to meet anyone affiliated with the PLO, the journalist suggested Sari Nusseibeh, a leading Palestinian activist who was not directly branded as a member of the organization. Amirav agreed.

Sari Nusseibeh, a philosophy professor from one of the oldest Jerusalem families, was deeply involved in the political struggle of his people. He recalls the moment he was approached by Ish-Shalom: 'He told me the Israelis were prepared to talk to representatives of the Palestinian people . . . Up until then, all their peace possibilities had gone through Jordan. Even the most dovish people in Israel thought along the Jordanian track.'

The first meeting on 4 July at Nusseibeh's house in the Jerusalem suburb of Abu Dis, went better than Amirav had anticipated. Amirav: 'I asked him, "Do you accept that Israel is a country you must recognize?" Nusseibeh: "Yes. We're willing to recognize it, but on a basis of mutuality". I said, "On a basis of mutuality, there's no problem. You'll recognize us, we'll recognize you, and then we'll start talking and reach a solution. It's a very promising beginning. We have something to talk about."' They agreed to meet again.

The second meeting, this time at Amirav's house in Ein Karem, another Jerusalem suburb, dealt with political and practical matters. By then, it was obvious that common ground could be found and that it was time to upgrade the talks. Nusseibeh suggested that Amirav should meet Faisal Husseini, the PLO's man in Jerusalem. Amirav said he would give his answer the following day. A little scared because he had been acting on his own initiative, he decided to tell his fellow party members about his activities. Amirav: 'We separated and I called a few friends in the Likud – Dan Meridor, Ehud Olmert, Micha Reiser – and told them about the talks I had had with Sari Nusseibeh. I said I had found a very positive approach and that I was going to meet Faisal Husseini. "I see this only as an intellectual exercise," I explained. "I don't see myself as a messenger of Likud. I haven't been appointed and I'm speaking only for myself". They all said, "Fine. That's the way to approach it". Dan Meridor said, "No problem. Tell me how it goes."'

For Amirav, this would be the first time that he had met someone affiliated with the PLO – a banned organization. Faisal Husseini himself had just come out of prison for engaging in activities related to the PLO. They met at Nusseibeh's home on 13 July 1987. Amirav: 'There was an immediate chemistry between Faisal and myself . . . I was very moved by his openness . . . He spoke about the pain and loss of Jaffa, and I spoke about the pain of losing Hebron. Both of us were in our mid-forties, both of us had been through enough wars in our lives.'

Once mutual confidence was established, the two men moved on to concrete issues. Husseini recalls: 'We discussed relations with what we called a Palestinian entity. We discussed refugees, settlements, the nature of military relations – whether there would be an army for this Palestinian entity; the economy . . . Our negotiations went so well, we soon reached the point where we were discussing a possible olive tree design for a Palestinian coin.'

Nusseibeh and Husseini were delighted by how quickly their talks were advancing, but both wondered if Amirav's position would be acceptable to the Israeli government. If both sides agreed, would Shamir sign an agreement on that basis? Although the extent of Amirav's involvement at an official level remained unclear, it was obvious that at least some Likud members were deeply involved. Nusseibeh: 'Moshe Amirav said that the people he was speaking to in the Likud, who were all connected with Shamir, were drawing up a document to represent their point of view. So we said we would like to see it. He presented us with the first draft, and we introduced amendments until we reached the stage that, from our point of view, was a step towards getting the Likud and the PLO leadership together.'

After several meetings, the final version of the two-page document was agreed by Husseini and Amirav on 25 August 1987. The following is an extract:

*Memorandum*

*. . . The PLO is the legitimate representative of the Palestinian people, and has the mandate and the authority to negotiate with the Israeli government, while the state of Israel, on the other hand, has the legitimate right to exist within safe and recognized borders.*

*We agree to the following:*
*1. There are to be two separate phases of negotiations . . . leading to the establishment of an interim agreement; the second phase leading to a final settlement.*

*3. The interim settlement will include the establishment of a Palestinian entity in the territories held by Israel since June 1967, with an administrative capital in the Arab parts of Jerusalem.*

*In due time, Israel will declare its recognition of the PLO, while the PLO will declare its recognition of the state of Israel.*

*Israel will announce and actualize a freeze on all settlement activity during the first phase of negotiations . . . the PLO will announce and actualize a freeze on all acts of violence.*[3]

Amirav was astonished that they had got this far. 'We wrote,' he said, 'that there should be recognition of the PLO as representative of the Palestinian state. My hand shook as I wrote this, but I knew we couldn't go on without it . . . We signed the document

185

and each of us went home and passed it on to the people close to us. I passed it to some of my Likud friends and Husseini sent his copy to Tunis [the PLO headquarters].'

Now, it was time to turn words into deeds. The idea was to have Amirav, as a representative of the Likud Party, to meet Yasser Arafat. But, to do this, Amirav needed an official mandate from Prime Minister Shamir. He tried to get this on 26 August 1987. Amirav: 'I gave the document to Tzachi Ha'negbi, who was Prime Minister Shamir's Chief of Bureau, to give to Shamir. He was very suspicious, and said, "We know all about Faisal. He's associated with terrorism, and is financing and distributing money for the PLO". I said, "I know, but that's what makes him Number One". Shamir didn't forbid me from carrying on talking.'

Apparently, as long as the talks remained secret, everyone was prepared to turn a blind eye. But then the news of the talks leaked, and the heavens caved in. Amirav: 'The next day Shamir ordered the arrest of Faisal Husseini on charges of contacts with the PLO and for leaking the document to Tunis. Husseini, believing that I had backing, had put his own credibility on the line and brought in Arafat. By arresting Husseini, Shamir was saying loud and clear, we do not agree with what Amirav has agreed. They left me hanging . . .'

For Nusseibeh the result was even more dramatic: 'I was due to give a lecture at the university. Four hooded Palestinian youths suddenly appeared and beat me up. I got no support – not from my colleagues nor from the PLO . . .'

By the end of August 1987, the first attempt by a Likud member to address the Palestinians directly had failed miserably. Amirav was kicked out of the Likud Party; Faisal Husseini was returned to prison; Nusseibeh spent an uncomfortable week in hospital.

*Chapter 27*

# The new equation

On 8 December 1987, the mood in Jabaliya refugee camp – the largest and most squalid in the Gaza strip – was sombre. Four Jabaliya youths had died in a road accident between an Israeli vehicle and a car carrying Palestinian day-labourers near the Israeli town of Ashkelon. It was not the first accident of its kind, but when the four shrouded bodies were carried down the dirt road leading to Jabaliya's main cemetery, the anger and tension were tangible. The funeral cortège was huge: tens of thousands of angry mourners had come to pay their last respects. For the inhabitants, this was no ordinary funeral. They believed rumours that the four youths had been deliberately killed by the relatives of Shlomo Sakel, an Israeli, who had been stabbed in the marketplace two days earlier. Israeli army units circled the cemetery area to keep the huge crowd under control. But the sight of Israeli soldiers merely exacerbated the tension.

At the funeral, Hatem El-Sissi, an eighteen-year-old, couldn't contain his anger. He bent down, picked up a large stone and lobbed it at one of the Israeli soldiers. The soldier fired back and Hatem El-Sissi was killed instantly. The road accident – and this death – were the last straw. Riots broke out in Jabaliya and spread, within hours, all over the Gaza Strip.

Qassem Kafarneh, a student at the West Bank University of Beir Zeit, was at home in the neighbouring village of Beit Lahya when the rioting started. A known political activist, affiliated with the PFLP (Popular Front for the Liberation of Palestine), Qassem couldn't believe what was happening. Despite the occasional eruption of riots in the occupied territories, he had not seen such deep anger and passion in Gaza for a long time. Only months earlier, he had tried to recruit people for civil disobedience, but no one was interested. After twenty years of occupation, apathy and desperation prevailed. The Arab countries, it seemed, had abandoned their cause and their PLO leaders – having been expelled from Lebanon in 1982 – had moved to Tunis where they now seemed content to lead a life of luxury. They – 'the insiders' –

felt like a forgotten people, and, until the morning of the funerals and Hatem El-Sissi's death, it seemed as though they were going to accept their lot.

'Everyone had had enough of political involvement,' Qassem recalls, 'people just wanted to get on with their lives. But this attitude changed once the rioting began. People began looking for me, asking if I was still recruiting. I wasn't. But, on the night of the rioting, I met with two colleagues and we asked ourselves – how are we going to use this enthusiasm? The next day [9 December 1987] we decided to block the entrance to Gaza. This would prevent Shin Bet [Israeli internal security] from entering, and would also stop [Palestinian] workers going into Israel itself. By four in the morning, we had gathered between fifty and sixty activists and blocked the entrance to Gaza with burning tyres and barricades. One person was killed, about fifteen wounded [Arabs].'

In the meantime, Israeli Defence Minister Yitzhak Rabin was attending a dinner in Tel Aviv for his Norwegian counterpart. News of the riots reached him, but he did not pay much attention. Riots in the occupied territories happened frequently enough, and then died down again almost immediately. He had no reason to believe that this riot would be any different. That same night, after the dinner, he was going on a trip to the USA and did not even contemplate postponing it. Eitan Haber, Rabin's aide was with him: 'We were going to purchase some Apache and Black Hawk helicopters . . . Rabin said of the riots: "We have had hundreds of such cases, there is nothing exceptional about these. It is more important to buy the helicopters for the next war than worry about a few beatings in Gaza."'

After the dinner, Rabin gathered his aides together and briefly gave them instructions about what to do while he was away. Haber: 'There were about twenty of us present, but not one person said, this is different, this is an *intifada*.'

The following morning the riots got worse and, in Gaza, Qassem and his colleagues didn't need to ask people to participate. Women, children, old men, shop-owners and labourers took to the streets – and everyone threw stones at the Israeli soldiers. It was an unpremeditated, unorganized, popular uprising – a true *intifada*.

Ehud Barak, the Israeli Deputy Chief of Staff, went to assess the situation and talk to his soldiers. 'It was clear,' he said, 'that this uprising was on a new scale, and that these people were not "terrorists", but the population itself. There was a real threat that they might overwhelm the Israeli soldiers who were there in very small numbers. If they did, this would leave the soldiers with only two possibilities: to run away, or to shoot. Both possibilities were bad . . . We were not technically prepared to deal with a violent popular riot on this scale.'

Barak returned to Tel Aviv and shared his anxieties with his fellow army commanders. Many questions had to be addressed quickly. Barak: 'The immediate need was to solve the dilemma of the troops in the field: what they should do in the face of such demonstrations without seeming to lose sovereignty or shoot into the crowd? We reinforced the troops by two or three times the numbers, and instructed them to act cautiously. We spent the first days concentrating on how to prevent a nightmare of wild shooting into the crowds, which we thought would cause us terrible damage.'

Another dilemma was whether Rabin should cut short his visit to the USA. Barak recalls the result of this debate among the commanders: 'We said, what can he possibly tell us that he can't tell us on the phone? So some of us recommended that he should go ahead with the visit. Looking back, that was a mistake.'

The unrest had not only taken the Israelis by surprise, it had also stunned the PLO. Although Abu Jihad – the top Tunis-based PLO leader of Yasser Arafat's Fatah faction, responsible for the occupied territories – had previously planned several civil disobedience scenarios, this uprising in which the demonstrators had practically taken control in Gaza with the riots now spreading throughout the West bank, was not of his making. However, the PLO, with all its different factions, jumped on the bandwagon.[4]

Abu Ali Shaheen, Abu Jihad's right-hand man in Tunis, had spent almost fifteen years in Israeli prisons in the occupied territories and was responsible for recruiting many of Gaza's young men into the ranks of the PLO. Released in a 22 September 1982 prisoner exchange, Shaheen was appointed as a Fatah-coordinator between Tunis and the territories. After a week of the continuous rioting, he got a phone call from Abu Jihad. Shaheen: 'He [Abu

Jihad] said, "Who do we have on the ground? Give me names. Contact our boys and find out who is behind this. We have to do something quickly."'

Shaheen immediately contacted his 'boys' through a Paris switchboard – direct calls between Tunis and Israel were banned – and started organizing cells to give the *intifada* political guidance. This did not take much effort – the clandestine political structure of the PLO in the occupied territories had been well established over the past decade.

However, for the first month of the *intifada*, it was left to Fatah's field leadership to make the decisions. Faisal Husseini (by now released from prison), the PLO's man in Jerusalem, was consulted: 'I got regular messages from the young people, asking me: "Do you advise us to continue or to calm down the situation because there are already heavy losses?". My suggestion was to go on, but to use stones instead of weapons. The best way, I felt, to paralyse the Israeli force was to give them no excuse to use their military power. If we used firearms, they would use machine-guns, planes or rockets, and would gain the upper hand with only a few soldiers involved. But, if we used stones they would only use plastic bullets or pistols, and would be obliged to use a bigger task force . . . '

The activists from the various PLO factions believed that if the *intifada* remained strong and lasted long enough, it could exert real pressure on the Israeli government. To achieve this, they knew that the different factions of the PLO would have to discard their usual rivalry and set up a unified national command. Qassem Kafarneh recalls: 'Marwan – my brother – was sent to see Tawfik abu Khousa, a Fatah activist, to see what could be done. Contacts were opened up between the PFLP and Fatah and other factions to plan simple activities, such as putting up slogans, making flags and placing these on top of buildings, printing leaflets *etcetera*.'

The frustration of the Israeli soldiers grew daily. When, on 21 December, Rabin returned from the US, the rioting had not died down and he decided to visit the troops in the field before working out how to proceed. Amram Mitzna, Commander of Israel's Forces in the West Bank, accompanied him. He recalls: 'Rabin said to the soldiers, "Tackle them". I then issued written instructions to the soldiers, saying that they had to use physical force to tackle them. From this, the soldiers got the impression that Rabin had said, "break their bones". He did not actually say that. [But] the problem was that the soldiers now felt they were allowed to use all the force at their disposal and some of them used Rabin's "break their bones" as a policy.'

The subsequent sight of Israeli soldiers breaking the bones of unarmed Palestinian youths, broadcast on television all over the world, accomplished in part what the *intifada* had set out to achieve: the questioning of the viability of Israeli rule over the occupied territories. But it took time for Rabin to come to this conclusion. While he was doing so, and while the soldiers were desperately trying to keep a lid on the situation, the tough measures taken by the army back-fired.

On 29 December, Rabin assembled his cabinet for the first serious discussion about the disturbances. Ezer Weizman, former Defence Minister, attended in his capacity as a Minister Without Portfolio. A hot-tempered man, he shouted at Dan Shomron, the Chief of Staff, who gave a situation report, 'Get out of Jabaliya and let them burn each other up!'[5]

Rabin was furious. For him, a withdrawal – even if it was from the most troublesome refugee camp in Gaza – was unthinkable. 'What are you talking about?' he said to Weizman. 'If they burn Jabaliya, then everything will go up in flames – it will spread in all directions.'

In mid January 1988, the Unified National Command decided that, without a clear political strategy, the *intifada* would run out of steam. Sari Nusseibeh, who had emerged as one of the *intifada*'s political thinkers, gathered some of the members of the Unified National Command together. Nusseibeh: 'We agreed that we had to come up with a strategy and a coherent political message to direct the *intifada*. We had to decide among ourselves where we wanted it to go. So, we held a meeting at the National Hotel [in East Jerusalem] and presented a fourteen-point plan.'

The fourteen points were divided between demands for Israeli concessions regarding self-determination; directives for the population on how to maintain the pressure through strikes and demonstrations; and a request – directed to the PLO – to include Palestinians from *inside* the occupied territories in the structure of the PNC – the Palestinian parliament in exile. The idea behind the latter was that if the PNC included people from *inside* the territories, then it would be easier for Israel to accept that the PNC was a council that represented all the Palestinians; and therefore easier for the Israelis to accept the need to talk with the PLO.

Nusseibeh explains the thinking during the first months of the *intifada*: 'We felt it was still possible to make use of the events in order to establish a bridge to talk to the Israelis, and to try to reach some kind of settlement. So we tried to make sure that our concerns were heard, and to warn the Israelis that if they were not, there would be an irreparable explosion. We even produced an alternative [to confrontation], by saying that the Israelis should move out of Arab-populated cities and towns and stop putting people in jail . . . If they did this, the Palestinians would see that there was a difference between a soldier beating them up and the Israeli court system. That was the alternative [to proceed by democratic and legal processes]. But the Israelis didn't pick it up. They decided to go ahead with confrontation.'

In Tunis, Abu Jihad, who had become the PLO's supreme guide of the *intifada*, was preaching escalation. Through the Paris switchboard, he introduced new elements to the strategy of the uprising. The Palestinians in the occupied territories should no longer go to their jobs in Israel; Israeli products should be no longer bought or sold, and the Arab population should boycott the Israeli civil administration, even when they needed identity documents. Nusseibeh recalls: 'Abu Jihad described how we could snip off, trim the edges, and slowly cut off ties that linked the occupied territories to Israel.'

Within three months of the outbreak of the riots, the link between the *intifada* and the PLO leadership in Tunis – especially Abu Jihad – could no longer be ignored by Israel. The situation was starting to affect Israeli morale. Something had to be done to end the vicious circle. The hijacking of a bus, carrying scientists working at the Dimona nuclear reactor on 7 March 1988, provided the pretext. This hijacking, which left three Israelis dead, had been approved by Abu Jihad.

## The killing of Abu Jihad

On 8 March 1988, the day after the hijacking, the Israeli inner cabinet met. Mossad recommended that Abu Jihad should be killed. This would not only be a suitable retaliation for the Dimona attack, it said, but would also send a clear message to the PLO that it would not be allowed to gain advantage from the unrest caused by the *intifada*. Four months into the unrest, the Israelis needed some sort of victory, and many believed that without Abu Jihad the *intifada* would rapidly die down.

Five weeks later, on 15 April, the cabinet convened for a half-hour meeting. An Israeli task force of four boats and an accompanying submarine had already set out for Tunis where Abu Jihad lived in a two-storey villa in the Sidi Bousaid suburb overlooking the Mediterranean. One minister – Ezer Weizman – opposed the operation and Shimon Peres was unenthusiastic about it. Yitzhak Navon, Minister of Education, attended the closed cabinet meeting. 'The discussions were secret,' he said. 'Each action that was to be taken by the army and by our intelligence service agents across the border was brought before the inner cabinet for approval. The cabinet consisted of ten members, five of my party – the Labour party – and five from Likud. We discussed various aspects of the situation and voted. As far as Abu Jihad was concerned, there was some discussion about the character of the action, but not about the actual action itself.'

The cabinet approved the operation, but decided that Israel would not claim responsibility for it. Mossad and the army were then given the green light to proceed.

That night, 15 April, the boats anchored just outside the territorial waters of Tunisia. Around 2 a.m., on 16 April, the assassination team went into action. Two commandos, dressed as women, approached a car where Abu Jihad's guard was sitting and killed him. Then the team broke into the villa and a twenty-year-old commando, whose task was to shoot Abu Jihad, rushed up the stairs to find him.[6]

Abu Jihad's wife, hearing the commotion, ran to the staircase to see what was happening. 'The first thing I saw,' she recalls, 'was three masked men with machine-guns. My husband brushed me aside, and the first of the men opened fire on him. He was wounded in his arm and heart. He turned around and fell to the ground.

Then four of them, as they started running down the stairs to leave the house, shot him in rotation. Hearing my screams, Hanan, my daughter, woke up. One of the men pushed her aside and said, "Go to your mother". There were about seventy-five bullets in Abu Jihad's body – eight of them in his heart.'

The assassination had taken five minutes from the moment the guard was killed until the teams left the house.

When Umm Jihad had last seen her husband alive, he was sitting at his desk preparing to write a letter of directives to the Unified National Command of the *intifada*. The Israeli raid succeeded in stopping this set of instructions from reaching the occupied territories, but the Israelis' main objective – ending the *intifada* by eliminating the man who was by now its mastermind – failed dramatically. As a result of Abu Jihad's assassination, the *intifada* immediately gathered some of the momentum it had started to lose during the previous few months.

### Rabin's eye-opener

The spiral of violence continued and, with every passing day, the morale of the Israeli soldiers declined. None of them had been trained to combat children throwing stones. Rabin sympathized with their dilemma, but had no idea of the extent of their frustration. Rabin's close aide Eitan Haber recalls an incident that occurred on one of Rabin's routine visits to the units in Gaza: 'The soldiers in Gaza were sitting on a dune. They seemed very tough. Rabin asked them, "What do you think of the orders?" They answered, "Everything is okay and under control". Rabin left happy.'

On return to the Defence Ministry, Haber found a document on his desk from the military censor, who, having read soldiers' personal letters, reported weekly to Rabin about the morale within the army. Haber: 'Going through the document, I identified, quite by chance, that the report was based on the very unit that we had visited that morning. I read the excerpts from the soldiers' letters to their families, and the questions that some of them were asking their parents and girlfriends were: "What are we doing here? Is it our duty as soldiers to chase ten-year-olds?" One of them wrote, "I punched a seven-year-old in his face, and asked myself: Is that why I was enlisted to the IDF?"'

Haber highlighted the relevant passages and took the report into Rabin. 'I was standing beside him when he read the document,' he recalls. 'It was very very hard for him – a completely different story from the one that he had heard that morning from the same soldiers. This was the turning point in his view of the *intifada*.'

Everything taken into consideration, Rabin now knew that a political solution must be found.

## *Chapter 28*

# Arafat's political initiative

On 15 November 1988, dressed in his usual black-and-white chequered *keffiyeh* and military fatigues, Yasser Arafat, Chairman of the PLO, walked slowly down the aisle of the main conference hall of the Club des Pins, a government residence on the outskirts of Algiers. As he climbed the steps to the podium, he looked tired and stood still for a few seconds, murmuring a prayer in front of a huge portrait of his assassinated comrade, Abu Jihad. This November session of the PNC – the Palestinian Parliament in exile which was the highest legislative authority of the Palestinians – was dedicated to Abu Jihad's memory.

It was past midnight when Arafat finally started reading from his prepared text: 'In the name of God, in the name of the Palestinian people, the Palestinian National Council proclaims the creation of the state of Palestine, with Holy Jerusalem as its capital!' His next words announcing the acceptance of UN resolutions 242 and 338 were drowned by the applause of 380 delegates singing the Palestinian national anthem, Biladi.

Arafat's acceptance of resolutions 242 and 338 (see chapter 26, page 178) was an extraordinary and bold move. At the heart of the two resolutions was that Israel should withdraw its armed forces from territories[7] it had occupied during the 1967 and 1973 Wars, and Arabs should recognize the right of Israel to exist and live peacefully in the Middle East.

While Israel, albeit reluctantly had accepted the principle of withdrawal, and Arab states such as Egypt and Jordan had accepted the resolutions, the PLO had, until now, refused. For them to accept the right of Israel 'to exist' would have meant giving up the Palestinian diaspora's claim to return to their homes in Palestine. On 23 November 1967, the PLO had issued a statement in Cairo rejecting resolution 242 and declaring, 'the determination of the Palestinian people to continue their revolutionary struggle to liberate their homeland'. It had also called on Arab states, 'to meet their national responsibilities and mobilize all their resources for this battle of destiny, with the support of all forces of liberation throughout the world'.[8] The PLO had also rejected resolution 338.

Since then, there had been intense international pressure on the PLO to accept the two resolutions because, if it did not, Israel would refuse to talk with the PLO, and the PLO would be unable to take part in peace negotiations.

But as Yasser Arafat, the leader of the PLO, stood on the podium in the hall of the Club des Pins, he was facing an altogether different situation. In the occupied territories, young Palestinians were in revolt against the Israeli occupation, and Arafat and the PLO leadership were aware that, if they did not take the initiative, a new leadership from *inside* the occupied territories could, in time, render the PLO's role obsolete. If the PLO were to survive, and if it were to exploit the momentum created by the *intifada* to bring about a political solution to the Palestinian problem, then it had to take a bold initiative.

Abu Mazen, a senior PLO official, recalls a discussion he had shortly before the November 1988 PNC meeting: 'I was sitting in my office in Tunis with a colleague and I said, "Do you agree with me that the *intifada* erupted to get the Israeli forces to withdraw from Gaza and the West Bank?" "Yes," he replied. I then asked him, "What do you think our people would do if we asked them to continue throwing stones until they succeeded in driving the Israelis out of the occupied territories, out of the beautiful places that were once ours – Haifa, Jaffa and Acre?" "They would throw the stones at us," he replied. "Then let's discuss what we can offer," This, recalls Abu Mazen, is how 'we began to consider the acceptance of resolutions 242 and 338 as a basis for a political process, which later became known as the Palestinian political initiative.'[9]

Thanks to this approach, the PNC delegates, along with the other delegations, endorsed Arafat's initiative at the 15 November meeting. After a few minutes of euphoria, when balloons painted in the colours of the Palestinian flag filled the hall, a general gloom engulfed the assembly. Everyone knew they were living through the end of an era: the days of their armed struggle were over. They had finally broken the taboo and recognized the right of Israel to exist. What they expected now was a positive response from Washington, and the lifting of the US ban on talks with the PLO which had been imposed fourteen years previously by Henry Kissinger, then Secretary of State, who had promised the Israelis that the USA would not talk to the PLO until it accepted resolutions 242 and 338.

But if Arafat thought that accepting resolutions 242 and 383 would satisfy the Americans, he was wrong. Kissinger added another condition for the lifting of the ban – that the PLO had to renounce terrorism, and Secretary of State George Shultz now made it clear to the PLO that it would have to do this publicly and unequivocally before it could proceed to talks.

### Arafat bites the bullet

On 6 December 1988, Arafat travelled to Sweden for a meeting with Swedish Foreign Minister Sten Andersson, who showed him a letter sent by George Shultz. In this, Shultz had proposed that the PLO should issue a statement renouncing terrorism. This, it added, would open the way for talks between the USA and the PLO. After much pressure from Andersson, Arafat promised that he would take this final step at a UN session to be held in New York on 13 December. The US administration, however, refused him a visa to enter the US, so the UN General Assembly agreed to move to Geneva.

Behind the scenes, Shultz had written the exact words he wanted Arafat to utter regarding the renouncing of terrorism. But Arafat was in a difficult position. If he said verbatim what the US was asking him to say, some of his close aides would regard this as an humiliation – especially after he had been refused entry to the USA. Secondly Arafat and his PLO colleagues regarded themselves as members of a Nationalist Resistance Movement, not terrorists. Thus, Arafat preferred to *denounce* rather than *renounce* terrorism, but Shultz would not consider even the slightest alteration. In the end, Arafat capitulated. In his memoirs,[10] Shultz recalls:

> On 7 December 1988, I received a signed statement: 'The executive committee of the PLO ... condemns individual, group and state terrorism in all its forms, and will not resort to it.' I also received word that Yasser Arafat would make a speech at Geneva saying exactly that. I said we would move promptly to be in touch with them – if he did say those words.

In the event, it was Mahmoud Darwish, a leading Palestinian poet, who wrote the UN speech. In the midst of lyrical prose about the *intifada*, and the suffering of the Palestinian people and their right to statehood, he carefully inserted the words that George Shultz wanted to hear. But the night before the speech, Yasser Arafat himself made some changes. He did not take out a single word that Shultz had stipulated, but he transposed them in a way that made the statement ambiguous. He thought he could get way with this. But Shultz noted the changes and was not satisfied. In his memoirs, he recalls how he responded to President Ronald Reagan right after Arafat's speech on 13 December:

> I told President Reagan ... 'In one place Arafat was saying 'Unc ... Unc ... Unc ... ' in another 'cle ... cle ... cle ... ', he has yet to cry 'Uncle'.

Arafat returned to his hotel suite, waiting for word from the US administration. Sten Andersson, Sweden's Minister of Foreign Affairs, who had acted as a mediator between the PLO and the US, arrived looking glum. He informed Arafat that the change in the order of the words had rendered the statement unacceptable. If he still wished to open a dialogue with the American administration, he would have to find another occasion and deliver Shultz's text verbatim. Arafat feigned indignation, said he would not go further and left to attend a dinner at the residency of the Egyptian Ambassador, Amr Moussa. There, it was agreed that Arafat should call a press conference on his return to the hotel and finally speak the required words.

At well past midnight, journalists were gathering for the press conference. Word had spread among them that something important was about to happen. Arafat was seated at an elevated table, flanked by his top advisers. He seemed irritable and was fiddling with documents laid out in front of him, waiting for the hall to fall silent. Finally he started reading from a small shrivelled scrap of paper: 'The executive committee of the PLO,' he said, 'condemns individual, group and state tourism'. He paused and smiled into the cameras lined up to capture the historic moment, and said, 'Sorry, I meant terrorism.' When he had finished reading Shultz's words, he stared into the cameras again and said, 'What more do you want me to do? Striptease?'

Arafat had finally complied with the conditions of the American administration. Shultz went to President Reagan and informed him that Yasser Arafat had finally said, 'Uncle'. Two statements were released – one by Shultz, the other by President Reagan – announcing the beginning of a dialogue with the PLO and the appointment of Robert Pelletreau, US Ambassador to Tunisia, to head the talks that would take place in Tunisia.

In Israel, Prime Minister Shamir listened to what Arafat had to say. Yossi Ben Aharon, the Director General of Shamir's office, recalls his boss's response: 'He made a movement with his hand, which meant that this doesn't meaning anything, so let's not waste time analyzing what he said.' After years of bitter conflict between Israel and the PLO, Shamir was making it clear that it would take much more than Arafat reluctantly reading out George Shultz's words verbatim to convince him and the Likud government that Arafat was sincere.

On 16 December 1988, talks to establish the future relationship between the PLO and the American administration commenced in Tunis, but did not get very far. In May 1989, a Palestinian group of Abul Abbas, the leader of the Palestine Liberation Front, one of the PLO factions, carried out a terrorist raid on the beach of Tel Aviv. The US suspended talks with the PLO, saying that this act had violated the conditions on which the talks were founded.

This put an end to the brave initiative by Yasser Arafat to end the deadlock and open the gates to talks with the Americans that he had hoped would lead to peace negotiations with the Israelis. Yet another historic attempt had failed.

*Chapter 29*

# Saddam Hussein's cunning linkage

On 2 August 1990, Saddam Hussein, President of Iraq, shocked the world when his armed forces crossed the border into neighbouring Kuwait, occupied and annexed it. His country was bankrupt following the eight-year war with Iran (1980–88) and if he were to carry on with his ambitious modernization programme, he needed money – lots of it. Kuwait, he decided, was threatening his projects by allowing the oil prices – on which Iraq largely depended – to crash to an all-time low. By invading it, not only would he command the largest pool of oil, he would be able to dictate the price and, as an added bonus, could help himself to some of the Emirate's riches.

President George Bush was determined that Saddam's act of aggression would not be tolerated. Worried that Saddam would also push on to invade oil-rich Saudi Arabia, Bush began sending his forces to the region.

Shortly after Saddam's invasion, the UN Security Council issued a series of resolutions. On 2 August, it issued resolution 660 condemning the Iraqi invasion, demanding Iraq's unconditional withdrawal and calling for immediate negotiations between Iraq and Kuwait. UN resolution 662 followed, condemning the annexation of Kuwait (which Saddam had declared to be 'the nineteenth province of Iraq'). On 6 August 1990, the UN issued resolution 661, imposing trade sanctions on Iraq.

Soon, however, it became evident that the trade sanctions would take at least a year to bite and even then might not force Saddam to comply with the UN resolutions without the threat of military force. Western forces joined the US forces to defend Saudi Arabia.

In addition to the US and western countries, Arab states also reacted strongly to Saddam's invasion of Kuwait. On 10 August, the Arab heads of state convened for an emergency summit in Cairo to decide how to react. The Arab leaders condemned Iraq's invasion and annexation of Kuwait, and called on Saddam Hussein to withdraw. They also decided to send troops to the region.

Egyptian troops began arriving on the day of the summit and Syrian troops the next day.

## The cunning linkage

Saddam's reaction to the mounting international and regional pressure was cunning. On 12 August, just two days after the Cairo summit, he proposed a comprehensive solution to 'all issues of occupation . . . in the entire region'. He suggested the immediate and unconditional withdrawal of Israel from the occupied Arab territories in Palestine, Syria and Lebanon, as well as the withdrawal of Syrians from Lebanon, and the withdrawal of Iran from the parts of Iraq which were still in dispute. Only after *all* these outstanding issues had been settled would 'the formulation of provisions relating to the situation in Kuwait' be discussed 'taking into consideration the historic rights of Iraq to this territory and the choice of the Kuwaiti people'.[11]

Saddam's introduction of an Arab-versus-Israeli dimension to the conflict appealed to the Arab masses over the heads of the Arab leaders who had condemned Saddam's invasion. The Palestinians in the occupied territories, in Jordan, and in other Arab states, cheered the Iraqi president as the 'New Saladin' (legendary Arab fighter who had defeated the Crusaders) who dared to stand up to – and face – the West.

The PLO leadership in Tunis recognized the danger in supporting Saddam, but, on the other hand, they did not want to go against the people's mood. Yasser Arafat, who had publicly supported Saddam Hussein, but who was also trying to find an answer to the PLO's dilemma, went to Baghdad. 'Please, Mr President, he pleaded, 'you cannot face all these forces.' But Saddam replied: 'Well, what will happen? We'll lose five million. It is not important'.[12] King Hussein, whose country had a large Palestinian population, refused to condemn Saddam and alienate the masses who were backing the Iraqi president.

The US, however, was determined that the issues should not be confused by a linkage between the Iraqi withdrawal from Kuwait and the Israeli withdrawal from the occupied territories. James Baker, Secretary of State: 'To avoid any suggestion of linkage, the UN Security Council resolutions stated: get out [of Kuwait] and get out unconditionally. And we were not about to negotiate these or water them down.' But the Americans, as they started to negotiate with the Arab states about joining the anti-Saddam Hussein coalition faced serious difficulties, especially when they tried to recruit Syria. Richard Haass, a member of the US National Security Staff, was involved in these negotiations. 'Syria,' he recalls, 'was important because it was the representative – almost the apostle – of Arab radicalism. If it were part of the coalition, it would legitimize the fight for the man in the street.' But Syria, which saw itself as the champion of Palestinian rights, could not ignore the linkage that Saddam had established. Farouk al-Shar'a, the Syrian Foreign Minister, recalls his country's position: 'We said there should be no double standards; that if we all supported the implementation of UN Security Council resolutions relevant to the Gulf War, then the same resolutions should be implemented regarding the Arab-Israeli conflict.'

President George Bush, who was working hard on forming the anti-Saddam coalition, found himself under severe pressure. In a speech to the General Assembly on 2 October 1990, after calling again for an unconditional Iraqi withdrawal from Kuwait, he announced that the Iraqi withdrawal would pave the way 'for Iraq and Kuwait to settle their differences permanently; for the Gulf states to build new arrangements for stability; and for all the states and peoples of the region to settle the conflict that divided the Arabs from Israel.'[13] The same line was adopted by British Foreign Minister Douglas Hurd, who said that the five permanent members of the Security Council should start arranging a Middle Eastern peace conference after Iraq left Kuwait. The linkage had been established.

On 23 November 1990, on his way back from a Thanksgiving Day meeting and lunch with his troops in Saudi Arabia, President Bush stopped off in Geneva to meet Syria's President Assad. This was an unusual move, for Syria was still on the USA's list of terrorist states. The priority now, however, was to persuade Assad to join the coalition. Richard Haass and Edward Djerejian, the US Ambassador in Damascus, accompanied President Bush to the meeting with President Assad: 'The key part of the conversation was that Assad needed reassurance that, if he joined the coalition, once all that was over and done with, we would turn to the peace process. By that he meant *comprehensive peace*.' Haass also recalls that Assad stated very clearly to President Bush: '"After the Gulf war, it is important to have stability in the Middle East. If you really want stability, then you have got to resolve the Arab-Israeli conflict by implementing the relevant United Nations' resolutions in exactly the same way that you are now pushing for the implementation of resolutions relevant to the Iraqi invasion of Kuwait."' Haass: 'Bush then said to Assad, "Once we are done dealing with Saddam, once we are done liberating Kuwait, you have my word that the United States will turn to the peace process, and will turn to it in a determined fair way".'

President Assad decided to join the coalition. He made it clear, however, that, although he was willing to work with the US, if Israel joined in the war, he would change camps. 'This was,' Syrian Foreign Minister Shar'a recalls, 'a very sensitive matter. We always said that if Israel interfered with Iraq, we would withdraw from the coalition; if Israel invaded Jordan to reach Iraq, we would stand with Jordan again Israel.'

On 29 November 1990, the UN passed resolution 678 – dubbed by the media as 'the mother of all resolutions' – which set a 15 January 1991 deadline for Iraq to withdraw its forces from Kuwait, and authorized member states to use 'all necessary means' to enforce Iraq's full compliance with all UN resolutions by midnight on this date.

### Scud missiles land in Tel Aviv

On the night of 16–17 January, the coalition attacked from the air. The next day, Saddam responded by launching five Scuds on Tel Aviv and three on Haifa. His rationale was that if he struck at Israel and Israel hit back, then the coalition forces would break down because the Arab states would find it difficult to fight shoulder to shoulder with the Israelis.

Israeli Defence Minister Moshe Arens was at home when he was informed that missiles had landed on Tel Aviv and Haifa. He recalls the moment: 'I had to get to the Defence Ministry as quickly as possible and didn't have time to wait for my driver or put on a gas mask.[14] It is usually a half-hour drive to Tel Aviv, but it took me less that fifteen minutes . . . I heard the explosions going off. It sounded like Tel Aviv was getting a beating.' Once in Tel Aviv, he immediately called US Secretary of Defence Richard Cheney.

In the US, the American National Security Staff were leaving the office. Richard Haass recalls: 'I had walked over to Brent Scowcroft's [National Security Adviser] office in the White House, just to check in before I went home. The secure phone behind Scowcroft's desk rang. He picked it up. It was Secretary Dick Cheney calling from the Pentagon. Cheney's message was simple. He had just gotten off the phone with Moshe Arens, his Israeli counterpart, who had essentially said, "We've been hit with Scuds, we've got to go in."'

Secretary of State James Baker tried to persuade the Israelis to show restraint. Haass: 'Baker was on one extension, I was on the other. We got the White House operator to place the call to Israel, but we couldn't get Shamir who was in a cabinet meeting. We asked if the Prime Minister could, please, call us back.'

In Tel Aviv, the Israeli cabinet had convened for an emergency session. Chief of Staff Ehud Barak recalls: 'There was a very tense atmosphere. Some ministers were in favour of taking action against Iraq. Sharon said that we should act as Israel had always acted throughout its history – we should use the air force to attack the missiles in west Iraq, and, if there was no choice, we should act by land; and, in the worst scenario, we should also take our ground forces through Jordan. I said, "The decision is a political one. Saddam Hussein wants us to attack Iraq because that would create serious cracks in the coalition . . . It's wiser to wait. We are in a very complex situation but, even if some missiles fall on Tel Aviv, we should not break the coalition while our enemy is being destroyed by it."' Prime Minister Shamir was torn.' It was not an easy decision,' he recalls. 'It was not our war. Everything had to be done by the international coalition, which would defend Israel, but this was not our tradition – and was against our main strategic objective to prove our own deterrent power. So how should we act?'

In the event, the cabinet decided not to retaliate, at least for the time being.[15] But when Shamir rang Washington back he did not give the Americans an easy time. James Baker recalls the conversation: 'Shamir said, "We've had a meeting and must retaliate". I said, "Prime Minister, you really can't do this, you'll be playing right into the hands of your number one enemy. And we would very much appreciate it if you would not."' President Bush then talked to Shamir. Richard Haass was listening: 'Bush said, "I am terribly sorry for what's happened, and now I am going to ask you as one head of government to another, not to act. I know, Mr Prime Minister, how difficult this is, but I really think it's in the best interest of Israel that the coalition should prevail against Iraq ... In return, I promise you that we will do everything possible militarily. We'll provide you with Patriot missiles; we'll send you the Deputy Secretary of State to see whatever else you need. Essentially you've got an open cheque. But, in return, I am asking you ... Please stay out of this war."'

Forty Scuds landed on Israeli cities during the Gulf War. Israel did not retaliate. On 24 February, after a month of intensive air raids on Iraq, the coalition opened up the ground offensive. After a hundred hours of fighting Iraq was defeated. Saddam Hussein agreed to a cease-fire and to a meeting of his military commanders with American commanders to arrange the Iraqi withdrawal from Kuwait.

President Bush, having led an international and regional coalition to a great victory, was now in a strong position to honour his promise to President Assad and turn his attention to the Arab-Israeli peace process. All the states in the Middle East were relatively weak and Bush knew that they would find it hard to resist the will of the one remaining world superpower. The PLO, which had backed the loser Saddam Hussein, was now bankrupt because Saudi Arabia and Kuwait had stopped sending it money. King Hussein of Jordan, who had also supported Saddam, was weak and marginalized. President Assad – who had supported the coalition, and who had finally faced the fact that the USSR, his traditional ally and patron, was breaking up – was ready to go along with the USA. Even Israel – which in the past had been of political importance to Washington in its struggle for dominance over the USSR in the Middle East – was now less vital to US interests and therefore weakened.

All in all, President Bush knew that this was the moment to honour his promise by bringing the Middle East leaders to the same negotiating table.

*Chapter 30*

# The long road to Madrid

A few days after the Gulf War ended, Secretary of State James Baker and some of his aides gathered in the office of National Security Adviser Brent Scowcroft. They had come to discuss ways of turning President Bush's pledge to tackle the Arab-Israeli conflict into an action plan. Dennis Ross, Baker's assistant, said that they should launch an immediate peace initiative. 'We have just experienced an earthquake [the Gulf War],' Ross said, 'and after an earthquake it takes a while for the earth to resettle . . . We have to act before the landscape out there resettles and solidifies. We don't have the luxury to wait.' Baker agreed: 'There really is a window of opportunity here,' he said.

On 6 March 1991, President Bush gave a Gulf War victory speech to Congress. He talked about a new order in the Middle East and added, 'We must do all that we can to close the gap between Israel and the Arab states, and between the Israelis and the Palestinians'. To achieve this, he sent Secretary of State Baker to the Middle East.

Baker carried with him a plan which he had dubbed 'an exercise in creative ambiguity'. 'The idea,' he recalls, 'was to give both the Arabs and the Israelis what they needed. The Arabs wanted an international conference supervised by other countries, the Israelis wanted bilateral face-to-face negotiations with their Arab neighbours.' To square this circle, Baker intended to suggest an international conference (Arab demand) as an opening session, which would then become face-to-face direct talks (Israeli demand).

After eight tours of the Middle East capitals between March and October 1991, Baker succeeded in cajoling the Israelis and the Arabs to sit at the same table.

## The events leading to the conference
In Israel, the news of the imminent arrival of James Baker with a new peace initiative caused Prime Minister Shamir to convene his cabinet. The Israelis feared that they would be cornered into a peace process which was not in Israel's best interests. Shamir, a

suspicious man by nature, thought the Americans likely to over-reward the Arabs for their efforts during the Gulf War.

On 6 March 1991, just six days before the arrival of Baker, Shamir and his cabinet discussed how they should face him. 'The major concern for all of us,' recalls Defence Minister Moshe Arens, 'was that Baker's peace initiative might degenerate into an international conference of the kind that Peres had backed [in The London Agreement], rather than lead to direct negotiations [between Israel and each of its neighbours]. There was also concern about who would represent the Palestinians. We didn't want the PLO to use this as an opportunity to appear on the scene as Palestinian representatives. Also [demands to stop the building of] settlements was – as it had always been – a cause for concern [for Israel].'

James Baker landed in Tel Aviv shortly before 3 p.m., on 11 March. At 8.30 a.m. the next morning, he met Prime Minister Shamir for a one-to-one meeting. Baker thanked Shamir for showing restraint during the Gulf War and for not reacting to Saddam Hussein's Scud provocations. He then outlined his idea for an international conference. Shamir resisted this. An international conference, especially with the planned Soviet co-sponsorship, he believed, would support the Arabs' demands and corner Israel.

He told Baker that Israel would prefer a regional conference with Egypt, Jordan, Saudi Arabia, and Syria.

Yossi Ben Ahron attended the meeting. He recalls: 'Baker said that we needed to negotiate with the Palestinian delegation, among which should be a representative of Jerusalem, and of the Palestinian exile [the PLO], and that this international conference must be under the auspices of the United Nations and the two superpowers. I was the one who said, '"Never".'

Ignoring Israeli resistance, Baker went to meet a delegation of ten Palestinians. Because Israel would not sit at the same table as members of the PLO, he knew he would have to bring to the conference local Palestinians, who lived in the occupied territories, to represent the Palestinian point of view. A group of new Palestinian leaders, thrown up by the *intifada*, had provided him with the opportunity.

During the few days before Baker's arrival, these Palestinian leaders had been debating whether or not they should meet him.

Hanan Ashrawi, a professor of English literature at Beir Zeit University, recalls the dilemma: 'The majority of us saw this initiative as an attempt to by-pass the PLO. And we, in the occupied territories, would not carry out any political steps without direct orders – instructions – from the PLO [in Tunis].' Saeb Erekat, however, another leading Palestinian, said that they must meet Baker. If they didn't, he argued, they would be 'offering Shamir on a golden plate what he wants. We must go, we must be a player. The whole Middle East is being reshaped.'

In Tunis, Yasser Arafat and his PLO colleagues were hesitant. Ever since the *intifada*, they had feared an alternative leadership arising to replace them. If they allowed the 'insiders' to represent the Palestinian people, this could further marginalize the PLO. But Arafat also understood that, having supported Saddam Hussein during the Gulf War, he stood no chance of taking part in the peace talks. After days of discussion, the PLO finally authorized the 'insiders': Faisal Husseini, the top Palestinian leader in the occupied territories, and Hanan Ashrawi, Saeb Erekat, and seven other Palestinian leaders to meet James Baker.

On 12 March, armed with a handwritten letter from Yasser Arafat, stating that the delegation was meeting the Secretary of State with PLO approval, the 'insiders' made their way to the US Consul General's residence in Jerusalem. James Baker walked into the room to find the ten Palestinians already seated. They handed him Arafat's letter. Baker looked at it and said, 'You are moderate people of good sense. You have to realize that we're not going to renew a dialogue with the PLO in the face of Arafat's embrace of Saddam Hussein'.[16] Baker then stated that he was meeting with them as Palestinians from the territories, not as representatives of the PLO. 'Wait a minute,' snapped Erekat, 'we've come here to discuss Palestinian participation in the peace process – the PLO participation in the peace process. We are the PLO's delegation.' Baker: 'Well, I'm not gonna argue whose delegation you are, but *I'm* not speaking to the PLO.' Erekat: 'Mr Baker, this meeting could not have taken place without the permission of the PLO.'[17] Baker: 'If you are from the PLO, then I am determined to stop talking to you.' Faisal Husseini: 'Mr Baker, as you know, the law of the PLO says that every Palestinian is, by birth, a member of the organization.' Baker: 'I accept that, but please don't say anything else! As far as I'm concerned I'm not sitting with the PLO.'[18]

'I reminded them,' Baker recalls, 'that the PLO, their organization and their Chairman [Yasser Arafat] had made a serious mistake in backing Saddam Hussein in the Gulf War and that this had made it far less likely for the United States to be sympathetic to the organization.' At this statement, the Palestinians became even more agitated. Erekat: 'If the US could get Iraq out of Kuwait, then they could get the Israelis out of the occupied territories!' Baker: 'That's absolutely correct. But we never would. And the reason, Mr Erekat, is that there are UN resolutions that deal with that issue. These call for Israel and Palestinians to negotiate the status of the territories. It is for that reason that I am here!'[19]

The acrimony of the meeting escalated. Erekat: 'I said to him if we make you angry, what can you do? We don't have assets in US banks that can be frozen by you; we don't have airlines that can be grounded by you; we don't have anything in the world that you can threaten us with. And, if you want to hit us with missiles, Jericho is adjacent to Israeli settlements, so you will not do that because you will be scared of hitting the Israelis by accident. So, court us, and we'll play positively.' Baker: 'For all their posturing, I knew they were at least relieved to be talking directly to us.'

## The thorny issue of the settlements

On 8 April, after a brief return to Washington, Baker landed in Israel and was met with a new problem. That day, the Israelis had declared that they were building a new settlement in the occupied territories. The Israelis were signalling to Baker that the West Bank was part of *Eretz Yisrael* and would not be given away. Baker was furious; he saw this as an attempt to sabotage his mission. He knew that it would infuriate the Arabs and Palestinians who were already incandescent about the settlements the Israeli government had built on the land it had occupied in 1967. Baker's assistant, Dennis Ross, recalls how his boss confronted Prime Minister Shamir: 'I'm working damned hard to try to produce a peace process that's going to serve your interests and, if you want me to be able to do it, you cannot confront me with a settlement every time I show up.' Shamir tried to belittle the action and said, 'Well, it's a small activity and, frankly, it's Sharon's doing.' Baker said, 'Then talk to Sharon. I don't appreciate it.'

If Baker didn't appreciate finding a new settlement each time he arrived in Israel, the Palestinians did not either. Hanan Ashrawi greeted the Secretary of State by saying, 'Mr Baker, maybe you should stop coming to visit us because we cannot afford to pay the price of your visits.' Faisal Husseini recalls: 'I brought him maps of the West Bank and Gaza. One map represented the situation before '67, and the other showed the present situation . . . a very ugly picture of how the settlements had expanded.' Hanan Ashrawi then said to Baker: 'If you want a Palestinian delegation in the talks, you should get us an immediate cessation of all settlement activities.' Baker recalls saying to Husseini: 'Let's talk about how we're going to get the negotiations going. If you want to stop the expansion of the settlements, then you had better engage immediately in the peace process. You have no other alternative . . .'[20]

## Calling on Assad

Syria was vital to the peace process and Baker knew he had to get President Assad to send a delegation to the proposed conference. On 13 March, he visited Assad in Damascus for a meeting that lasted seven hours. Afterwards, he cabled President Bush, saying, 'Assad gave me the clear impression that he is serious about pursuing peace, but that he will be a tough nut to crack.'[21]

On 23 April, Baker flew again to Damascus to see Assad. Edward Djerejian, US Ambassador to Syria, who met and briefed him about what to expect from the meeting, reminded him of Assad's style of negotiating. 'Nobody can predict how long this meeting's going to last,' Djerejian said. 'So, be careful how much you drink. Assad will not leave the room. If you drink too much, the forces of nature will overcome you!'

This was good advice. The meeting lasted nine hours, forty-six minutes *without* a break, and took place, as Baker recalls, in 'a room rendered stifling by too little air-conditioning and sealed bullet-proof windows concealed behind drab olive-coloured drapes.'[22] Baker also recalls another detail which Djerejian had forgotten to mention: 'Assad would sit in a chair at one end of the room and you would sit in a chair at 180 degrees away from him on his right, so, in order to speak to him, you had to crane your neck and, at the end of a seven- or eight-hour session, you'd invariably have a terrible neck ache!'

Djerejian, who had not followed his own advice, felt severe discomfort six hours into the meeting. He passed a note to Baker saying, 'Secretary, it's okay if you want to take a break'. To Djerejian's distress, Baker replied, 'Ed, I don't want a break'. It took another hour for the Secretary of State to change his mind. 'I pulled out a white handkerchief,' Baker said, 'and waved it at Assad. "I give up," I confessed, "I have to go to the bathroom."'[23] Baker had been defeated by bladder diplomacy!

The reason the meeting lasted so long was that President Assad was refusing to budge on his principal procedural demands. Syrian Foreign Minister Farouk Shar'a recalls Assad's position and Baker's response: 'President Assad said, "It is important to have the United Nations as a co-sponsor alongside the Americans and the Soviets, and also to have the Europeans as a partner in the sponsorship." He then added, "A peace conference should not be convened just once and then disappear. The conference should be re-convened whenever necessary". Baker: "Mr President, the Israelis will not accept the United Nations – they hate the United Nations."'

To break the deadlock, Baker came up with an offer that was more remarkable in substance than procedure – an offer, which he knew Assad would find difficult to turn down. Dennis Ross: 'After going around and around for hour upon hour, he [Baker] finally said to him [Assad], "Why are you focusing on procedural questions, the real issue here is whether the Israelis are prepared to withdraw from the Golan Heights. You don't have a chance to get your land back if they're not prepared to withdraw, and they'll only withdraw if they feel they're secure and an American guarantee could provide that." He then added, "We'd be prepared to provide such a guarantee, which we have not offered in the past."'

Baker's proposal, however, was conditional. Ross recalls: 'Baker said, "I'm prepared to go to President Bush to see if he's prepared to authorize me to provide such a guarantee. But I'm not going to do this unless I know that it's going to take care of your procedural objections and you will go along with what we need."'

On 3 May, Djerejian reported to Baker that Assad had agreed to a UN observer (which, by now, Israel had also accepted) and that, only by consensus, would the conference be re-convened. This was good news.

Baker was convinced that Shamir would like his idea of security guarantees. 'The principal Israeli argument for keeping the Golan,' he said, 'was that it was needed for [Israeli] security purposes. The ultimate security guarantee, I thought, would be an American military presence. Prime Minister Shamir, however, was not too happy with the idea of an American military presence on the Golan because that removed the argument that the territory had to be kept for security reasons.'

On 11 May, Baker returned to Damascus to find that the Syrians had retreated from their previous pledge. 'President Assad,' Baker recalls, 'surprised me and my colleagues by interpreting my suggestion that the United States might guarantee the security of a negotiated border between Israel and Syria on the Golan as being a guarantee of a return of the Golan, which was clearly not what I had said, and it didn't make any sense.'

Baker was getting angry. He could see months of shuttling between the capitals going to waste. However, such a misunderstanding – if indeed it was one – could not be tolerated. Dennis Ross: 'Assad said to Baker, "Well, you promised to guarantee their [Israeli] withdrawal". Baker said, "*If* I promised to guarantee their withdrawal, why would I be talking about having negotiations? We wouldn't need 'em at all. I didn't promise anything of the sort . . . " And Baker started quoting, "Here's what I said . . . ". They went back and forth in their competing versions. Baker was pretty angry.'

The Syrians genuinely believed that Baker had back-tracked. Foreign Minister Shar'a: 'I personally concluded that he had had difficulties with the Israelis on this point and that's why he was wavering and backing away from his previous commitment.'

The meeting had reached a dead end. Djerejian recalls how it reached its climax: 'I was sitting to the right of Secretary Baker. He looked straight at Assad, slammed his leather-bound dossier shut, and said, "Mr President, I don't think we can do business together."'

When Baker returned to Washington, it was clear that his

attempt to bring the parties together was failing. Despite all the minor compromises he had managed to wrench from each of them, they were still not prepared to sit around the same table. However, he had invested too much time and energy to let the whole initiative collapse. An additional measure, he decided, had to be taken: President Bush should intervene by sending letters to all the parties involved.

### Twisting arms

On 31 May, President Bush sent letters to Shamir, Assad, President Mubarak of Egypt, King Hussein of Jordan, King Fahad of Saudi Arabia and Faisal Husseini (Palestinian leader from inside occupied territories), urging them to demonstrate flexibility. Six days later, Shamir responded. 'In his letter to President Bush,' Baker recalls, 'Shamir basically said we're not going to be there.' That was not an encouraging response to what Baker had hoped would be a re-launch of the conference process. Baker: 'The only leverage a Secretary of State has in this kind of situation is the ability to blame one party or the other for the collapse of the peace process. And there was a bit of an opening in Shamir's letter. They didn't want to be blamed for the collapse of the peace process.'

Baker was hoping for a 'yes' from Syria that would then force Shamir to be positive. Syrian Foreign Minister Farouk Shar'a recalls: 'Baker told President Assad, "Your position is very important. If you accept the American initiative, then the whole world will stand by Syria and will blame Israel. Perhaps, then, the Israelis will be embarrassed and will agree to go to the conference.'

The key to breaking the deadlock now lay in Damascus. Baker could only sit and wait.

On 14 July, US Ambassador Djerejian was summoned to see Foreign Minister Farouk Shar'a who handed him a letter from President Assad to President Bush. Djerejian: 'I read it and then re-read it.' Foreign Minister Shar'a said, "What's taking you so long?" I said, "I want to make sure I understand it. This is a very important letter." Then I said, "Mr Minister, you can convey to President Assad that he has made an historic decision for peace". Shar'a smiled, and repeated, "But what took you so long to read it?" I said, "I was looking for the Syrian loophole!"'

Djerejian was delighted and immediately phoned Washington to convey the good news. Baker's assistant Dennis Ross took down the wording of Assad's reply. Ross: 'Baker was squinting over my shoulder trying to read my writing. "Dennis," he kept saying, "I can't read this". I kept replying, "Let me finish ... " When he [Djerejian] got about two-thirds of the way through it, I said, "Uh-huh. He's giving us a 'yes' and it's not qualified!" As I finished writing, Baker got on the phone and said, "Well done, Ed."'

Now it was time for Baker to see Shamir. On 21 July 1991, he returned to Jerusalem. Yossi Ben Aharon, Director General of Shamir's office, recalls what Baker said to the Israeli Prime Minister: 'I am giving you, Mr Shamir, a positive answer to the conditions you have presented to go [to the peace conference]. There will be no PLO, no United Nations, no prolonged conference.' Shamir listened, but was still suspicious, wondering what had made President Assad agree to attend. Defence Minister Moshe Arens recalls the Israelis' concern: 'Obviously Baker had wrung some concession out of the Arabs. The question was: how had he done it and what had he told them? Maybe there was some secret commitment that had brought about this change? It was obvious that the Golan Heights had been discussed and our suspicion was that either he [Assad] had been told that he would have American support for the Golan Heights being put under Syrian control or maybe, more ambiguously, he had been told that the Americans supported the formula of territories for peace.' Shamir said to Baker, 'We need a little time, but you will get your answers and you won't be disappointed.'

On 31 July, while Baker was in Moscow, he talked with Shamir on the phone. Baker: 'I want you to be able to stand up with me after a short meeting and say "yes" ... There is still the Palestinian representation issue to work out. You will be saying "yes" to everything but that.'[24] Shamir, in a quiet voice said, 'yes'.

## The Palestinian delegation
'Getting an agreement for the composition of the Palestinian delegation,' Baker said, 'was the hardest thing we had to do because the Israelis wanted nobody from East Jerusalem, nobody from the diaspora, nobody from the PLO.' To find a way around

the problem, Baker revived the idea of a joint local Palestinian-Jordanian delegation that had been first mooted by King Hussein and Shimon Peres in London in 1987 (see chapter 26). The Palestinians hated this idea. Baker had touched a sensitive chord: the Palestinians had always suspected that Jordan was bent on representing the Palestinian people and killing the idea of an independent Palestinian entity.

Djerejian was at the meeting with the Palestinians when Baker put forward the idea of a Jordanian-Palestinian delegation. Djerejian recalls, 'He put his body in a very strange posture at the negotiating table, which surprised us all, and said: "What you are trying to do is analogous to a tailor trying to fit a suit to a man who has been contorted into a strange position."' To illustrate the situation the Palestinians were in, Husseini said, 'A man was given an ill-fitting suit as a present from his wife. The suit only looked good if the man twisted one of his arms, like Dr Strangelove, and made the other arm look foreshortened and withered. Persuaded by the tailor to accept this, he went out into the street where two girls looked at him and felt terribly sorry for him. One said to the other, "Look at that poor fellow – his body is deformed – but God has helped him by giving him a clever tailor."' Husseini then looked at the US Secretary of State and said, 'Mr Baker, it's a strange suit that you have tailored for us!'

'It was,' Baker recalls, 'a lively and animated discussion.'

It would take him a further three months to unravel problems with Israel, and to get the Palestinians to agree to be part of a Jordanian-Palestinian delegation and come up with names of delegates which would satisfy the Israelis.

He succeeded. On 31 October, the Israeli and Arab delegations met in Madrid.

*Chapter 31*

# The Madrid conference

On the first day of the Madrid conference, Saeb Erekat, the Vice-Chairman of the Palestinian delegation, walked into the ornate hall of the Spanish Royal Palace with a mischievous smile on his face. He ignored the surprised looks from the other delegates and settled into his chair behind Dr Haidar abdel-Shafi, the head of the Palestinian delegation. Like the majority of those present, Erekat was wearing a dark suit, but around his neck hung a black-and-white chequered scarf – a *keffiyeh* – on the edge of which was embroidered the Palestinian flag. This addition to his attire was intentionally provocative.

Erekat had given much thought to this gesture. 'Shamir,' he recalls, 'had once said that the Palestinians didn't exist. How could we tell this man, I asked myself, that we, Palestinians, were here in Madrid? The only thing that symbolizes Palestinians is the *keffiyeh*, which President Arafat wears all the time, so I decided to put it on my shoulder. Some of my colleagues objected and said, 'Saeb, we don't wanna break up the conference.'

US President Bush was already at the podium to read his opening speech. As he talked about the mission to work on a just and comprehensive settlement in the Middle East, Erekat looked across the rectangular table into Israeli Prime Minister Shamir's eyes. Erekat: 'The angle of my seat was engineered by God. It was perfect. He was looking at me and was furious about the *keffiyeh*. I nodded my head; he shook his head and averted his eyes . . . The next time he looked at me, I smiled and winked at him. He made a tut-tutting sound.'

Shamir was shifting uneasily in his seat, not only because of Saeb Erekat, but because President Bush's words were making him uncomfortable. Although the Israelis and Americans had agreed, in advance, that the US President would not refer to the 'Land for Peace' formula in his speech, President Bush had found a way around this by talking about 'territorial compromise'. 'We believe,' President Bush said, 'that territorial compromise is essential for peace. Boundaries should reflect the quality of both security and political arrangements.'

Sensing the tension, Secretary of State James Baker knew he had to calm the situation. The first step would be to get Saeb Erekat to take off his *keffiyeh*. Immediately after the session ended, he sent John Kelly, one of his assistants, to reproach Erekat. 'After the session,' Erekat recalls, 'every one surrounded me – John Kelly of the United States, Prince Bandar, Saudi Arabia's Ambassador [to the US], and said, "Why are you doing this? We don't want the conference to collapse". I said to Prince Bandar, "You're wearing a *keffiyeh*, why don't they make a fuss about that?" Then I saw Rubinstein [an Israeli delegate], and said, "How about if I make a deal with you? You take off your *kippa* [skull cap] and I'll take off my *keffiyeh*. Why are you making such a big fuss? We are not here just to be photographed with you. We, Palestinians, are the key to your peace process and you must accept this as a fact of life."'

Erekat would not relinquish his *keffiyeh*. That evening, Baker spoke to Faisal Husseini about the matter. 'I said, "You know it would be better if he [Saeb Erekat] were not a member of the formal delegation". The Israelis had told us they would not return if he remained a member of the delegation.'

It was PLO Chairman Yasser Arafat who resolved the crisis. In constant telephone contact with the delegation from his head-quarters in Tunis, he ordered the Madrid delegation not to include Erekat in the following session – to avoid a diplomatic incident.[25]

That night, the steering committee of the Palestinian delegation gathered for a 'co-ordination' meeting in the home of Essam Kamel, the PLO's representative in Madrid. Every aspect of their speech and position had to be approved by the PLO. The members of the committee were ready to start work, but the PLO representative was stalling. Suddenly he announced that the location of the meeting would have to be changed because he feared the place was bugged. Ghassan Khatib, a member of the steering committee, recalls: 'We were taken by car to an unstated destination. On arrival, we found ourselves in front of a plane. Only when we were on board the plane were we told that we were going to Tunis. It was a 100-seater plane, but we were only eight people! On arrival in Tunis we were taken to the house of the PLO Ambassador, and there we found Arafat and the whole Palestinian leadership. Arafat said, "Where are the others?" Somebody said, "We thought you only wanted the steering committee." "No, no," Arafat said, "I wanted all the delegation!"'

The steering committee was returned to Madrid at 3 a.m., and each of them crept back to his hotel room under the cover of darkness. Yasser Arafat had made his point. If he could not go to Madrid, then the Madrid delegation would come to him – every night of the conference if he chose.

The following night – the second day of the conference – the whole episode was repeated. But, this time, the full 100-member delegation was taken to meet Arafat in Algiers. Hanan Ashrawi, the spokeswoman of the delegation, recalls: 'We were taken to an auditorium and the grievances started coming out. It was a griping session.'

Instead of talking strategy or positions, Arafat addressed the delegates' grievances. One of the main problems was telephone bills. Most of the delegates were from inside the occupied territories where they had no opportunity to telephone friends and relatives living in Arab countries, because, with the exception of Egypt, Israel had no telephone system connected to Arab countries. Once, in Madrid, the delegates had used the telephones freely, and the delegation administrators were now complaining to Arafat that they could not cover the cost of the calls. Ghassan Khatib recalls: 'During his response Arafat said, "Do you know that, because of all our international telephone calls, they call us Palestinians the zero-zero people. But these calls just reflect that we are a scattered nation." He then ordered his administrators to pay for the calls.

Once again the delegation returned to Madrid under the cover of night.

On Thursday, 31 October, Prime Minister Shamir had been invited to deliver the first speech. 'We pray that this meeting will mark the beginning of a new chapter in the history of the Middle East,' he said. Shamir then talked about the history of the conflict, and how he saw the way forward: 'We know our partners to the negotiations will make territorial demands on Israel, but, as examination of the conflict's long history makes clear, its nature is not territorial. The conflict raged long before Israel acquired Judaea, Samaria (West Bank), Gaza and the Golan in a defensive war. There was no hint of recognition of Israel before the 1967 War, when the territories in question were not under Israel's control.'[26]

In his speech, the Syrian Foreign Minister Al-Shar'a then called on Israel to withdraw from the Golan Heights, from the West Bank, Gaza and from South Lebanon.

The next morning, a Friday, was devoted to responses. Shamir asked to be the first to talk because he wanted to reach Israel before the Sabbath. He said: 'I could recite a litany of facts which demonstrate the extent to which Syria merits the dubious honour of being one of the most oppressive, tyrannical regimes in the world.' He then went on to say that Syria was nothing but a terrorist state. His words echoed around the hall and the tension was tangible.

Edward Djerejian, the US Ambassador to Syria, leaned forward in his seat to look at Farouk Al-Shar'a. The Syrian Foreign Minister, who was heading his country's delegation, was obviously furious. Djerejian: 'I saw immediately that he was extremely tense. He froze, then called one of his aides over.'

Farouk Shar'a had called to Walid Moualem, the Syrian Ambassador to the US, with whom he had spent seven hours the previous night writing the Syrian speech. They had spent ages labouring over the tone so that it would not sound too hostile nor too conciliatory towards Israel. But Shamir's words had triggered a war of words. Farouk Shar'a recalls: 'He made a bitter attack on Syria and accused it of being on the list of terrorism. I was very angry. I didn't *want* to create a problem in the conference but, at the same time, I could *not* accept these false accusations and a distortion of history, so I lay aside my prepared speech.'

The previous evening, Walid Moualem had shown Farouk Shar'a a 1948 newspaper clipping – given to him by a member of the Lebanese delegation – that contained a photograph of Yitzhak Shamir in his youth with the word WANTED[27] written across it in bold letters. Farouk Shar'a now asked Moualem if he still had the photograph. The Ambassador slipped the photograph out of his suit pocket and handed it to Shar'a.

Edward Djerejian, who was keeping an eye on what was happening, recalls: 'He [Shar'a] literally tore up his prepared script for his speech.'

As Shar'a went to the podium, with only the photograph in his hand, Shamir left the hall to catch his plane back to Israel in time for Sabbath. He left his delegation to listen to what Shar'a had to say: 'I will just show you, if I may, an old photograph of Mr Shamir. Why was this picture distributed? Because he was WANTED. He helped, as I recall, in the assassination of Count Bernadotte, the UN mediator in Palestine in 1948. He kills peace mediators!'

Yossi Ben Aharon, the director of Shamir's office, recalls: 'We were furious. I took off my earphones and started to bang on the table. "What's going on here?" I asked Baker. He just looked very uncomfortable.'

Baker was only thankful that the incident hadn't taken place on the first day of the conference when it might have aborted all his efforts. 'It wasn't going to go anywhere,' he recalls, 'if the parties insulted each other, which is exactly what they were doing – beginning with Shamir's speech which was quite incendiary – and followed by Foreign Minister Shar'a's speech which was perhaps even more incendiary.'

Baker addressed the gathering, urging them to act more responsibly during the second phase – that of direct negotiations 'If you do not seize this historic opportunity,' he said, 'no-one else will. The continuation and the success of this process is in your hands. The world still looks to each of you to make the choice for peace.'

A new crisis erupted almost immediately. As far as the Syrian Foreign Minister was concerned, the coming phase was a concession Syria had made to satisfy Israel. Syria had agreed to direct negotiations, provided that the beginning of talks between the different Arab delegations and Israel be held at the *same venue* and at the *same time*. Thus, when Baker informed Shar'a that the direct negotiations would be held in *different* venues at *different* times, Shar'a categorically refused to accept this. US Ambassador Djerejian recalls: 'We heard that Foreign Minister Shar'a's plane was being geared up on the runway to go back to Damascus – and that this was a sort of brinkmanship.'

The Americans soon devised a compromise. The direct negotiations between Israel and the Arab delegations would take place at the same hotel but at *different* times. President Assad gave the go-ahead. The last-minute threat to face-to-face talks was averted.

The years of mistrust that had boiled over during the Madrid conference would not fade away easily. But, to James Baker's satisfaction, the launch of the peace process had not been derailed. The Madrid conference, to a large extent, had been a ceremonial opening to the direct negotiations that were to follow. These would be held in Washington.

PART

# 6 PEACE AT LAST?

## Introduction

The Madrid peace conference of 30 October to 1 November 1991 was the biggest breakthrough in Arab-Israeli relations since President Sadat's historical visit to Israel on 19 November 1977 which itself led to the first-ever peace agreement between Israel and an Arab state.

At the Madrid conference, under the auspices of America and Russia, Israeli and Arab leaders sat down at the same table to begin the negotiations. But often throughout the two-day gathering, these seemed more like the continuation of war than the dawn of a new era of peace.

What was important, though, was that the conference created a two-track mechanism for future negotiations. The first track was multilateral, in which Israel, regional Arab states and other states outside the region, could join in discussions about five key Middle East problems: water, environment, arms control, refugees and economic development. These multilateral talks, initiated at the Madrid conference, commenced in Moscow in January 1992.

The second was the bilateral track, in which Israel would negotiate in Washington with each of its Arab neighbours – Syria, Lebanon, Jordan and the Palestinians. The latter two were united into one 'Jordanian-Palestinian' delegation and, since Israel would not talk with the PLO which it considered a terrorist organization, it insisted that the Palestinian group should be composed of indigenous people from the West Bank and Gaza, none of whom could be a member of the PLO. The Israelis hoped that this local Palestinian leadership would gradually gain stature, sideline the 'outsiders' – the PLO of Tunis – and conclude a deal with Israel. But this proved wishful thinking. The local Palestinian leadership remained dependent on the PLO's instructions and, after each round of the Washington talks, travelled to Tunis to discuss their next move and receive orders from Abu Mazen, the PLO official who co-ordinated the Palestinian side of the talks in Washington. Furthermore, if Israel thought that the local Palestinians would be more flexible they were wrong. At the negotiating sessions, Dr Haidar Abdel Shafi from Gaza, Hanan Ashrawi from the West Bank town of Ramallah, the spokeswoman for the Palestinian delegation, and others, insisted on discussing the most sensitive issues, most notably the status of Jerusalem.

So, the talks in Washington moved at a snail's pace. Even agreeing the agenda proved to be a nightmare. Initially the Israeli and Palestinian negotiators refused to convene in the same room and conducted instead what became known as 'corridor diplomacy'. Often, they communicated only by exchanging memorandums. When they did sit around the same table, it was for the exchange of declarations rather than for negotiations.

In the summer of 1992, as general elections approached in Israel, Yitzhak Rabin, the leader of the Labour Party, made a pre-election promise that would, when the Washington talks became totally deadlocked, cause him to do the unthinkable – to talk directly with the PLO of Tunis, and then stand on the same stage with the man he despised, the PLO leader Yasser Arafat, and shake his hand in front of the world.

*Chapter 32*

# Deadlock in the Washington talks

'*Should* I form the next government,' promised Yitzhak Rabin, the leader of the Israeli Labour Party, just before the 1992 General Election, 'I undertake to reach an agreement with the Palestinians in the [occupied] territories within six to nine months of taking office.'

Shortly after delivering this speech, Rabin won the election and sent Yitzhak Shamir into retirement. The new Prime Minister kept the Defence Ministry for himself but, bowing to party pressure, gave the Foreign Ministry to his arch rival, Shimon Peres. In his 1979 memoirs,[1] Rabin had called Peres an 'indefatigable intriguer' and Peres had never forgiven him. As Peres accepted Rabin's offer, he said, 'If you are seeking peace, you can rely on my support. But if you move away from that path, I will reach my own conclusions. You are too pessimistic and I am too optimistic. Together, we can create the right balance. It is our responsibility to take unpleasant decisions and clear the way to peace, so that the younger generation can enter a field without treading on a land-mine.'

Rabin and Peres soon saw the promised deadline of six to nine months approaching without any real progress having been made. The talks in Washington between Israel and the Palestinians from the occupied territories were deadlocked. The Palestinians thought Israel was offering too little; Israel thought their opponents were asking too much – notably to have East Jerusalem, which Israel had occupied in 1967 and annexed after the war, as the capital of their future Palestinian state.

Then came an incident which stopped the talks altogether. On 13 December 1992, Nissim Toledano, a twenty-nine-year-old Israeli border policeman, was kidnapped as he was leaving home in Lod. Six hours later, two masked men entered the office of the Red Crescent[2] in the West Bank town of El Bira. Having announced that they were members of Hamas (the Islamic Resistance Movement), they left a photocopy of Toledano's identity card and a letter for the Israeli authorities demanding the release of Sheikh

Ahmed Yassin who, since 1989, had been serving a life-sentence in an Israeli jail.[3]

Sheikh Yassin, a quadriplegic, was a fundamentalist clergyman and leader of Hamas, which he had established in February 1988 in the Gaza Strip. The Sheikh rejected the state of Israel and was against peace talks with it. He was also a rival of the PLO. Sheikh Yassin called on his activists to help him establish an Islamic state in Israel, Gaza and the West Bank. Responding to his call, his Hamas followers attacked, killed and kidnapped Israelis. In retaliation, Israel captured and jailed the Sheikh, hoping that Hamas would collapse without his leadership. The Sheikh's followers then kidnapped Toledano to force Israel to release their leader.

The Israelis asked the kidnappers to give them proof that Toledano was still alive. There was no response. Two days later, a Bedouin woman found Toledano's body. He had been knifed and strangled, and his hands were tied behind his back.

Ehud Barak, the Israeli Chief of Staff, was in bed when the telephone rang. Prime Minister Rabin was on the line. 'I am going to convene a cabinet meeting,' Rabin said, 'a special meeting [to discuss the killing of Toledano]. Can you expel them this evening?' By 'them' Rabin meant the 415 Hamas activists who had been rounded up by the Israeli security forces after the kidnapping. Now that Toledano was dead, the expulsion of the activists would be a clear signal that Israel would not tolerate such killings. Barak telephoned his deputy, Amnon Lipkin-Shahak, gave him the necessary instructions and went to the cabinet meeting.

At the meeting, Rabin demanded that the cabinet should support him in his decision to expel the Hamas activists, but not all the ministers agreed. Justice Minister David Libai pointed out that the expulsion would be illegal, while Minister Amnon Rubinstein thought that the move was politically unwise and would transform the activists from terrorists who killed Israelis into deportee 'victims' who might win international sympathy. It was a long and tense meeting in which Rabin tried to change the minds of the ministers who were against the expulsion. Chief of Staff Barak, who kept going out to ensure that preparations were being made for the expulsion if the cabinet agreed, recalls: 'Yitzhak was angry with the wishy-washy ministers who seemed to be trying to be nice to everyone and were unwilling to give him the necessary support'.

Meanwhile in Washington, Hanan Ashrawi, the Palestinian delegation's spokeswoman, was also informed that, 'there were rumours of an intended mass deportation of Palestinians'. That night, she appeared on CNN's *Larry King Live* programme and warned: 'If the deportations are carried out, there will be no Palestinian delegation at the Washington talks'. King: 'But they're Hamas people, opposed to the peace process.' Ashrawi: 'They're Palestinians.'

In Israel, Foreign Minister Peres, just back from an official visit to Japan, was furious. Rabin had not informed him of his intention nor had he invited his deputy, Yossi Beilin, to attend the crucial cabinet meeting. Peres went to see Rabin. 'This is a mistake,' he said. 'It won't lead us anywhere.' But it was too late. The Israeli Supreme Court of Justice had approved the expulsion, and the 415 activists were already being unloaded from the twenty-two buses that had carried them to South Lebanon.

In Washington, the Palestinian delegation walked out of the peace talks. 'We will not come back,' its members warned, 'until the Hamas deportees are returned.'

*Chapter 33*

# Secret talks in Oslo

On 4 December 1992, a group of Palestinians, Israelis, delegates of other Arab states, and from other countries such as India, Greece, China and America, were gathered in London for yet another round of the peace talks. This round consisted of the steering committee which was established after the 1991 Madrid conference to co-ordinate the multilateral peace talks. Ahmed Qurei, known as Abu Ala'a, a man in his fifties and the PLO's finance chief, was present, but not allowed to sit at the negotiation table because Israeli law banned direct contact with PLO officials. Behind the scenes, however, he was the prime mover on the Palestinian side. Also present was Yair Hirschfeld, a forty-nine-year-old Israeli professor from Haifa University.

Hanan Ashrawi, the Palestinian team's spokeswoman at the Washington talks, who knew both Abu Ala'a and Hirschfeld, had suggested that, as both the men were interested in the links between economic issues and the Middle East peace process, they should meet while in London.

The first meeting between them took place at the Cavendish Hotel, near Piccadilly Circus, on the morning of 4 December 1992. Hirschfeld arrived early to meet Terje Rød Larsen, a Norwegian Socialist with good contacts in Norway and a passionate interest in Israeli-Palestinian relations. Larsen promised Hirschfeld that if, after meeting Abu Ala'a, he wanted to continue the contact, then he would make the necessary arrangements for them to meet in Norway. Larsen then left, leaving Hirschfeld to wait for Abu Ala'a. Hirschfeld was nervous. He was breaking Israeli law by meeting a PLO official. Abu Ala'a, on the way to his first-ever face-to-face meeting with an Israeli, was also nervous. He recalls: 'I was looking to my left and right, afraid of being seen.'

They talked for more than two hours. Having discussed how they could help break the stalemate in the Washington talks, they agreed that it was important to meet away from media attention where there was no temptation to play to the gallery. Hirschfeld told Abu Ala'a that, although he was just an academic, he was a good friend of Yossi Beilin, Foreign Minister Peres's deputy. They agreed to meet again later that evening.

Excited, Hirschfeld consulted Yossi Beilin, who was also in London representing the Israeli government on the steering committee. As a Deputy Minister in Rabin's government, Beilin could not approve an illegal meeting with a PLO official, so he said, 'I will say nothing'. With that silent blessing, Hirschfeld and Abu Ala'a agreed to meet again – this time in Oslo. Terje Larsen would make the arrangements.

### Washington out, Oslo in . . .

Back in Tunis, Abu Ala'a wrote a three-page report for Yasser Arafat who then passed this on to Mahmoud Abbas, known as Abu Mazen, the PLO official in charge of Palestinian-Israeli affairs. Abu Ala'a also gave Abu Mazen an oral report, outlining his impressions of Hirschfeld. 'There's no such thing as "just an academic" in Israel,' Abu Mazen replied, 'they all work for either

Mossad or the Foreign Ministry.' Since the Washington talks were going nowhere, Arafat and Abu Mazen agreed that it was worth giving the informal talks a chance.

Abu Mazen and Abu Ala'a then decided that two other people should join Abu Ala'a in Oslo: Hassan Asfour from the PLO in Tunis, who was secretary to the negotiations committee supervising the Washington talks; and Maher al-Kurd, an economist, who spoke fluent English, and who had worked as an economic adviser in Abu Ala'a's department. Abu Mazen then gave Abu Ala'a advice on how to deal with the Israelis. 'Don't talk politics during the first half an hour or an hour,' he said. 'Talk about human things . . . Ask: "How many children do you have?", "Are you married?", "Where do you live?", etc.'

Meanwhile, in Israel, Hirschfeld – who was not a Mossad agent – was preparing himself and Ron Pundak, one of his former students, to go to Oslo.

### 'Can we forget history for now?'

On 21 January 1993, Hirschfeld and Pundak landed in Oslo on the day the Knesset – against the wishes of Prime Minister Rabin – abrogated the law that forbade meetings between the Israelis and the PLO. This was a great relief for Hirschfeld and Pundak, for, even if nothing came of their meeting, at least they would not be in trouble. From the airport, they were taken straight to the Norwegian Foreign Ministry.

Abu Ala'a and his colleagues, though, had a bumpy landing. With no visas, they were held up at passport control for more than an hour. Taken to security and questioned, Abu Ala'a lost his temper and threatened to return to Tunis. But, once passport control had received the necessary clearance, the Palestinians met Terje Larsen and his wife, Mona Juul, who took them to a secluded manor in the small town of Sarpsborg, some 80 kilometres south of Oslo.

The next afternoon, Hirschfeld, Abu Ala'a and their teams met for their first session. Abu Ala'a opened by reading a speech in Arabic, which Maher el-Kurd translated into English. 'We are going through a fateful and important phase that requires courage and daring,' he read. He then presented ten points which he saw as the basis for a Palestinian-Israeli peace agreement. He added some practical advice: 'We can talk history forever without convincing each other or getting anywhere,' he said. 'So, can we forget history for now and talk about the conflict?'

It was Hirschfeld's turn. 'What I am hearing now is extremely important,' he said. 'It expresses a determination to achieve peace.' He added, 'Let's focus on Gaza first . . . ' The idea of starting with Gaza, and handing it over to the Palestinians so that they could rule themselves, had been floating around for some time. Shimon Peres had suggested this, but it had been rejected by the Palestinians who suspected that the Israelis wanted to give them Gaza, which was riddled with problems, and hold on to the West Bank. The Palestinians remembered that, in September 1992, Prime Minister Rabin had said that his dream was to wake up one morning and find that Gaza had disappeared under the sea. They feared that when the Israelis spoke about 'Gaza first', they actually meant 'Gaza first and last'. 'What about East Jerusalem which is very important for us Palestinians?' Abu Ala'a asked. On this subject, Hirschfeld knew he had little to offer – at least at this stage. Jerusalem was the most combustible issue for the Palestinians and the Israelis. The Palestinians were claiming that Eastern Jerusalem would be the capital of their eventual state, while the Israelis were adamant that Jerusalem East and West would remain their eternal undivided capital. 'We can hold unofficial talks on Jerusalem,' Hirschfeld said to Abu Ala'a. 'We do appreciate that Jerusalem needs to have a special status. But, for Israelis, Jerusalem must remain united. At the same time, we do understand that Jerusalem's Palestinians must not become part of Israel.'

All in all, it was a reasonably good discussion and, after two more days, the delegates left Oslo and returned home. In Tunis, Abu Ala'a and his team reported to Yasser Arafat and Abu Mazen that the Israelis were serious.

## A first Declaration of Principles (DOP)

Hirschfeld reported to Yossi Beilin who decided that, for the time being, he would not share the secret with his boss, Foreign Minister Peres. Relations between Peres and Rabin were, as usual, soured by mutual suspicions. If Peres felt obliged to tell Rabin about the talks, he might stop them altogether. Alternatively, if

Peres kept the information to himself, this might eventually lead to an explosive situation and, once again, Rabin might stop the talks. So, Beilin simply said to Hirschfeld, 'Why don't you draft a Declaration of Principles (DOP) as an academic exercise?' Hirschfeld agreed. A DOP would concentrate the minds of the Israeli and Palestinian negotiators in Oslo. But Hirschfeld had no idea how to produce such a document. He consulted Hanan Ashrawi, the Palestinian team's spokeswoman at the Washington talks. Keeping her in the dark about the secret contacts in Oslo, he told her that he was 'doing a project with students about the peace process', and asked her if he 'could borrow a sample Declaration of Principles'. She gave him a copy of something that had been drafted in Washington. 'She never suspected why I needed it,' Hirschfeld said, 'and there I was working for a peace negotiation that was competing with hers!'

On 11 February, Hirschfeld and Pundak brought their document to the second meeting in Oslo. It had three parts. The first contained fourteen principles to guide the parties towards the signing of an intermediate agreement to establish a Palestinian Interim Self-Government Authority in Gaza. The second part concerned an annex dealing with Israeli-Palestinian co-operation over water, land and other areas. Then there was an annex which concerned a Marshall Plan for Gaza, so that the impoverished and over-populated area could be developed.

After breakfast, the two groups sat around the table and Hirschfeld offered the Palestinians the draft DOP. Abu Ala'a looked at the document, and said, 'This is very comprehensive. We will need three or four hours to read it'. To allow them to do this, Hirschfeld and Pundak went for a walk in the woods. It was a crucial moment. If Abu Ala'a and his team accepted the suggested document as a working paper, then they could develop it into a fully fledged agreement. After three hours, the Palestinians were still studying the document, but then when Hirschfeld and Pundak came in, Abu Ala'a said, 'Let's sit down and start work'.

### 'I'll go along with Oslo . . . '
In Israel, Yossi Beilin told Peres that Hirschfeld and Pundak had now been twice to Norway to meet with the 'Palestinians from

Tunis'. Peres: 'Who were the Palestinians?' Beilin told him the names. Peres had never heard of Abu Ala'a and was not impressed. In his long political career, he had witnessed so many initiatives and secret meetings and contacts, why should this one be any different? Beilin then told Peres about the DOP that Hirschfeld and Pundak had discussed in Oslo. 'Okay,' said Peres. 'Leave the document with me and I will see if it is interesting.'

With the talks in Washington deadlocked, and with the approach of Rabin's self-imposed pre-election deadline coming ever closer, Peres went to see Rabin. 'The talks in Washington,' he told him, 'have no chance. They're dead. Washington's become a place for exchanging declarations, not for negotiations.' He then told Rabin of the 'two *meshugoim*' (crackpots) who were meeting Palestinians from Tunis in Oslo. Although unimpressed, Rabin instructed Peres not to stop the talks. Rabin was embarrassed that the fiasco of the Hamas expulsion had halted the Washington talks just at the moment when the US's newly-elected President, Bill Clinton, was entering the White House. He wanted them back on track. He said that he would not like anyone else, apart from him and Peres, to know about Oslo. But then added, 'I will go along with the Oslo talks as long as they are running parallel to the Washington talks'.

In Oslo, Hirschfeld said to Abu Ala'a, 'We cannot meet again unless the Washington talks are renewed – run parallel'.

### 'Don't just think about yourselves'

In Tunis, Arafat received this message and was worried. If his delegation did not return to the Washington negotiations, the other Arab delegations might continue the talks and leave the Palestinians out in the cold. It was important for Arafat to keep the two channels – Washington and Oslo – on track and, for this, he needed the co-operation of his Washington delegates. But the delegates, all residents of the occupied territories, were under pressure from the families of the 415 deported Hamas activists not to return to the negotiations until Israel brought their relatives back from Lebanon. A group of women had come to Ashrawi's house in Ramallah when Faisal Husseini was visiting. 'In the name of your father, the great freedom fighter and martyr Abdel-Kadir Husseini,' they had said to Husseini, whose father a

Palestinian leader was killed in 1948, 'we ask you not to go back to the talks. Bring our men back!'.[4] Saeb Erekat got a blunt message when his family was physically threatened.

Inspite of all this, Arafat needed the delegates back in Washington. 'You are coming with me,' he said to Ashrawi. 'Meet me at the airport at 6 o'clock.' He gave the same instruction to Saeb Erekat, and then instructed the rest of the Washington team to drive from the West Bank and Gaza to meet him in the Intercontinental Hotel, Amman. 'We will take the decision together,' he said.

Arafat flew to Syria and met with President Assad in Latakia. Assad urged Arafat, who was flanked by Ashrawi and Erekat, to send his delegates back to Washington. Arafat wanted Ashrawi and Erekat to witness this pressure on him, so that when they reached the Intercontinental Hotel, Amman, the two West Bankers would advise the rest of the delegation to return to the negotiating table in Washington. But, once in Amman, Erekat said to his colleagues, 'I *don't* think we should go back'. Arafat lost his temper. 'Other leaders,' he shouted, 'just issue instructions to their delegations and they obey. I have to cajole, persuade and argue with you.'[5] He turned to Ashrawi: 'Don't only think about yourselves, think about others. This is a responsibility you have undertaken. You must go back'. Then, turning to Saeb Erekat, he cajoled: 'Come on! You know we have to think politics, and not just run on emotions. Stop living in your small world. If you don't, you'll break the peace process. Come down to earth!' Haidar Abdel Shafi, an elderly doctor from Gaza who was heading the delegation, requested Arafat to let the delegation deliberate in private. Arafat swept out. At dawn, after a long stormy meeting, the delegation agreed to go back to Washington.

### 'I want the big fish'

On 27 April 1993, the ninth round of the Washington talks started, but again led nowhere. In Oslo, three days later, the Israelis and the Palestinians met, but Abu Ala'a was playing tough. Turning to Larsen, the Norwegian facilitator who, by now, had become father-confessor to both camps, he said, 'I want the big fish.' Pointing at Larsen, he threatened, 'If you are not able to persuade the Israelis to upgrade these talks, then this is the last time you will see me . . . ' He then added, 'We've presented what we have to offer and if Israeli government officials do not come to these talks then our mission is over.'

By now, more than three months after the start of the Oslo talks, Abu Ala'a and his supervisors in Tunis – Abu Mazen and Yasser Arafat – were still not sure if Hirschfeld and Pundak were officially representing Israel or bluffing and simply running their own show.

Abu Ala'a's message was passed on to Israel, where Peres discussed it with Rabin on 13 May 1993 – the day Rabin's promise to conclude a deal with the Palestinians within six to nine months of being elected had run out of time. 'We have to upgrade the level of the Oslo talks,' Peres said, adding, 'The best thing is for me to go there so I can run the negotiations myself.' Rabin: 'That will present a problem. You are a cabinet member. If you go, it will mean that we have officially recognized the PLO. If the talks do not succeed, we must maintain our ability to deny this.' Accepting what Rabin had said, Peres suggested that they send their highest civil servant – Uri Savir, the Director General of the Foreign Ministry. Rabin agreed and Peres asked Uri Savir to come and see him in Jerusalem. 'Uri,' Peres asked him, 'what do you think about spending a weekend in Oslo?' Savir: 'Pardon?'

### 'Your public enemy number one'

On 20 May 1993, Savir left Israel, but did not go straight to Oslo. The talks were still a secret and he had to ensure that they remained so. He flew to Paris, checked into the Baltimore Hotel, told the Israeli Ambassador that he was going to meet his wife at the Cannes Film Festival and that he did not need an escort. He then scattered some towels around the room to make it look lived in, left 'Don't Disturb' on the door-handle, took a cab to the airport and flew to Oslo. There, Larsen and Hirschfeld were waiting to take him to the meeting with Abu Ala'a and his team.

Larsen was deeply disappointed with Savir: 'He looked like a bureaucrat with no sense of humour'. Savir was unimpressed with Larsen, the 'tall-slim man wearing a long raincoat, sunglasses who looked like a Nordic character in a French spy movie'.

'We will need to break the ice,' Larsen said to Savir in the car. 'When introducing Abu Ala'a to you, I will say, "This is your public enemy number one". Then, likewise, I will say to Abu Ala'a, "This is your public enemy number one". Then you will have to take it from there.' Larsen, looked at Savir, awaiting his response, but Savir – poker faced – did not say a word.

He drove Savir to a house. When the three Palestinians entered, Larsen jumped up to do his 'public enemy number one' speech. Savir stood looking at Abu Ala'a, surprised by his appearance. 'Abu Ala'a,' he recalls, 'looked more like a European businessman than my idea of a senior PLO official.' Abu Ala'a looked at Savir. From the information the PLO had gathered in Tunis, he knew that Savir was one of the brightest men in the Labour Party; that his father had been an ambassador; and that Savir had been Consul General in New York.

They shook hands and sat down at a small table. The atmosphere was chilly and no one said a word. Larsen tried again to break the ice: 'Take off your jackets and ties, guys, and roll up your sleeves.' No one moved. Larsen gave up and left the room. Surprisingly, this eased the tension.

Savir started by reading from a paper he had prepared. The Palestinians took notes. 'Jerusalem is not on the agenda,' read Savir, 'because if we discuss Jerusalem, we will not be able to proceed. We regard Jerusalem as Israel's united capital.' Instead, Savir suggested that, 'The first item for discussion should be Gaza'. He then went on, 'No matter what happens between us in the future, no matter what our disagreements are, there should be no obligatory international arbitration – everything should be resolved through negotiation.' Savir then turned to what he deemed the most important issue for Israel – security. 'Throughout these negotiations,' he emphasized, 'Israel will insist on reliable security arrangements. Our leadership,' he added, 'is following these talks closely, but insists on maintaining secrecy, and does not consider them a substitute for the Washington negotiations.'

It was now Abu Ala'a's turn: 'As far as Jerusalem is concerned,' he said, 'we will have to check with our leadership in Tunis. As far as Israeli security is concerned, Arafat has instructed me to be flexible.' Then he said, 'But tell me, Mr Savir, what are you afraid of? You have nuclear reactors, bombs, the best aeroplanes and tanks – the most modern war machine in the world. Why are you worried? We, Palestinians, have only stones and light-resistance ammunition.' Savir: 'You are a threat to us, Mr Abu Ala'a, because you want to live in our houses. You, the Palestinians, have rejected the right of the state of Israel to exist. You have said that Israel is your national home and have given the whole Arab world a pretext to fight us from the day we became an independent state.' Abu Ala'a replied, 'Where are you from, Mr Savir?' Savir: 'From Jerusalem – and where are you from, Mr Abu Ala'a?' 'Jerusalem. And where did your father come from?' Savir: 'My father was born in Europe.' Abu Ala'a: 'But my father was born in Jerusalem!' Savir: 'Do you want to go back to the time of King David?' Abu Ala'a, laughing: 'Let us agree that we will never agree on the past, but we will make an effort to agree on the future.'

By now, it was 4 a.m. 'Well?' asked Larsen anxiously as they came out of the room. 'We are going home, we have nothing to talk about,' said Abu Ala'a and Savir in unison, and then they burst into laughter. Larsen and his wife then took Savir to their flat in down-town Oslo. 'He's a wise guy,' said Savir, referring to Abu Ala'a, 'I can do business with him.'

The next morning, Abu Ala'a and Savir took a short walk in the forest. By now, Abu Ala'a had spoken with Abu Mazen in Tunis. 'You can tell Rabin and Peres,' he said to Savir, 'that we agree not to raise Jerusalem in these talks. We will discuss it at a later stage when we discuss the final status of the territories. Regarding international arbitration – okay, we accept that everything should be mutually agreed between us. As far as Gaza is concerned, we will not settle only for Gaza. We need something on the West Bank as well – something symbolic in Jericho.' The idea of adding Jericho, the sleepiest West Bank town, to Gaza and forming a Palestinian self-rule area, was not new. In November 1992, Foreign Minister Peres had suggested this to Egypt's President Hosní Mubarak and asked him to pass it on to Arafat.

Back in Israel, Savir gave a positive report to Peres. 'Here, we have a serious partner,' he said, and suggested that they should go ahead with the secret negotiations and add a legal adviser to the Israeli team.

### 'An un-baked cake'

In Washington DC, the telephone rang at Joel Singer's office in the Sidley & Austin law firm. In the 1970s, while serving in the Israeli Defence Forces' legal department, he had worked on

Israel's Disengagement Agreements with Egypt and Syria, and on the Camp David Accords. On the line was someone from the Israeli Foreign Ministry. 'Can you come to Israel on a matter that is too confidential to discuss on the telephone? Shimon Peres wants you to come and Rabin has approved the visit. Could you just get on a plane?' The instructions for Singer were simple: check in at the Holiday Inn Hotel, Jerusalem, where 'someone who talks with an Austrian accent will meet you. He'll hand to you a document which you should read carefully. Half an hour later, walk to the Foreign Ministry and give Shimon Peres a thorough legal analysis of the document'.

At the Holiday Inn, Singer met the man who said, 'I am Professor Yair Hirschfeld and I have here a Declaration of Principles that we have been discussing with the PLO in Oslo for more than four months'. Having read it, Singer went to the Foreign Ministry where Yair Hirschfeld was waiting with Ron Pundak, Uri Savir and Yossi Beilin. Singer was blunt: 'This document,' he said, 'is an un-baked cake and shouldn't be signed.' He then went to Peres's office and gave him the same advice. He criticized many things, but, in particular, the plan to let the United Nations administer Gaza as a trusteeship for an interim period until the Palestinians took over. He also asked the question nobody else had dared to ask: 'How can you talk with the PLO without recognizing it? Inevitably, this will be found out and will be embarrassing.' He then flew back to Washington convinced that nothing was going to come of the matter.

### Rabin suspends the Oslo talks

On 6 June 1993, while Singer was on his way back to America, Peres went to see Rabin to discuss the Oslo talks. By now, and inspite of Singer's criticism, Peres was convinced that the Oslo channel stood a good chance of succeeding. But when Beilin saw Peres walking out of Rabin's office, ashen faced, he realized that something had gone wrong. 'How was the meeting?' he asked. 'Rabin is not happy with some of the points in the document,' Peres replied, 'and, for the time being, wants us to do nothing about it and not to return to Oslo.'[6] Beilin was shocked. But, worse, was to come.

The next day, a courier came to the Foreign Ministry bringing a sealed envelope addressed to Peres. The sender was the Prime Minister. Rabin, not trusting Peres, had sent a him a formal two-page letter in which he summarized their previous day's talk. In the letter, he described the 'Oslo contacts' as 'dangerous' to the peace process, and said that 'the radical PLO-Tunis leadership' was trying to torpedo the negotiations between Israel and the 'moderate Palestinians in Washington', and that for this they were also using the Oslo channel. Rabin ordered that the contacts should be stopped until his next meeting with Peres. He also said that the DOP was 'unacceptable', and expressed his dissatisfaction that it had been presented without his having been consulted.[7]

The Israeli-Oslo team were plunged into despair. As a last resort, Beilin and Peres decided to call Joel Singer and ask him to come back to Israel. Only Singer, they decided, could persuade Rabin that all was not lost, and that the DOP could be amended. If this plan failed, the Oslo peace initiative would be dead.

### 'A new boy is coming'

On 10 June, four days after the disastrous Peres-Rabin meeting, Singer was driven to a meeting with Rabin. Just before arriving at Rabin's office, Beilin said to Singer, 'I don't want to put you under too much pressure, but you should know that the entire fate of the Oslo negotiations now rests on your shoulders'.

Prime Minister Rabin opened the meeting and, surprisingly, the atmosphere was good. There was no mention of the letter he had sent to Peres three days earlier. They discussed the Oslo documents and Singer said that, although he had many reservations, documents could be changed. The discussion then took another direction. Rabin wanted to know if Israel could use the Oslo talks to stop the Palestinian *intifada*, which had been dragging on for five years and was a heavy burden on Israel. Singer leapt on this opportunity and said that, in order to do this, Israel must first recognize the PLO because only the PLO had the authority to stop the *intifada*. This was a brave suggestion. Beilin, sitting in the meeting, thought Rabin would react by kicking them all out of the room, but he did not. He just looked at Peres and asked, 'What do you think, Shimon?' Peres: 'I don't think we should recognize the PLO as yet.' Rabin: 'I agree.' But Singer did

237

not give up. It did not make sense to him that they should continue talking with the PLO without officially recognizing it. 'Suppose I suggest this in Oslo, but make it clear it is my personal suggestion?' he asked. 'Offer whatever you like in your own name.' Rabin replied, adding, 'I want you to go to Oslo, meet with the PLO people, and then come back and report to me.'

The Oslo channel had survived – at least, for the time being. Singer sent Hirschfeld and Pundak ahead of him to Oslo to warn the Palestinians that he was coming. 'Tell them,' he told the two academics, 'that a new boy is coming and is going to ask a lot of questions. Tell them they should do their utmost to answer in the most positive manner, because, for the first time, this guy is reporting to Prime Minister Rabin. If they convince me, I will convince Rabin'.

In Oslo, as requested, Hirschfeld and Pundak prepared the Palestinians for the new arrival. Hassan Asfour, a Palestinian delegate, recalls what they said, 'A lawyer is coming, and we hope that you will work with him quietly and positively. Prime Minister Rabin has a lot of confidence in this man. There's no need to be tense or nervous.' In the event, the last remark added to the tension. The Palestinians realized that the meeting would be crucial. Singer was representing the Prime Minister of Israel.

### 'More like an interrogator than a negotiator'

On 13 June, just before going into the first meeting with the Palestinians, Singer said to Hirschfeld and Pundak, 'Take notes of everything they say. Don't participate in any exchange. Just maintain a poker face'.

The 1 a.m., meeting, which took place at Larsen's home in Oslo, was a shock for the three Palestinians. Singer had brought with him more than forty hard-hitting questions: 'How will the different aspects of the civil administration on the occupied lands be organized after the Israeli withdrawal?' 'Will the person taking over be a politician, a technocrat or a professional?' 'What will Gaza's status be after the Israeli withdrawal?' 'If an agreement is reached on the Declaration of Principles who will sign it in Washington? Will it be the Palestinian and Israeli delegations or the joint Jordanian-Palestinian and Israeli delegations?' 'Is it possible for you to commit yourselves to collecting all the weapons in Gaza and the West Bank?' 'Is it possible for you to call for the halting of the *intifada* after the Declaration of Principles is signed?' 'Can you commit yourselves to us, as you have to the Americans, to recognize Israel and renounce terrorism?', and so on.

There was more than enough here for Abu Ala'a: 'Is this a test – an exam paper?' he demanded. 'Are you here to perform an examination of us?' Singer: 'No, I am here on behalf of Yitzhak Rabin and his government to ask you all these questions.' He then finished reading out the list.

They met again the next day for a session that began at 10 a.m., and went on until 6 p.m. Abu Ala'a was trying to answer Singer's questions. Hassan Asfour, No 2 man of the Palestinian delegation, was shocked: 'I was very angry about Singer's manner,' he recalls. 'His questions were tough and provocative. He was more like an interrogator than a negotiator.' As the session went on and on, the answers provoked more questions. At one point, Larsen put his head round the door, saying to Singer, 'You'll have to hurry, the plane is leaving soon'. Singer, not wanting to leave questions unanswered, rushed through the remainder, and Abu Ala'a felt under even more pressure. Singer then wrote down the answers and concluded the session by saying, 'I will now go back to Rabin and Peres and get their replies'.

After the meeting had ended, Abu Ala'a came up to Larsen and complained: 'This is absolutely crazy. We cannot continue like this. He is impolite and destroying everything'. But, at the end of this outburst, he smiled and added: 'I learned a hell of a lot from his questions!'

Back in Tunis, Abu Ala'a and the team reported to Abu Mazen and Arafat that, although they were frustrated by the session, they realized that Singer was Rabin's man and that the talks were now at a critical stage. If they did not succeed, the Oslo channel would be shut down.

From Oslo, Singer and Savir flew straight to Vienna to report to Foreign Minister Peres who was on an official visit there. On the way, Singer said to Savir, 'The Palestinians are a serious group. We can do business with them and reach an agreement. But when we see Shimon, we must speak in a hesitant manner, mustn't over-do our responses or be too enthusiastic'.

'How did it go?' asked Peres coming into the room where

Singer and Savir were waiting. Singer [in a very enthusiastic voice!]: 'If we don't make a deal with these people we will be jackasses . . . ' and he gave a detailed report of the meetings. After they had left, Savir turned to Singer and quipped: 'Joel, how *do* you sound when you get enthusiastic?'

Back in Israel, Singer reported to Prime Minister Rabin and recommended that they should continue the negotiations. 'Well,' said Rabin, 'go ahead, revise the document.'

It took Singer five days in his New York office to write the revised agreement. He then flew back to Israel and showed it to Rabin. The revised DOP was now very different from what it had been before. Trusteeship in Gaza – a main feature of the previous DOP had disappeared altogether – and many other issues had been amended. The main idea, at this stage, was for the Israeli forces to leave Gaza and Jericho before the Palestinian elections took place, in which the leadership would be chosen through democratic processes. After the elections, the Palestinians would start to control their own daily life and the Israeli forces would be deployed to other duties in phases. Parallel to this, the Palestinians and the Israelis would start 'Permanent-Status Negotiations' to resolve outstanding issues. Rabin approved the document, saying to Singer, 'Go back to Oslo and negotiate it'.

As, on the previous occasion, Singer sent Hirschfeld ahead of him to prepare the Palestinians and say, 'Joel has somewhat revised the agreement, but the changes are only cosmetic. You will like them. They are good. The document has been approved by the Prime Minister of Israel'.

### A subtle play on words
On 27 June 1993, they met again, this time at the Headquarters of the Norwegian Institute for Applied Social Sciences (FAFO), Oslo. Larsen, who co-ordinated everything, kept changing the venue so that no one would find out about the secret meetings. It was the eighth round of talks in Norway. More than five months had passed since the two Israeli academics had met Abu Ala'a for the first time under very different circumstances.

Singer took out the thick DOP document, and said to Abu Ala'a and his team, 'We are authorized to put forward these proposals so that we can arrive at a final agreement'.

Having read the DOP, the Palestinians were bitterly disappointed. They had been warned that there were some 'cosmetic' changes, but this looked like a totally new document. Asfour, usually a quiet man, lost his temper: 'Now we have to start from scratch,' he snapped at Singer. 'You have come here with a clear mission to destroy the peace process. You are full of hostility towards the Palestinians. You're living in the past, in the ghetto, and it's difficult for you to see the future and look forward.' Abu Ala'a tried to calm him down, but Asfour, raising his voice and pointing at Singer, said, 'This man has come to these talks with the mentality of an interrogator.' Singer interrupted him at this point, 'Listen,' he said. 'Everything I've added, I've taken from *your* answers to my questions. These are *your* words. Check *your* notes. This is what *you* told me, so how come you can't sign it? Either you didn't tell me the truth then or you are not telling the truth now . . . All I have done is put down what *you* told me.' Singer *had* used the answers that the Palestinians had given him in the 'Questions Session', but, as an experienced lawyer, he had played with the words and altered the text.

It took a break to calm things down. When they resumed, Singer presented Abu Ala'a with his 'personal suggestion' that, pending the PLO's acceptance of some relevant conditions, Israel should recognize the PLO as the legitimate body representing the Palestinian people. He then read out the relevant conditions, some of which had been accepted by the PLO in 1988: The PLO will recognize the right of Israel to exist and commit itself to peaceful co-existence with it; the PLO will renounce the use of terrorism and other acts of violence; the PLO will declare that, in the light of the peace process, it considers that those articles of the Palestinian Covenant which are inconsistent with the peace process are inoperative and no longer valid; the PLO will call on the Palestinian people to halt the *intifada* and on the Arab countries to suspend the Arab boycott of Israel . . . and so on. There were nine conditions in all. But the recognition of the PLO, Singer emphasized again, was his 'personal proposal', not Rabin's.

## Tit-for-tat crisis

On 11 July, when Savir and Singer returned to Oslo to find their Palestinian counterparts smiling, it was a pleasant surprise. But they were soon in for a shock when Abu Ala'a said, 'We have prepared our position in a comprehensive and objective draft that takes into consideration all the previously discussed factors and issues.'

Savir looked at the document and immediately realized that it contained more traditional hardline PLO positions – Jerusalem was mentioned, and, for the first time, the words '*National* rights of the Palestinians' were written instead of '*Political* rights of the Palestinians'. There was a demand for an extra territorial corridor between the West Bank and the Gaza strip, which would pass through Israeli territory, and a reference to the 'Jericho area' rather than the 'town of Jericho'. In addition, the words 'Palestinian Liberation Organisation – PLO' were written in where the word 'Palestinians' had been before.

Savir asked for a break and led his team out of the room. After a short consultation, they returned. Savir: 'The reference to '*National* rights of the Palestinians' is a matter that pertains to the state and is unacceptable.' He then added, 'At first, you asked for Jericho to be a symbol, but now you are talking about an *area*'. Abu Ala'a: 'Well, we drew up a document with Hirschfeld and then you came up with a new proposal. We felt, then, as you are feeling now. We have the right to do to you what you did to us.'[8]

### 'I want kissing points'

In spite of the latest crisis, Rabin and Peres still felt that they were on the way to concluding a deal with the Palestinians. Rabin was meeting Peres, Singer and Beilin every Friday afternoon to co-ordinate the talks. To maintain secrecy, they sometimes met in Rabin's Tel Aviv office, sometimes in his Jerusalem office, sometimes at the Acadia Hotel. Nobody else from Rabin's office was involved – not even his trusted Chief of Staff Ehud Barak. Rabin was playing all his cards close to his chest, afraid of a leak or any opposition to the Washington peace talks.

He and Peres now wanted assurance that Arafat himself was in the picture. It would be embarrassing, they decided, if it ever emerged that, while the Prime Minister and Foreign Minister of Israel were personally involved, the man at the top of the Palestinian hierarchy was not. The Norwegians were asked to check that Arafat was fully involved in the Oslo talks and that he understood what the draft agreement was all about. They were also asked to persuade Arafat to take a step back from the tough draft that the Palestinians had presented at the last Oslo meeting – and thus avoid plunging the talks into a bigger crisis.

Since becoming Norwegian Foreign Minister, in April 1993, Johan Joergen Holst had been deeply involved in the talks. At this point he happened to be on a formal visit to Habib Ben Yahia, the Foreign Minister of Tunisia. Mona Juul, Larsen's wife, who was Holst's bureau chief, was also there and Larsen joined them in Tunis. Arafat agreed to meet them on 16 July 1993. After the formal meeting, Holst asked for a private chat with Arafat to which he also took the Larsens. At this meeting, they went through the document to see if Arafat was familiar with the details. They found him enthusiastic. Going into a side-room, he returned with a map of Gaza, the West Bank and Israel, and started pointing at the border lines they were discussing. Then, pointing to the map, he said, 'And I want kissing points'. Holst looked questioningly at Terje and Mona Larsen, but they, too, were puzzled. 'Do you mean crossing points or checkpoints?' Holst asked, somewhat sheepishly. 'No, no,' said Arafat, 'I mean kissing points.' To demonstrate, he moved his lips and made kissing noises. They were bemused, but then realized that Arafat was referring to extra-territorial roads – 'kissing points' – between Gaza and the West Bank where people and goods could move freely. This demand was one of the reasons the previous Oslo meeting had plunged into crisis. Holst put pressure on Arafat to give up this idea, and to accept instead 'a safe passage' for people and goods on the existing roads. Eventually, Arafat agreed.

Holst prepared a handwritten report for the Israelis, explaining that Arafat was fully aware of the details. Larsen and Mona then took the letter and flew to Tel Aviv. 'We were taken to a hotel suite,' Larsen recalls, 'and, to our amazement, everybody was there – Uri Savir, Joel Singer – all Shimon Peres's close crew – and Peres himself.' It was a scrutinizing interview that lasted for hours. Peres wanted every detail of the Larsens' conversation with Arafat. 'How did Arafat express himself?' 'What did he say?' 'How close is the relationship between Abu Ala'a and Arafat?' 'Is Abu Ala'a sufficiently high level to take part in the Oslo discussions?' 'Does he have Arafat's confidence?'

At last, the Israelis were satisfied – Arafat was in the picture and had shown that he was willing to be flexible. Confident that Abu Ala'a and his team would also be flexible, they decided to go back to Oslo.

### 'I want to say goodbye to you'

On 25 July, the next meeting, in Halvorsbole, near Oslo, started badly. 'We did not get a good reception in Israel after our last round,' Savir said to Abu Ala'a. 'And now we are hoping that you have some new ideas for us.' After Holst's meeting with Arafat in Tunis, Savir was expecting the Palestinians to be flexible, but they were not. The draft document that the Palestinians had brought back from Tunis was just as tough as the previous one. Savir: 'Quite frankly, if we were to present these amendments to our leadership, I believe this would be the end of this channel. But let's review the document article by article.'

After a fifty-six hour marathon, they were all exhausted and impatient. They had not succeeded in bridging at least sixteen essential differences between the Palestinian and Israeli drafts. 'Sir,' snapped Savir to Abu Ala'a, 'you have gone back on your word, and this is no way to negotiate. This is unacceptable.' Savir was about to put his things away when Abu Ala'a asked them to remain seated because he wanted to make a personal announcement. Slowly, casting glances at the Israelis and his own colleagues, he said in a low tone that was in sharp contrast to the previous shouting, that he was resigning. 'I am sure,' he added, 'that Chairman Arafat will replace me. And I hope that my replacement will succeed better than I did. I personally would like to thank you all for your work.' Then, with tears in his eyes, he added, 'I want to say goodbye to you'. When he had finished speaking, there was silence around the table. Savir recalls sitting there, wondering 'whether Abu Ala'a, such an experienced negotiator, was pulling some kind of trick or being absolutely genuine'.

The resignation was genuine. While Savir and Abu Ala'a and their teams were trying to bridge the differences, Asfour, one of the Palestinian delegates, had gone back to Tunis to consult the leadership. But when he met with Arafat at Abu Mazen's home in Tunis, he was in for a shock. He recalls: 'Arafat accused us [the Oslo team] of trying to defend the [Oslo] track instead of defending the contents of the draft document. I replied, "I will carry out your instructions, but, if we adopt this attitude, it will close the channel and the Israelis will not continue, because they will not believe we are serious."' Arafat: 'These are our instructions, whether the Israelis like it or not. They can take it or leave it.'

Asfour phoned Abu Ala'a. 'I am coming back to Oslo,' he said, 'but things are not what they should be.' When he arrived, he told Abu Ala'a of Arafat's uncompromising approach. 'Let's not do it,' Asfour said. Abu Ala'a: 'No. If they [the Tunis leadership] are going to play tough – and that's what they want us to present – we have to present it, no matter what happens later.' Abu Ala'a then decided that he was going to resign.

Savir, of course, knew none of this: 'I am sorry you are leaving,' he said to Abu Ala'a. 'We will gladly work with your replacement, but I think you are making a big mistake. When Abba Eban said that, you, the Palestinians, never miss an opportunity to miss an opportunity, he was speaking the truth.' When Savir finished, Hirschfeld asked to speak. With tears in his eyes, he looked at Abu Ala'a and said, 'This is the blackest day of my life. We are losing an historical opportunity which may never come again. I am very upset.' They all gathered up their things, and left the room.

Abu Ala'a retreated into another room. Larsen, despairing at how the whole enterprise was disintegrating, tried to join him, but Abu Ala'a shouted, 'Get out! I don't want to talk to you!'. Larsen refused to go. Taking the Palestinian's hand in his, he pleaded, 'Abu Ala'a, please do it for my sake. I've slaved day and night all these months. Give it one more shot. Do this for me'.

While this was going on, the Israelis were considering how to proceed. Singer, recalls: 'All the Israelis were convinced that this was the last day of the negotiations, particularly Hirschfeld.'

To save the day, the Israelis tried to come up with a dramatic new formula. They decided to divide the points of contention into two groups of eight and to propose to Abu Ala'a a swap-deal. The Israelis would yield on the eight points they could most easily concede and the Palestinians would also yield on eight points. To sweeten the pill, the Israelis would offer to recognize the PLO as the sole representative of the Palestinian people.

While he and Singer were considering how to offer this proposal to Abu Ala'a, Larsen rushed into the room. 'Uri,' he said, 'you *must*

go to see him. He is sitting alone in a room, staring straight ahead.'
Savir: 'I'll try.' Along with Larsen, he crossed the hall to the room
where Abu Ala'a was sitting. Seating Savir on a chair in front of
Abu Ala'a, Larsen said, 'Look, gentlemen, it's up to you. I don't
want to have to come in here again. It's your problem.' On this note,
he left the room.

Savir: 'How are you?' Abu Ala'a: 'Very bad. Very bad.' Savir:
'Listen, Abu Ala'a. If we can't manage this small thing of an inter-
mediary agreement, let's try to do the big thing. Let's talk about
mutual recognition?' Abu Ala'a's eyes lit up. But Savir had his
conditions. Taking out of his pocket the piece of paper, listing
the eight points, he said to Abu Ala'a, 'Just do me one favour,
write down the following points. If you persuade Mr Arafat to
accept these, which are crucial to Israel as they are, I promise I
will persuade the Israeli Prime Minister and Foreign Minister to
recognize the PLO'. Abu Ala'a looked at Savir and said, 'I'm going
to try'.

In Tunis, Arafat accepted the eight points in return for mutual
recognition. But there were still some points that needed a political
decision. The next crucial moment arrived on 18 August 1993.

## A seven-hour telephone call between Stockholm, Tunis and Tel Aviv

Foreign Minister Peres, who had a pre-scheduled trip to Sweden
and Norway, said to Singer, 'Joel, bring all your documents and
come with me. We are going to conclude the agreement'. From
Stockholm, Peres called Larsen in Norway. 'You have to come to
Stockholm and play host.' In Israel, Yossi Beilin, Peres's deputy,
called Norwegian Foreign Minister Holst who was in Iceland.
Waking him up, he asked if he could meet Peres in Stockholm.
'No problem,' said Holst, 'I'll be there.'

Late on the night of 17 August, Holst and Larsen arrived at
Peres's hotel. 'We have to finish this business,' Peres said. 'I want
to sign the agreement with the Palestinians when I arrive in Oslo in
two days time.' Larsen: 'The Palestinians love drama. Let's finish it
tonight.' Peres: 'If you think my presence will add to the drama, you
can mention it.' Then, to put some pressure on Arafat, Peres added,
'Tell Arafat that if there is no signature forthcoming from the
Palestinians in Oslo, we will give up the Palestinian option and go

to the Syrian option . . . ' This threat meant that Israel would re-direct its energy to signing a treaty with the Syrians.[9] To Foreign Minister Holst, Peres said, 'I don't want to speak on the phone myself to Arafat. I would like you to be my mouthpiece'.

Meanwhile, Larsen was trying to contact Abu Ala'a in Tunis, but he was not at home so Larsen tried Arafat. 'Abu Ammar,' he said, 'I have the two fathers here.' ('Father' was the code name for Foreign Ministers.) 'My father and the other father, and they want to finish everything tonight, but I am not able to get hold of Abu Ala'a, so what do we do?' Arafat: 'Call me back in fifteen minutes.' Arafat located Abu Ala'a and also summoned Abu Mazen, Yasser Abd Rabbo and Hassan Asfour.

With Arafat's team lined up in Tunis, and Peres's team lined up in Stockholm, they were ready to start negotiating the sticking points that had prevented the signing of the Israeli-Palestinian agreement. Some of these concerned issues that would be discussed in the later permanent status negotiations. Once again, the Israelis did not want to specify these at this stage, but the Palestinians were insistent because they wanted to ensure, in advance, that such issues as Jerusalem, refugees and settlements, would be on the agenda of the later status talks. Another sticking point was the control of the crossing points from Egypt and Jordan to Gaza and Jericho. Israel wanted to be in control of these, to ensure that no weapons and 'unwanted' people crossed into the territories it handed over to the Palestinians for self-rule. However, as control of the borders was a symbol of sovereignty and, as Israel would only accept auton-omy for the Palestinians rather than a future state, the Palestinians would not concede on this. There were also three or four other issues involved.

At 10 p.m., they started the negotiations. Holst conveyed the Israeli position to Abu Ala'a in Tunis and they then waited for him to ring back after conferring with Arafat and others. In the interest of security, Holst tried to veil his references, but kept forgetting himself and saying 'Israel'. Eventually, he decided to say 'blurp' for Israel, which at least brought some light relief to the proceedings.

This climax of the Oslo peace channel was an exercise in compromise and barely contained excitement. 'The room we were sitting in [in Tunis],' recalls Abu Mazen, 'was thick with cigarette smoke and the aroma of Arabic coffee; coffee cups were strewn all over the tables and ashtrays were overflowing. The telephone would ring and we would carry on with the discussion of yet another point.'

In Stockholm, at one point, an exhausted Peres left the negotiations to get some sleep, leaving his assistant and Singer to carry on, but he was present at the most crucial moments to make the decisions. 'I could almost hear Arafat sighing,' recalls Peres, 'almost hear their tears of excitement!' They were all eager to conclude the deal and, although both sides maintained some positions, they also compromised. In the case of the list of issues to be covered by permanent status negotiations, the Palestinian demand was accepted and these issues were specified. In the case of control of the crossing points leading to the Gaza Strip and the Jericho area, an ambiguous formula was accepted. This said that: 'The agreement [between Israel and the Palestinians] will include arrangements for *co-ordination* between both parties regarding passages.'

'In the morning [after seven hours of telephone calls], recalls Peres, 'we agreed. I think the phone bill was paid by the Swedish government and, to this day, we still owe it the money!' Abu Mazen recalls that, 'It was after five in the morning when the last telephone call ended. In Tunis, we all stood looking at each other in amazement, unable to believe the finale had occurred.'

### 'Son, such things always take far more time'

The next evening – 19 August – Peres was in Norway, staying in the government's official guesthouse. He went to an official dinner, but his thoughts were elsewhere. Later that night, he would be attending a secret historical ceremony at which the agreement concluded in the previous night's telephone conversation would be signed. (After his call Abu Ala'a had flown to Norway.) When the dinner ended, Peres pretended he was tired and refused an invitation to go to the bar. Instead, he went up to his room. 'One by one,' he recalls, 'the lights went out on the ground floor. At midnight, I got up, dressed again, and quietly slipped upstairs.' Around that time, the Israeli and Palestinian delegates – who, had spent all the time in between hammering out remaining problems with the wording of the agreement – were smuggled out of the service entrance of the hotel and driven in a van to the official guesthouse.

Under Larsen's supervision, the Israelis, Palestinians and Norwegians went into separate rooms. The Norwegians hauled a famous desk – Norway's 1905 secession from Sweden was signed on it – to the hall. At 2.30 a.m., Peres, Holst and Mrs Holst took their place in the receiving line. The Israeli delegation came in, shook hands with the Norwegians and Peres, and joined the reception line. Then the Palestinian delegation entered, and the first handshake between Abu Ala'a and Peres took place.

Savir and Abu Ala'a initialled the agreement, which, because Israel had not yet officially recognized the PLO, said that the agreement was between: *The government of the state of Israel and the Palestinian team in the Jordanian-Palestinian delegation to the Middle East peace conference representing the Palestinian people* – meaning the Palestinian delegation to Washington.

On his way back to Israel, Yair Hirschfeld, the academic who had started it all, stopped off in Vienna where his parents were living and hinted that peace between Israelis and Palestinians might be close. 'Son,' said his mother, 'you don't understand. Such things always take more time.'

**'He spoke two sentences and smiled once – he is very enthusiastic'**
Peres went to Rabin: 'After we've initialled,' he said, 'we'll have to tell the Americans.' He suggested that Rabin should go to Washington to tell President Clinton about the agreement and to get his blessing. Rabin replied that too many questions would be asked and that it would be better if Peres reported to Secretary of State Warren Christopher.

Peres had dreaded this. He had already had a traumatic experience with former Secretary of State George Shultz who, in 1987, had failed to support his 'London Agreement' with King Hussein. Peres asked Larsen and Norwegian Foreign Minister Holst to join him on his trip to America. The Norwegians agreed and sent a government plane to pick up Peres and his team from a military base in Israel. They then met in Geneva, boarded the Transatlantic-capacity plane that the Norwegians had rented and flew to the Point Magu Marine Base, California. Meanwhile, Christopher had cut short his holiday to meet Peres. On the way, Peres and Holst discussed how to present the agreement to Christopher.

249

On 27 August 1993, they landed at the American naval base and were taken into the Admiral's office. Standing there, with their backs to the American, Israeli and Norwegian flags, were Secretary of State Warren Christopher and his Special Middle East co-ordinator Dennis Ross.

Peres opened the meeting and explained what had happened in Oslo. Then Holst took over and, stressing the American role in the overall peace process, reminded Christopher of how he had briefed him about the Oslo negotiations. (This was true. But, acting on the advice of Deputy Foreign Minister Beilin, Holst had actually volunteered very little information, and had not informed Christopher that Israel had upgraded the talks by adding Uri Savir to the delegation.) Singer then took fifteen minutes to go through the details of the agreement. When he stopped, there was momentarily a dead silence in the room. 'Dennis, what do you think?' asked Christopher. 'I think it's great,' Ross replied. This was a magnanimous response from a man who had tried so hard to persuade the Israelis and the Palestinians to come to an agreement at the Washington talks.

Peres now suggested that the agreement should be made public, but that it should be portrayed as an American initiative. This was the only way in which the agreement could be signed without revealing that Israel and the PLO had jointly negotiated it in Oslo. Christopher was unsure about this, and said, 'I'd like to have a few minutes alone with Ross so we can discuss it and give you our reaction'. Peres, Holst and the others left the room.

Throughout the session, Christopher had been solemn and silent, and Larsen was worried. On the way out of the room, Larsen whispered to Peres, 'How do you read him?' Peres, who knew Christopher well, whispered back, 'He spoke two sentences and smiled once. He is very enthusiastic!'

Alone in the room, Christopher asked Ross, 'Do you think it makes sense for us to have this as an American initiative?' Ross: 'No, it doesn't. Once it comes out, it will be known [that it was agreed in Oslo] and we will lose credibility. We can back the agreement, we can support it, but we have to tell them it's not an American initiative.' Christopher: 'That's my feeling.'

When the others came back into the room, Christopher said to Peres, 'We're prepared to support this, but it cannot be an

American initiative'. He agreed, though, that the agreement could be signed at a ceremony on the White House lawn.[10]

On 9 September 1993, Yasser Arafat sent a letter to Prime Minister Rabin confirming that the PLO recognized the state of Israel, was committed to the peace process, and renounced the use of terrorism and other acts of violence. Arafat also affirmed that those articles of the Palestinian Covenant which denied Israel's right to exist were inoperative and no longer valid.[11] In response, Rabin replied, 'Mr Chairman, I wish to confirm that, in the light of the PLO commitments outlined in your letter, the Government of Israel has decided to recognize the PLO as the representative of the Palestinian people and will commence negotiations with the PLO within the Middle East peace process'. The Israeli government and the PLO, having formally recognized each other, could now publicly sign the agreement.

### 'Enough of bloodshed and tears. Enough.'

In Israel, there was a last-minute discussion between Rabin and Peres about who should represent Israel at the signing ceremony. Peres said he should go because Arafat did not yet deserve to shake hands with the Prime Minister of Israel. Rabin accepted this and decided to send Peres. But when Christopher rang to say that Arafat was coming to the signing ceremony and that Rabin should come as well, Rabin agreed and asked his aide, Eitan Haber, to inform Peres about the change of plan. Before Peres had the opportunity to discuss this, Rabin's visit to Washington was announced on radio. Peres was furious and telephoned Giora Eini who acted as their go-between. 'I brought him the Oslo Agreement. Why does he always put me down? Tell him,' he added, 'he can go to Washington. I'm not going, and I'm now considering resigning from the Foreign Ministry. This *shmok* has given me enough troubles.'[12] In the end, they went together.

In Washington, on 13 September 1993, crises continued to the last minute. Eitan Haber, a close associate of Rabin, recalls: 'I was told that Arafat was coming to the ceremony with a pistol and that he would give it to Clinton as a gesture of his willingness to make peace. I said, 'In that case, Rabin should also come with a pistol and shoot Arafat!' But symbolic gestures were not the only problem – there was a bigger crisis looming.

The Declaration of Principles had been initialled in Oslo on 20 August 1993 *before* Israel had officially recognized the PLO in Rabin's letter to Arafat and, as a result, the wording of the agreement stated that it had been made between: *The Government of the state of Israel and the Palestinian team in the Jordanian-Palestinian delegation to the Middle East peace conference representing the Palestinian people.* But, because, since then, Rabin and Arafat had exchanged letters of recognition, Arafat was insisting on having the words *Palestine Liberation Organization* inserted on the documents about to be signed.

At 5.30 a.m., Arafat telephoned Ahmad Tibi, an Israeli Arab, who was on good terms with the Israeli leadership and a confidential adviser to the PLO, and summoned him to his suite. Tibi recalls: 'Arafat said, "Ahmad, there is a problem. The text still refers to the Palestinian delegation, but we have agreed on mutual recognition – us of Israel, them of the PLO. Go and solve the problem, otherwise I will not sign."' Tibi rang Itamar Rabinovich, the Israeli ambassador in Washington, who said, 'It's too late now to change the wording on the document'. Tibi remained insistent. He went to the hotel where the Israelis were staying and met with Peres, Rabinovich and other members of the Israeli delegation, all of whom said, 'No change'. Peres then said to Tibi, 'We will turn up at the signing ceremony on our own and the whole world will know who is to blame for destroying the peace process'. Tibi retorted, 'Our plane is ready to take off.' With the Israelis still insisting on no changes to the wording, Tibi returned to Arafat.

At 8.45 a.m., Arafat consulted the Palestinian delegation. Fifteen minutes later, James Baker, the former US Secretary of State, came over for a visit. When Arafat informed him of the latest crisis, Baker said, 'When is the Accord to be signed?' Arafat: 'At eleven o'clock.' Baker: 'The Israelis will agree to the amendment at 10.58.'

Arafat instructed his delegation members to go to the White House, but he remained at the hotel with Abu Mazen and Hayel al-Fahoum, a member of the Palestinian team. He then sent Ahmad Tibi again to the Israelis. At 10 a.m., Abu Mazen asked Arafat, 'What will we do if the amendment is not made?' Arafat replied, 'We will not sign the Accord.' At 10.10 a.m., the telephone rang in Arafat's suite. On the line was Tibi who confirmed that Peres had agreed to include the words *Palestine Liberation Organization* on the document, and the text now read, *The Government of the State of Israel and the Palestine Liberation Organization* . . . Arafat was delighted: 'Two kisses,' he replied, 'one for you, one for Peres.'

## A momentous occasion

On the White House lawn, a worldwide audience was waiting in the blazing sun. Behind the scenes, Arafat and Rabin were standing well apart from each other. But when the time came for the ceremony, they moved closer together and Rabin said to Arafat, 'We are going to have to work very hard to make this work'. 'I know,' Arafat replied, 'and I'm prepared to do my part.' They then walked slowly across the lawn for the historic signing. Peres and Abu Mazen signed the agreement, and Rabin – speaking emotionally and directly to the Palestinians – said, 'We, who have come from a land where parents bury their children, we who have fought against you, the Palestinians, say to you today in a loud and clear voice, enough of bloodshed and tears. Enough'.

Arafat, wearing an olive-green uniform and black and white *keffiyeh*, said, 'My people are hoping that the agreement that we are signing today marks the beginning of the end of a chapter of pain and suffering which has lasted throughout this century . . . Our people want to give peace a chance'.

After a few seconds in which nobody moved, the moment that millions of people were waiting for, came. With Rabin standing on President Clinton's right, and Arafat on the President's left, Arafat made the first move and stretched out his hand to Rabin. Clinton, placing his hand on Rabin's back, gently encouraged the Israeli Prime Minister to move closer to Arafat and shake his hand. Peres recalls this moment: 'Rabin didn't want to shake Arafat's hand. It was terrible. The whole world was watching – and could see from Rabin's body language that he did not want to look at Arafat. Finally, though, Rabin shook his hand and Arafat, who is an expert in these matters, hung on to it. After he had finished shaking Rabin's hand, Arafat turned to me, and Rabin whispered in my ear, "Now it's your turn". He had gone though hell; now it was my turn to go through hell.'

Sitting in the crowd on the White House lawn were two unknown people – Yair Hirschfeld and Ron Pundak. They had not been invited to attend the signing ceremony and had had to make their own arrangements. Later, when Peres was asked why he had not included them on his list of guests, he replied, 'Nurses and midwives were not invited'.[13]

### Just the beginning

The signing was over, but the efforts that had gone into the agreement had resulted in no more than a framework, a Declaration of Principles. It was now necessary to transform this into an action plan.

The first item to be negotiated, after the Washington signing, was the withdrawal of the Israeli forces from Gaza and Jericho, and the hand-over of these areas to the Palestinians. Two months after the signing of the Gaza-Jericho agreement on 4 May 1994, Arafat returned to Gaza to take over and control Palestinian affairs from his headquarters there. Even more complicated, though, were the negotiations concerned with the Israeli withdrawal from the West Bank. The talks to achieve this started in early 1995 and became known as the Oslo II Talks. Whereas, in Gaza, there were only a dozen or so Jewish settlements, and very few in and around Jericho, there were about 140 on the rest of the West Bank. A further complication was that the West Bank included Hebron, after Jerusalem the most sacred town for the Jews and an important holy site for Muslims. Four hundred Jews lived there alongside an overwhelming Arab population, and the situation was highly charged. (On 25 February 1994, Baruch Goldstein, a Jewish settler, had walked into the tomb of the patriarchs, the holiest site in Hebron for both Muslims and Jews, and sprayed the Arabs praying there with bullets. He killed twenty-nine. The Arab community – and, indeed, most of the Israeli community – were incensed. Between 6 and 13 April 1994, Hamas retaliated by placing bombs on Israeli buses.)

In complicated negotiations, the Israelis and Palestinians worked together to divide the West Bank into three areas – one to be under Palestinian control (Palestinian populated areas), the second under Israeli control (Israeli settlements and military sites), and a third area in which the Palestinian police would be responsible for public order, while Israel would have over-riding responsibility for security. By mid-August 1995, hundreds of Israelis and Palestinians were working in the Israeli Red Sea resort of Eilat, trying to hammer out a deal. Ten intensive days were then needed in September for Foreign Minister Peres and Chairman Arafat to take personal charge and sort out the most complicated matters, notably the deal concerning Hebron.[14]

On 28 September 1995, the 300-page Oslo II Agreement was signed in Washington and, during the following months, Israeli troops began to withdraw from six major West Bank cities and hundreds of villages. This huge operation – except for the redeployment of Israeli forces from Hebron – was completed in about three months.

When Rabin came to office in June 1992, he had promised to reach an agreement with the Palestinians within six to nine months. Although he failed to meet his self-imposed deadline, his premiership had succeeded in reaching a momentous deal with the Palestinians that resulted in Israeli forces withdrawing from Gaza and from many West Bank cities and villages.

# 7 TALKS WITH SYRIA

## Introduction

On 7 March 1923, the border between Syria and Palestine was agreed between France and Britain, the two victorious powers at the end of the First World War. Twenty-five years later, with the departure of the British forces from Palestine, Israel and Syria became sworn enemies. In the spring of 1948, the Syrian army joined other Arab armies – Egyptian, Jordanian, Lebanese, Iraqi – and invaded Israel. Syria captured three areas which were previously part of Palestine.

After the guns fell silent, Israel concluded armistice agreements with all its neighbours. Syria was the hardest nut to crack. The Israel-Syria armistice agreement was finally signed on 20 July 1949. Syria withdrew its forces from the areas it had occupied, allowing these to become three demilitarized zones without either country having sovereignty. In these zones, it was agreed that Israeli farmers and Arab villagers would continue to co-exist, that both states should have police forces, but no military personnel.

Although Israel signed on the dotted line, the Israelis were unhappy with this agreement and, during the nineteen years leading up to the 1967 War, took actions to expand its control over the demilitarized zones. These tactics were intended to provoke the Syrians, so that the resulting border clashes could be exploited to increase Israel's influence in the areas. Moshe Dayan, a former Chief of Staff and Defence Minister, admitted in an interview published in *Yediot Aharonot*, an Israeli newspaper that, 'It used to go like this: we would send a tractor into the demilitarized zone knowing, in advance, that the Syrians would start shooting.

If they refrained, we would instruct the tractor to keep on advancing, until the Syrians lost their temper and started shooting. Then we would use our canons and, later, also our air force.'[1]

While Syria was responsible for some of the border clashes, Moshe Dayan also admitted in the interview quoted above that Israel was responsible for at least eighty per cent of the clashes that occurred in the demilitarized zones between 1949 and 1967.

Water was another key issue that led to clashes between Israel and Syria. In 1953 Israel had been forced by the UN to abandon its plan to divert water from the Jordan River in the central demilitarized zone along the border with Syria to the Negev desert in the south. In 1959 it began to build a National Water Carrier to convey water from the Sea of Galilee in the north of Israel to the Negev, and this project was completed in 1964. But the Syrians, who controlled the main source of this water, started to divert the supply so that it would not reach Israel. The Israelis then brought in tanks and destroyed Syria's water-diversion equipment. When the Syrians moved this beyond the range of Israeli tanks, Israel sent planes to continue the destruction.[2]

In 1967, Israel went on the offensive, consolidated its hold on the demilitarized zones and took the Golan Heights.[3] However, fearing international pressure to withdraw from all the occupied territories, Israel took the initiative and, on 19 June 1967, offered to sign a peace treaty with Syria based on the international border agreed in 1923. Israel also offered to withdraw from occupied areas of Golan Heights, provided this also became a demilitarized zone, and provided that Syria would not divert water before it reached Israel. Syria rejected this peace offer, but, even before they did this, Israel took action to turn the Golan Heights into *de facto* Israeli land by starting to build settlements on the Heights, and, from the autumn of 1967 up to mid-1968, systematically destroying Arab houses and villages.

In 1973, President Assad of Syria sent his forces to try to regain the Golan Heights. He failed.

When, in 1979, Egypt signed a separate peace deal with Israel, President Assad realized that, with the Egyptians no longer actively on his side, it would be even more difficult for him to regain the Golan Heights by force. (To defeat Israel, the Arabs would need to attack from more than one direction.) Then, in the late 1980s, when

257

the Cold War ended, resulting in the disintegration of the USSR, Assad also lost his main patron and supplier of weapons.

By 1991, when the USA led an international coalition of UN forces against President Saddam Hussein of Iraq who had invaded Kuwait (see chapter twenty nine), Assad realized that the only way he could regain his land was by talking with the Israelis. He then agreed to take part in the 1991 Madrid conference and, for the first time, he allowed his representatives to sit face-to-face with the Israelis in peace negotiations. But they led nowhere because the right-wing Likud government headed by Yitzhak Shamir regarded the Golan Heights as an important strategic asset and refused to trade it.

The June 1992 general election was won by the Labour party and Yitzhak Rabin's new government kept open the possibility of withdrawing from occupied areas of Golan Heights in return for full peace with Syria. But the keystone that might have completed the arch of a Middle East peace failed to fall into place.

## Chapter 34

# A vicious circle

The bilateral talks between Israel and Syria started immediately after the 1991 Madrid conference, but, from November onwards, no progress was achieved. Yossi Ben Aharon, the Director General of the Prime Minister's office, represented Israel, and Muwafiq el-Allaf represented Syria. They spent most of the time arguing about past events. Once, Allaf brought along a UN report to prove that Israel rather than Syria provoked the pre-1967 border incidents. But Ben Aharon did not want to listen to that. He left the table, made himself a cup of tea and, when he returned, sat banging the teaspoon on the table. Allaf, ignoring these antics, continued reading the document aloud. Ben Aharon then stood up and started dancing. 'Remember,' he said, 'I am originally from Alexandria – from Egypt. I know Arabic dances.' When Allaf finished reading the document, Ben Aharon said: 'I didn't hear a word, I was too busy dancing'.

But then, in June 1992, Shamir was defeated in Israel's general elections and succeeded by Rabin.

## The vicious circle of Articles 5(a) and 7

The first meeting between the Syrians and the Israelis representing the new Rabin government took place in Washington on 24 August 1992. Allaf led the Syrian delegation and Professor Itamar Rabinovich – a leading scholar of Arab history and a friend of Rabin – represented Israel. They met in a State Department conference room, and there was no handshake as they entered. Since there was also no chairperson, Rabinovich decided to open the discussion. He read a speech, which Prime Minister Rabin had approved. Israel not only wished to negotiate peace, it also understood that it would have to return land for peace. 'We recognize,' Rabinovich said, 'the applicability of Security Council resolution 242 in all its parts in the negotiations with Syria.' This statement marked a fundamental shift in Israel's position. Whereas the Shamir government had rejected the principles of trading the Golan Heights for peace, the Rabin government accepted it.

Just before the meeting, Rabinovich had inscribed a book, *The Road Not Taken*, that he had published about the failure of the Arab-Israeli peace talks in 1949, for Ambassador Allaf. The inscription read, *To Ambassador Allaf, hoping that this time the road will be taken*. When Rabinovich finished his opening speech, he took out the book, handed it to Allaf and stretched out his hand. Allaf took the book and Rabinovich's hand and shook it. It was an excellent start.

They met again the next week. The atmosphere was good, and Allaf was so encouraged that he felt he could do what President Assad had instructed him to do if the meeting were positive – present a new working paper.

This paper, entitled *Draft Declaration of Principles*, was prepared in Damascus between May and August 1992, and was an agenda for the talks with Rabin's new government. It consisted of four pages: the first three outlined a comprehensive peace plan for Israel and its Arab neighbours. The rest only concerned Israel and Syria. The following key extracts are published for the first time:

*The peace process is entering its eleventh month without any
meaningful advance ... We feel that it is about time – if we
really want to realize the objectives of the peace process – to
spell out clearly and without ambiguity, in an even and
balanced document, the basic principles without which no
peace can prevail ...*

*5(A). Machinery of Implementation:*
*Total Israeli withdrawal from the Syrian Golan occupied in
1967; the evacuation and dismantling of all the settlements
which have been established on the occupied Syrian territory
since that date in contradiction to the Geneva Conventions,
the principles of international law and UN resolutions.*

*7 Security Arrangements and Guarantees:*
*... the two parties declare their disposition to undertake and
accept the necessary measures to guarantee their security in a
parallel and reciprocal manner, including the possibility of
establishing on both sides and on equal footing demilitarized
zones or zones with reduced armaments, and to obtain from
the Security Council, from particular states or from both,
security guarantees without any prejudice to the sovereignty
of any party nor to the principle of equal rights for both.*

Allaf placed the paper in front of Rabinovich, who requested
half an hour to read it. Syrian Ambassador Walid Moualem, a
member of the Syrian delegation, recalls: 'The Israelis always use
mobile phones and Rabinovich went into another room to ring
Prime Minister Rabin and to read him some of the articles of
the document.' Rabinovich did want to clear some things with
Rabin, but he also wanted to ensure that the Prime Minister heard
about the new Syrian document from him – and *not* from the
correspondents outside the State Department.

The two men soon turned to the issues relating to Syrian-Israeli
relations, which began with Article 5(a). Rabinovich, however,
flicked past this to Article 7, which was concerned with security
arrangements and guarantees. 'No,' snapped Allaf, 'we need to start
with 5(a).' An argument ensued. Allaf obviously wanted to establish Israel's stance on the withdrawal from the Golan Heights

*before* he took matters further; Rabinovich wanted to discuss security arrangements *before* he gave details of Israel's view on the withdrawal. This was the beginning of a long, fruitless period: 'All the negotiations from August 1992 till August 1993,' recalls Moualem, 'were entirely focused on whether we should begin by discussing Article 5(a) or Article 7. There was no progress whatsoever. It was a vicious circle.'

## Rabin's bold gambit

On 4 August 1993, in an effort to break the deadlock, America's Secretary of State Warren Christopher went to Jerusalem to see Prime Minister Rabin. Ross and Rabinovich were also present as note-takers. 'The four of us came into the room,' Rabinovich recalls, 'and sat clustered around a small table. After some give-and-take, Rabin suddenly surprised us all with a dramatic gambit. "Mr Secretary", he said to Christopher, "when you go to Damascus, I would like you to ask President Assad – and I emphasize that this is a hypothetical question – that, should he be satisfied on what he is after, [i.e., Israeli withdrawal from the Golan Heights] would he be willing to make peace with us?"'

Christopher, a meticulous corporate lawyer, asked, "What would this mean with regard to your negotiations with the Palestinians?"

Rabin: "If Assad were to come forward and an Israeli-Syrian deal were to be made, then this would be supplemented by a small Palestinian deal. If Assad's response is disappointing, there will be no Israeli-Syrian breakthrough, so then there would be a major Israel-Palestinian agreement."'

At this time – August 1993 – the Oslo talks between Israel and the Palestinians (see chapter 33) were about to be finalized. Rabin was trying to decide whether to go the extra mile in Oslo and sign an Israeli-Palestinian agreement, or make a bid for the Syrian option and – if it proved to be a reality – sign with Assad first. He was hedging his bets.

Christopher left the room knowing that he had been given a significant mandate. Rabin was thinking about full peace with Syria in return for *total* withdrawal from the Golan Heights. Overnight, Christopher went to see Assad whose response was positive. Syria was willing to offer peace for withdrawal. But, in Christopher's detailed breakdown of Assad's answer, it emerged

261

that Assad's response was a 'yes, *but* . . . '. Rabin had wanted the process to take five years, Assad had said six months; Rabin had said adequate security arrangements and Assad had said, 'Yes, but on the basis of equality on both sides of the border', which Rabin could not accept because this would mean that the price for peace would be removal of Israel's troops from half its frontier region of Galilee. Assad also opposed the normalization of Israeli-Syrian relations *before* Israel had made a significant withdrawal of its forces from the Golan.

Assad's lukewarm reaction to his gambit had clinched the matter for Rabin. Disappointed, he decided, at least temporarily, to put the Syrian option on hold and concentrate instead on concluding the Israeli-Palestinian talks in Oslo. Having decided to do this, he said to Rabinovich, 'I cannot raise these two flags simultaneously'.

As Christopher and Ross returned to Washington, they did not know that soon their summer vacation would be interrupted by the unexpected visit of Israeli Foreign Minister Peres and Norwegian Foreign Minister Holst, bringing news of a breakthrough in the Oslo talks between the Israelis and Palestinians.

### An exchange of gestures

During the autumn of 1993, the Americans called for a summit in Geneva between Presidents Clinton and Assad. Before this took place, they asked the Israelis: what is the single most important concession you want us to extract from Assad at the meeting? Rabinovich: 'The answer was: let's get him to agree to the concept of normalization.'

The five-and-half-hours meeting took place on 16 January 1994 and was followed by a press conference. To reassure the Israelis that he was serious about making peace, Assad had agreed with the Americans that he would use the term 'Normal Peaceful Relations' between Syria and Israel in his statement. Speaking in Arabic, Assad said: 'We want the peace of the brave, a genuine peace that can survive. If the leaders of Israel have sufficient courage to respond to this kind of peace, a new era of security and stability, in which there will be Normal Peaceful Relations among all, will dawn.'[4]

Rabin, unimpressed by Assad's public gesture, planned his next move. Rabinovich explains: 'He said, "Okay, Assad, if this is what you call a public gesture, I'll give you my own public gesture."'

The next day Rabin announced that whatever deal Israel agreed with Syria would be placed before the Israeli public in a referendum. The Syrians, however, did not like the idea of a referendum.

### 'Four legs of the table'

On 28 April 1994, Secretary of State Christopher, having made another visit to Damascus, came once again to Israel. He told Rabin that Assad had surprised him by saying that he wanted more from Rabin. He wanted him to clearly define the line of withdrawal from the Golan Heights as meaning to the lines of 4 June 1967. The Syrians had started to suspect that when Rabin made his offer he meant withdrawal to the 1923 border, not to the 4 June lines which were to the west of the international border. Rabin was angered by the request and offered nothing more.

It took three months of American persuasion before, in July 1994, Rabin decided to go the extra mile and accommodate Christopher by offering a formula that showed that he was willing to withdraw to the 4 June 1967 line. He talked of a 'table with four legs': that Israel's withdrawal to the 4 June line was only *one* of the four legs; that the other three were normalization of relations between the two countries; the timetable for withdrawal (which Rabin wanted to be five years so that he could monitor whether the Syrians would give normalization in return for land); and adequate security arrangements (for the Israelis to ensure that Assad would not use the returned land to launch an attack on Israel). But his offer to withdraw to the 4 June line, Rabin emphasized, was not an offer to Assad but to the *Americans*. It must not, said Rabin, be put to Assad as Rabin's offer to him, but as an *American* offer. Rabin called it a 'deposit' in the hands of the Americans.

Rabin told Christopher: 'You can tell him that he has every reason to believe [that I will go back to the line of the 4 June 1967 border], but that the Israelis will not spell this out before all our needs are met.'

Christopher: 'I'll keep it in my pocket, not put it on the table.'
On the basis of that comment, the code name of the talks became
'File Pocket'.[5]

Christopher then went to Damascus for a meeting with
President Assad. Christopher ignored Rabin's instruction not to
put his 'deposit' to the Syrian President as a firm proposal, and let
Assad understand that he was conveying to him an Israeli offer.
When Rabin learned of this betrayal of confidence he exploded.[6]
He considered that Christopher, by revealing to Assad Israel's
bottom line, had severely weakened Israel's bargaining position.

Assad was thrilled. Believing that Rabin had made a real
concession, he gave the green light for a meeting to take place
between his Washington ambassador, Walid Moualem, and
Rabinovich, with Dennis Ross present. Two meetings followed at
Ross's house during September. The atmosphere was good, but
those present felt that the issues at stake required further talks
between the military professionals.

## Blair House, Washington

The following month, President Clinton arrived in Damascus –
the first time an American President had visited Syria since
Richard Nixon's 1974 visit. 'Mr President,' said Clinton, 'now
that Rabin has committed himself to a full withdrawal to the 4
June 1967 line, we want to move ahead fast.'[7] Assad said he was
ready to do this, and President Clinton asked for the next round
of negotiations to focus on security arrangements.

Assad agreed and sent Ambassador Walid Moualem to meet
Chief of Staff Ehud Barak. When Moualem reported that he was
impressed with Barak's attitude towards making peace, Assad
decided to send his most senior military man, Hikmat Shihabi,
not only Chief of Staff of the Syrian Army, but one of Syria's
senior political figures.

Assad plainly thought that a breakthrough was at hand and that
Israel would agree to a full withdrawal to the 4 June 1967 line at
the next meeting. So he sent a representative who could talk frankly
and practically about the consequent security arrangements. But
he was wrong. Despite Rabin's so-called 'commitment' deposit to
the Americans, the Israelis had other ideas in mind. They wanted
to talk in generalities around the table and use the interim periods

for informal converations to establish how flexible the Syrians were prepared to be.

Wearing wigs, so that they would not be recognized on the El Al plane, Israel's Chief of Staff Ehud Barak and his aides arrived at Blair House.

The next day, 21 December 1994, Barak, Shihabi and their colleagues, and an American delegation led by Christopher, met for the first session in a small conference room.

Barak laid out a comprehensive plan of Israel's needs. These ranged from early-warning systems to separation zones to reduce any future friction between the armies and reduce the probability of war. Shihabi, in turn, talked about the need for limited security arrangements, but tried to convey to the Israelis that they had nothing to fear from Syria; that, in fact, Syria had more reasons to fear Israel. 'Look at the map,' Shihabi said to Barak, 'and see who is really under threat. Who has more military force, more atomic bombs? Who carries out surprise attacks? You! You say you are afraid of our attacks, but we are afraid of your air force attacks. It was you who attacked us in 1967 – four days after the war began. You say you want early-warning systems, but we want security arrangements to protect us from your air force.' Barak was frustrated and disappointed. 'The meeting,' he recalls, 'failed to meet both our expectations. They were waiting to hear a final concession from a man who was close to Rabin, while we had come with the expectation of meeting a high-ranking man who would reveal, when nobody else was around, how flexible they were prepared to be.'

Upset by the failure of the Chiefs of Staff meeting, Assad said to the Americans: 'Unless both sides reach an agreement of *principles* concerning the security arrangements, it will be unproductive to let the Chiefs of Staff discuss things in general. As politicians we need to establish a framework for the military to work within'. He then insisted on talks that would focus on the principles. When Rabin gave his consent to this, President Clinton sent a letter to Assad requesting that Ambassador Moualem should discuss the principles involved with Rabinovich, Israel's ambassador to Washington and chief negotiator.

This round of intensive discussions between Moualem and Rabinovich resulted in a paper entitled *Aims and Principles of*

*Security Arrangements* (agreed on 21 May 1995). It tackled the main stumbling point concerning equal security arrangements on both sides of the border between Israel and Syria. The door was then open for a meeting in Washington between General Shihabi and Israel's new Chief of Staff, Amnon Lipkin-Shahak, to discuss the details.

They met in June 1995 at the National Defence University, but the result of their two-day meeting was disappointing; the military Chiefs of Israel and Syria were still driven by mutual mistrust.

## Chapter 35

# The rise and fall of Shimon Peres

On 4 November 1995 in Tel Aviv, at a rally in support of the peace process, Prime Minister Yitzhak Rabin was assassinated by a Jewish right-wing zealot. Israelis – and millions in the international community – were shocked and horrified. The following is the testimony of Foreign Minister Shimon Peres[8]:

> When we came to the rally Yitzhak [Rabin] could not believe his eyes. It was an immense rally attended by tens of thousands of people. And he was overjoyed. I had never, in my life, seen him so happy. We had known each other for fifty years and he had never, never hugged me. At the rally, for the first time in his life, he hugged me. I had never heard him singing before. But, at the rally, he stood and sang. The three of us, the singer Miri Alonie, Yitzhak and myself, sang. Yitzhak was given a paper with the words of the 'Song of Peace' written on it. After we had sung, he folded it and put it in his jacket pocket. During the rally, Yitzhak came up to me and said that there was some information about the Hamas intending to make a terrorist attack on the rally and that we should not walk down the stairs together because of the danger. When the rally was over, I asked Yitzhak where he was going. He said, 'Tel Aviv'. I said I was going

*to Jerusalem. We said goodbye to each other. I began to
descend the staircase. My car was parked a little way in
front of Yitzhak's and I asked his driver, "Where is
Yitzhak?" "He's over there," he said. I turned to look and
saw him about fifteen metres from me walking down the
staircase. I got into my car, closed the door and then
suddenly heard three shots."Stop!", I said to my driver. I
wanted to get out. But my security men said, "Absolutely
not!" And, sounding the sirens, they drove away wildly. We
didn't know yet what had happened. We only knew that
Yitzhak was being taken to hospital. I demanded to be taken
there immediately. The head of the hospital came to me and
said that Yitzhak was no longer alive. We went to the room
where he was lying on the bed. His body was covered with a
sheet up to his shoulders. On his face was an expression of
peace – and an ironical sort of a smile; a special smile.
I kissed his forehead and said, "Goodbye". I was very
shocked.*

## Flying high

Peres was appointed to the top post and, like Rabin and many of
his predecessors, kept the role of Defence Minister for himself.
'One man needs to direct both peace and security,' he said. Time
was short, for in about a year's time there would be a general
election.

After Rabin's funeral, President Clinton held a one-to-one
conversation with Peres. This took place just half an hour after
Ambassador Rabinovich had briefed Peres about the Israeli-
Syrian talks. It was only then that Peres realized what Rabin had
been doing behind his back. He had known nothing about
Rabin's commitment to the Americans to withdraw from the
Golan Heights to the 4 June 1967 line if the 'other three legs of
the table' were agreed. Nevertheless, now that he knew, Peres told
President Clinton that he would fulfil, 'everything Yitzhak Rabin
had said, whether in writing or orally'.

About two weeks later, on 19 November 1995, Dennis Ross,
the American peace co-ordinator, arrived in Israel to give Peres
a fuller briefing on the Israeli-Syrian talks. Ross found Peres in a

buoyant mood, eager to conclude a deal with Assad. For years, Peres had pursued peace with Israel's neighbours, but his quests had either failed at the last minute or the glory had gone to someone else. In 1987, he had concluded his 'London Agreement' with King Hussein, only to see it sabotaged by Prime Minister Shamir.[9] In 1993, he had worked hard on the Oslo talks, but the credit had gone to Rabin. Now, this was his opportunity to join the gallery of Israeli peace-makers – Menachem Begin, who had concluded peace with Egypt in 1979, and Rabin who had recently shaken the hands of Arafat and King Hussein of Jordan. 'I suggest,' he said to Ross, 'that, if we reach an agreement with the Syrian President, we should also meet with all the other Arab leaders and announce that the conflict is over. Then we can sign a comprehensive agreement to end the war in the Middle East.'

To convince President Assad that he was serious, Peres wrote him a letter in his own handwriting and asked Ross to deliver it. It was, recalls Peres, 'a letter of goodwill in which I expressed my willingness to negotiate with honour and with equality'. Having studied the letter, Assad said to Ross, 'It's a good letter'.

When Christopher and Ross then assured Peres that Assad was also serious about the peace agreement, Peres said, 'If Assad wants to sign an agreement in 1996, before the [Israeli] elections, I am willing to do that, but we will have to upgrade the negotiations to a higher level'. He then suggested that there should be, 'a meeting between myself and Assad'. He also asked Christopher to tell Assad, who was a former pilot, that, 'A well-known French author had written that mothers, whose sons are pilots, always pray that their sons will fly low and slowly. They don't understand that flying high and fast is much safer. Ask Assad,' he added, "What do you want – to fly high and fast or low and slowly?"'

Assad's response to Christopher was not encouraging, 'I understand,' he said, 'that there must be a meeting between Peres and myself during the negotiations, but I can't give you a date'. Peres was bitterly disappointed. But lower-level talks continued in the US.

**'Building a bridge'**
**(First round: Maryland, 27 December 1995)**
To head his negotiating team, Peres chose Uri Savir, the young diplomat who had played a major role in negotiating both the Oslo I deal and Oslo II agreements, which had turned the negotiations into an action plan. He also added Joel Singer, another key figure in the Oslo talks, who was by now the Foreign Ministry's legal adviser.

Peres was convinced that the previous talks had become deadlocked because Rabin had insisted on concentrating mainly on the security issues. So, to expand the scope of the negotiations, he decided to implement one of his own suggestions that Rabin had rejected. He instructed his team to put *all* the issues – not only the security arrangements – on the table and explore *all* the elements of a future agreement. These included normalization of Israeli-Syrian relations, water issues, and whatever else was necessary to peaceful co-existence between neighbouring states.

Before the first meeting, Savir said to Dennis Ross, 'Go back to Washington and find an isolated location in some woods where there are no phones – a place where we can be together, take walks and create some kind of chemistry'. Savir wanted to repeat the Oslo atmosphere. After checking this out with Assad, Ross found a 1100-acre former plantation overlooking the Wye River, about 80 kilometres east of Washington. The delegations would stay there for three days and two nights. The talks would mark the first meeting for six months between the two countries.

Once inside the villa, Savir went downstairs to lunch, wearing his usual chief negotiator's 'uniform' – jeans and a sweat-shirt – and was pleasantly surprised to find that the atmosphere was relaxed, and that everybody was dressed informally. A man (the Syrian Ambassador) stood up to greet him, smiled, and said, 'I am glad to meet you. My name is Walid Moualem'. He then invited Savir to join him for lunch.

Savir was delighted. He had hoped to deal directly with Ambassador Moualem with the minimum of American intervention and suddenly this seemed possible. 'I have to tell you,' he said to Moualem, 'that the best way for us to do business is to do it on our own.' But Moualem disagreed. To convince him, Savir told him a story of a man who fell head over heels in love with a

young girl. But he was so shy, he did not know how to tell her
that he loved her, so he wrote her a love letter every day. A year
later the girl married the postman! Moualem laughed heartily, but
remained unmoved. 'I'll be glad to sit with you privately,' he told
Savir, 'but, when negotiating, my instructions from President
Assad are to negotiate only when the Americans are present.' He
explained that Israel and Syria needed a bridge to enable them to
communicate, and that the bridge was America which should be
involved both in the negotiating process and the implementation
of any agreement that resulted. The Israeli team was not enthusiastic. As Singer recalls: 'We wanted a direct interconnection. They
[the Syrians] said, "No, we can kiss, but only through a third
party."'

There were only three items on the Syrians' normalization
list: opening embassies in both countries, cancelling of the Arab
boycott on Israeli goods, and allowing Israeli tourists to pass
through Syria to visit Turkey. The Israelis' list for normalization
had eighteen points which included: opening the border to Israeli
and Syrian tourists, open trade between the countries, the interconnection of roads, telecommunication and electricity systems.

In the end, after Singer had used every trick in the book to try
to achieve his eighteen normalization points, they managed to
agree on eleven. Secretary of State Christopher then contacted
President Assad to see if the military people could now join in and
discuss security matters.

### 'Take your hands off Damascus'
### (Second round: Maryland, 24 January 1996)
Assad sent two of his officers – Chief of Military Intelligence
Ibrahim Omar and Major-General Hassan Khalil to join
Ambassador Moualem. One Israeli question that echoed round
the room throughout the discussions was: where would the Syrian
army be deployed in peacetime? If the Israelis gave back the
Golan Heights, a strategic, high asset, they wanted reassurance
that the Syrian troops would be deployed as far away as possible
from their border. Moualem replied, 'This is a sovereign decision
that only President Assad can decide.'

When the discussion moved to the proposed demilitarized
zone, Moualem asked General Uzi Dayan of the Israeli Defence

Force, 'Where do you want the demilitarized zone to be?' Dayan leaned over the table and, placing his hand on the map, said, 'Here'. Moualem sat back: 'Where is Damascus in relation to your hand?' he asked. Dayan looked down and said, 'Well . . . it's just under my palm'. Moualem: 'Did you hear that? General Dayan has just said that our capital, Damascus, is under his palm?' Then: 'Take your hand off Damascus!', he shouted at Dayan. 'Take it off at once! If you don't, I will leave the room.' And he stormed out.

Dennis Ross followed him to his bedroom. 'He didn't mean what you thought,' he said to Moualem. 'It's just a habit of his to put his hand on maps when he's explaining to his soldiers.' 'I am not his soldier,' snapped Moualem. 'This is my capital, my city, my country.' Savir joined them: 'I know Uzi Dayan,' he said to Moualem, 'he's very forthright, but he didn't mean what you thought he did.' Moualem: 'I will not return to the table unless he agrees never to put his hand on the map like that again.' Savir, placatingly: 'I'll teach him to keep his hands in his pocket.'

Moualem recalls the moment he lost his temper: 'When he put his hand on the map, I felt as if I was in the company of an aggressor . . . The way he did it reminded me of the way conquerors used to put their hands on other countries' maps. I could not tolerate this.'

### All comes to nothing
In Israel, Prime Minister Peres concluded that things were moving too slowly. President Assad had clearly rejected his idea to 'fly high and fast'. With a maximum of ten months to go to the elections, and with too many complex issues still to be resolved, he decided to bring the date of the elections forward.

Back at the Wye plantation, Secretary of State Christopher arrived by helicopter. It was Ramadan, the thirty days in the ninth month of the Muslim year when Muslims fast from sunrise to sunset, and he came at 5 p.m. to have *Iftar* (the first meal after a day's fast) with the delegates. He was in good spirits, cracking jokes, telling stories. He took Moualem to a side room. 'I have some unpleasant news for you,' he said. 'Prime Minister Peres has informed me by telephone that he is going for early elections.'

President Assad was unhappy about Peres's decision, but did

not want to be seen as the person who sabotaged the talks. Nor did Peres. They sent their delegations back to the Wye Plantation. Nevertheless, the meeting came to a sudden end. In Israel, Hamas had renewed a bombing campaign in Jerusalem, Ashekelon and Tel Aviv, leaving scores of Israelis dead and wounded. Israel was in shock. Uri Savir talked on the phone with Peres, but the Prime Minister was aghast at the bombings and no longer in a mood to discuss peace. It was agreed that their Wye plantation delegation should return to Israel.

On 29 May 1996, Prime Minister Peres lost the general elections and Benjamin Netanyahu came to power.

Why didn't Israel and Syria conclude a peace deal? Why didn't Assad move faster when he was told that Rabin was willing to give back the Golan Heights? Did he think that the price for this, in terms of what he would have to concede for normalization of relationships and security arrangements, was too high? Or was it simply not in his character to move in anything other than slow incremental steps? Was he also confused by Rabin who had conducted two channels – one through the Americans in which he had made the commitment to give back the Golan Heights if all his conditions were met, and the other through his military when his offer had been more restrictive? And why, after Rabin's assassination, didn't Assad move faster when Prime Minister Peres was prepared to honour Rabin's promises? We do not know. Perhaps we never will.

*Chapter 36*

# Benjamin Netanyahu – a new man at the helm

The new Prime Minister's manifesto slogan *Peace with Security* was well received by Israelis, shocked to the core by the Hamas bombing campaign. Israel's ninth Prime Minister, Benjamin Netanyahu, aged forty-six, affectionately known as Bibi, was articulate and, conducted himself more like an American than an Israeli. Once in office, he surrounded himself with tough Likud party ministers, such as Ariel Sharon, the architect of the 1982 Lebanon War, Rafael Eitan, formerly Sharon's Chief of Staff, and Benjamin Begin, the son of the late Menachem Begin.

Netanyahu and his new team had little trust in Arafat, and found implementing the agreement that the previous Labour government had signed with him a bitter pill. At the time of the signing, Peres had said to Abu Ala'a, the Palestinians' chief negotiator, 'We may have been miserly in the [Oslo] formula, but we will have to be much more big-hearted in the implementation of the agreement. It's better to promise little and give more, than to promise much and give little.'

For Netanyahu, though, when Peres promised little, he promised too much. Netanyahu saw no reason to be 'bigger hearted' in the implementation. On the contrary, he took steps that killed the spirit of Oslo and infuriated the Palestinians. Less than three months after being elected, he ordered the opening of a second entrance to an archaeological tunnel in Jerusalem that ran alongside the western foundation of what is known as the Temple Mount by the Jews and elAqsa mosque by the Arabs – the site of one of Islam's holiest places and mosques. This sparked off a battle between the Israelis and Palestinians which endangered the whole peace process, and forced an American intervention and a summit in Washington (29 September 1996) to calm things down. The expansion of the settlements did not help either. Netanyahu agreed to pull out of Hebron, as agreed by the previous government, but on terms which ran against the spirit of the Oslo talks.

On the Syrian front, Netanyahu was reluctant to accept the commitment that Rabin had deposited with the Americans to withdraw to the 4 June 1967 line. 'Statements,' he said, 'made in the course of negotiations, which are not written down, are not part of a formal commitment, are *not* formal commitments . . . I will only honour formal commitments.'

In July 1996, Dennis Ross tried to revive the Israeli-Syrian talks on the basis of a Syrian formula that suggested continuing 'the peace talks with Israel on the commitments that had been reached before'. But Netanyahu rejected the formula: 'No,' he said, 'I am only willing to resume the peace talks without any pre-conditions.'

At the time of writing, Israel has signed peace agreements with Egypt and Jordan, has a peace agreement with the Palestinians that seems daily to be under threat, but no agreement with Syria.

The fifty years war between Israel and the Arabs is not yet over.

# Notes on sources

This book, which accompanies the BBC television series, is based mainly on filmed interviews with the chief participants in the conflict – Arabs, Israelis, Palestinians, Americans, Russians and Europeans. We have also drawn on other interviews which cannot – at the insistence of the interviewee – be directly attributed to a named person. In these instances – to respect the need for anonymity – we have summarized what was said. The following, in alphabetical order, is a list of people we have interviewed:

**Israelis:** Amos Amir, Moshe Amirav, Meir Amit, Moshe Arens, Ehud Barak, Yossi Beilin, Yossi Ben Aharon, Benyamin Ben Eliezer, Ben Zion Cohen, Avraham Dar, Uzi Dayan, Robert Dassa, Ziamah Divon, Abba Eban, Miriam Eshkol, Yeshayahu Gavish, Benjamin Givly, Eitan Haber, Yair Hirschfeld, Mordechai Hod, Amram Mitzna, Shimon Monita, Uzi Narkiss, Yitzhak Navon, Benjamin Netanyahu, Marcelle Ninio, Meir Pail, Dan Pattir, Shimon Peres, Itamar Rabinovich, Gideon Rafael, Ran Ronen (Peker), Uri Savir, Amnon Lipkin-Shahak, Yitzhak Shamir, Ariel Sharon, Joel Singer, Yisrael Tal, Yair Tzaban, Ezer Weizman, Ezra Yachin, Eli Zeira.

**Palestinians:** Mahmoud Abbas (Abu Mazen), Ahmed Suleiman Qurei (Abu Ala'a), Hassan Asfour, Hanan Ashrawi, Saeb Erekat, Khaled Fahoum, George Habash, Faisal Husseini, Um Jihad (Intissar Wazir), Abdullah Khaled al-Ghoul, Said Kamal, Ghassan Khattib, Mohamad Labadi, Spear el-Monaier, Sari Nusseibeh, Yasser abed Rabbo, Mohammed Asaad Radwan Al Yassini (Abu Mahmoud), Abu Ali Shaheen, Jamal Sourani, Salah Tamari, Abu Tawfik Yassini, Ahmad Tibi.

**Lebanese:** Jonny Abdo, Salim al-Hoss, Chafiq al-Hout, Hussein Husseini, Walid Jumblatt, Joseph Abu Khalil, Karim Pakradouni, Chafiq Al-Wazzan.

**Jordanians:** Mashour Haditha, King Hussein, Taher al Masri, Queen Noor, Hazem Nusseibeh, Zaid el-Rifai, Prince Zaid bin Shaker.

**Egyptians:** Shams el-din Badran, Salah Bassiouny, Ahmed Fakher, Muhammed Fawzi, Abdel Ghani Gamasy, Boutros Boutros Ghali, Kamal el-din Hussein, Mohsen Abdel Khalek, Mustapha Khalil, Zakaria Mohiedin, General Bahy Edin Noufal, Adel Sabit, Jihan Sadat, Abdel Rahman Sadeq, Saad el-Shazly.

**Syrians:** Walid Moualem, Farouk al Shar'a, Mustapha Tlas.

**Russians:** Pavel Akopov, Karen Brutenz, Anatoly Dobrynin, Victor Israelyan, General Kirpichenko, Evgeny Pyrlin, Vassily Reshetnikov, Victor Sukhodrev.

**Americans:** James Baker, Dean Brown, Zbigniew Brzezinski, George Bush, Jimmy Carter, Clark Clifford, Edward Djerejian, Hermann Eilts, Richard Haass, Alexander Haig, Henry Kissinger, Robert McNamara, William Quandt, Elliot Richardson, Dennis Ross, Eugene Rostow, Walter Rostow, George Shultz, Joseph Sisco.

**Others:** Terje Larsen, Jafaar Numeiry.

# Select bibliography

Abbas, Mahmoud (Abu Mazen), *Through Secret Channels* (Reading, Garnet Publishing, 1995).

Abu Sharif, Bassam, and Mahnaimi, Uzi, *Tried by Fire* (London, Little, Brown and Co., 1995).

Arens, Moshe, *Broken Covenant* (Simon & Schuster, New York, 1995)

Ashrawi, Hanan, *This Side of Peace* (New York, Simon & Schuster, 1995).

Baker III, James A. with Defrank, Thomas, M., *The Politics of Diplomacy, Revolution, War and Peace 1989-1992* (New York, G.P. Putnam's Sons, 1995).

Beilin, Yossi, *Touching Peace* (Tel Aviv, Yediot Aharonot, 1997).

Ben Caspit et al., *Committing Suicide,* (Tel Aviv, Ma'ariv, 1996) (Hebrew).

Black, Ian, and Morris, Benny, *Israel's Secret Wars* (New York, Grove Weidenfeld, 1991).

Carmel, Hesi, and Derogy, Jacques, *Le Siècle D'Israel: Les Secrets D'Une Epopée 1895-1995* (Paris, Fayard, 1994).

Clifford, Clark, *Counsel to the President* (New York, Anchor Books, 1991).

Dayan, Moshe, *Story of My Life* (London, Weidenfeld & Nicolson, 1976).

Eban, Abba, *An Autobiography* (New York, Random House, 1977).

Enderlin, Charles, *Paix ou Guerres* (Paris, Editions Stock, 1997).

Fisk, Robert, *Pity the Nation: Lebanon at War* (Oxford, Oxford University Press, 1992).

Frankel, Glenn, *Beyond the Promised Land* (New York, A Touchstone Book, Simon & Schuster, 1996).

Freedman, Lawrence et al., *The Gulf Conflict* (London, Faber & Faber, 1994).

Friedman, Thomas, *From Beirut to Jerusalem: One Man's Middle Eastern Odyssey* (London, HarperCollins, 1990).

Gilaad, Z. (ed), *The Book of the Palmach* (2 vols; Tel Aviv, 1963) (Hebrew).

Green, Stephen, *Taking Sides* (London, Faber and Faber, 1984).

Haber, Eitan, *Today War will Break Out* (Tel Aviv, Edanim Publishers, 1987) (Hebrew).

Heikal, Mohamed, *The Road to Ramadan* (London, Harper Collins, 1975).

Heikal, Mohamed, *Secret Channels* (London, HarperCollins, 1996).

Ismail, Hafez M., *Amn Misr Al-Kawmy* (Cairo, Ahram, 1987).

Khalaf, Salah, *Falastini Bila Hawiya* (Tunis, Official Press of the Tunisian Republic, 1991) (Arabic).

Kissinger, Henry, *The White House Years* (London, Little, Brown and Co., 1979).

Kissinger, Henry, *Years of Upheaval* (London, Weidenfeld & Nicolson and Michael Joseph, 1982).

Laqueur, Walter and Rubin, Barry (eds) *The Israeli-Arab Reader: A Documentary History of the Middle East Conflict* (London, Penguin Books, 1995).

Luckas, Yehuda (ed), *The Israeli-Palestinian Conflict, A Documentary Record, 1967-1990* (Cambridge, Cambridge University Press, 1992).

Marcus, Yoel, *Camp David: The Door to Peace* (Tel Aviv, Schocken Publishers, 1979) (Hebrew).

Meir, Golda, *My Life: The Autobiography of Golda Meir* (London, Weidenfeld & Nicolson, 1975).

Mohi El Din, Khaled, *Memories of a Revolution* (Cairo, American University Press, 1995).

Morris, Benny, *Falsifying the record: a fresh look at Zionist documentation of 1948,* Journal of Palestine Studies, Spring 1995 (XXIV, no. 3), pp. 44–62.

Morris, Benny, *1948 and After* (Oxford, Oxford University Press, 1990).

Noufal, Mamdouh, *Al-Inkilab* (Amman, Dar Al-Sherouk, 1996) (Arabic).

Peres, Shimon, *Battling for Peace, Memoirs* (London, Weidenfeld & Nicolson, 1995).

Quandt, William B., *Peace Process* (Berkeley, University of California Press, 1993).

Rabin, Yitzhak, *Pinkas Sherut,* (2 vols; Tel Aviv, Ma'ariv, 1979) (Hebrew).

Rabin, Yitzhak, *The Rabin Memoirs* (London, Weidenfeld &

Nicolson, 1979).

Rafael, Gideon, *Destination Peace: Three Decades of Israeli Foreign Policy, A Personal Memoir* (London, Weidenfeld & Nicolson, 1981).

Randal, Jonathan, *The Tragedy of Lebanon* (London, The Hogarth Press, 1990).

Raviv, Dan, and Melman, Yossi, *Every Spy a Prince* (Boston, Houghton Mifflin Cy, 1990).

Sabit, Adel M., *A King Betrayed* (London, Quartet Books, 1989).

Sadat, Anwar, *In Search of Identity: An Autobiography* (New York, Harper & Row, 1977).

Sadat, Jihan, *A Woman of Egypt* (London, Bloomsbury, 1987).

Savir, Uri, *The Process* (New York, Random House, 1998).

Schiff, Ze'ev et al., *Intifada* (London, A Touchstone Book, Simon & Schuster, 1985).

Schiff, Ze'ev et al., *Israel's Lebanon War* (London, George Allen & Unwin, 1985).

Shalew, Aryeh, *Israel and Syria: Peace and Security on the Golan* (Tel Aviv, Tel Aviv University, 1993) (Hebrew).

Shamir, Yitzhak, *Summing Up* (London, Weidenfeld & Nicolson, 1994)

Sharett, Moshe, *Personal Diary,* (8 vols; Tel Aviv, Ma'ariv, 1978) (Hebrew).

Sharon, Ariel with Chanoff, David, *Warrior: The Autobiography of Ariel Sharon* (London, Macdonald & Co Publishers Ltd, 1989).

Shazly, Saad, *The Crossing of Suez: The October War* (1973) (London, Third World Centre for Research and Publishing, 1980).

Sheffer, Gabriel, *Moshe Sharett: Biography of a Political Moderate* (Oxford, Oxford University Press, 1996).

Shultz, George P., *Turmoil and Triumph,* (New York, Charles Scribner's Sons, 1993).

Snow, Peter et al., *Leila's Hijack War* (London, Pan Books, 1970).

Teveth, Shabtai, *Ben Gurion's Spy* (New York, Columbia University Press, 1996).

# Notes

## PART 1: Palestine, Egypt and the New State of Israel

### Introduction
1   The eleven members of the United Nations Special Committee on Palestine (UNSCOP), listed here in alphabetical order, were: Australia, Canada, Czechoslovakia, Guatemala, Holland, India, Iran, Peru, Sweden, Uruguay and Yugoslavia.

### Chapter 1
2   After the Second World War, Britain recognized the Jewish Agency as the body representing the Jews in Palestine.

3   Chaim Weizmann was deposed as the head of the Zionist movement at the Basel Congress of 1946, because members of the organization did not approve of his pro-British views, and considered the British government repressive and anti-Jewish.

4   Hesi Carmel and Jacques Derogy, *Le Siècle D'Israel* (Fayard, Paris, 1994), pp. 403-4.

5   Ibid., p. 403. For further reading, see Larry Collins and Dominique Lapierre, *O Jerusalem*, (Bnei Brak: Steimatzky, 1982), p. 16. This book states that Harvey Firestone contacted President William Tubman of Liberia, saying that if Liberia did not change its vote, his company would reconsider plans to expand its acreage in Liberia.

6   Ibid. For further reading, see *O Jerusalem*, p. 16. This states that two justices of the Supreme Court cabled President Carlos Rojas warning, 'the Philippines will isolate millions of American friends if they continue in their efforts to vote against partition'. The Philippine ambassador was also called to the White House to a 'blunt and intensive briefing'.

7   Ibid., p. 403. Abba Eban, in *An Autobiography* (New York, Random House, 1977) pp. 95-7, makes a brief reference to attempts to convince Haiti.

8   *O Jerusalem*, p. 17, states that President Carlos Rojas intervened personally, saying to the delegation that 'in the higher national interest' of the Philippines, they should switch from 'against' to 'for' partition.

9   'By the morning of November 29, the Thai delegate, Prince Wan,

had prudently departed for Bangkok on the Queen Mary, ostensibly on the grounds that a revolutionary situation existed in his country, but actually in order to avoid having to cast a vote against partition.' Eban, *An Autobiography*, p. 97.

10 Weizmann had sent a cable to Leon Blum, a French Socialist statesman, urging France not to abstain but to vote for partition.

11 The Arab League's inaugural pact was signed by Egypt, Syria, Lebanon, Jordan, Iraq, Saudi Arabia and Yemen. The rest joined later.

12 Palmach was founded in 1941 as Haganah's élite force. Haganah (the Hebrew word for defence) was the underground Jewish militia in Palestine that became the nucleus of the Israeli Defence Forces (IDF) in 1948.

13 In the battle for Kastel, the volunteers came mainly from Iraq. But in general, volunteers also came from Egypt and Syria.

14 Irgun was a dissident militia group, established in 1936, with the aim that Jews should control all of Palestine and Transjordan. Lehi (also known as the Stern Gang after its leader Avraham Stern) broke away from Irgun and Haganah during the Second World War, because it objected to their policy of ceasing to fight the British while the Allies were fighting Nazi Germany.

15 Pail's friend would not have known that Pail's job was to fight dissidents. All the organizations, including the Haganah, were underground and secretive.

16 Person chosen by villagers to act as local governor.

17 At this time, the British Government – even though it had started pulling out its soldiers – was still the governing body in Palestine. Both the Arabs and the Jews, however, had their own leadership which – until the total withdrawal of the British on 15 May – were theoretically clandestine but functioned quite openly. The leadership of the Jews was in the hands of the Jewish Agency, which was in control of the militia – Haganah. The leadership of the Arabs was the Arab High Committee whose main leader, Haj Amin al-Husseini, was in exile in Egypt. The Arab High Committee had local National Committees that functioned within each town in Palestine.

18 Z. Gilad (ed), *The Book of the Palmach* (2 vols; Tel Aviv, 1963) (Hebrew).

## Chapter 2

19 In the event, trusteeship did not replace partition. But, for further

information about how the US State Department could overrule President Truman after the partition vote had been taken, see Clifford Clark, *Counsel to the President* (New York, 1991), pp. 8-9.

20 Quotation taken from David K. Shipler, 'Israel bars Rabin from relating '48 eviction of Arabs', *New York Times*, 23 October 1979.

21 This question, `What to do with the Palestinians?' that reflects Israel's internal policy regarding the Palestinians at this time, was never posed in public. It has only come to light since Israeli documents, relating to this period, have been declassified.

### Chapter 3

22 Tito, who had a close relationship with Nasser, was a perfect mediator because he also had a close but independent relationship with the USSR and Israel. Together, he and Nasser created the Non-Aligned Movement.

### Chapter 4

23 Gabriel Sheffer, *Moshe Sharrett: Biography of a Political Moderate* (Oxford, 1996), p. 634.

24 Stephen Green, *Taking Sides*, (London, 1984), p. 105.

### Chapter 5

25 The Unit 131 text is based on filmed interview with Robert Dassa, 24 January 1997, Israel.

26 The squabbles between the Muslim Brotherhood Group and Nasser's Government were about internal affairs - mainly the role of religion in the 'new Egyptian society'. Both were opposed to the British presence in the Canal Zone, but the Muslim Brotherhood regarded itself as an 'opposition party within Egypt'. Nasser later banned the group and imprisoned all its leaders.

### Chapter 6

27 The relationship between Egypt and the US did not sour until September 1955 when Nasser signed an arms deal with Czechoslovakia. From then onwards, and throughout the 1960s, when Nasser's policies were orientated towards the USSR, the US considered him a USSR ally. From the late 1960s onward, the US regarded Israel as its main strategic ally in the Middle East.

28 Twenty-nine countries attended the first Non-Aligned Summit,

including sixteen newly-independent states that had ended colonial rule. The aim of the summit was to create and co-ordinate a solidarity movement by setting down principles aimed at remaining neutral in the Cold War between East and West.

## PART 2: The 1967 War

### Chapter 7

1  This text is based on Miriam Eshkol's testimony and Yisrael Lior's memoirs, see Eitan Haber, *Today War Will Break Out. The Reminiscences of Brig.Gen. Yisrael Lior Aide-de-Camp to Prime Ministers Levi Eshkol and Golda Meir* (Tel Aviv, 1987), p. 147 (Hebrew).

2  The Civil war in Yemen broke out on 26 September 1962. Egypt intervened in the war, seeing it as an opportunity to teach King Saud of Saudi Arabia, who had led a campaign against Egypt, a lesson. Egypt supported the Republicans, and Saudi Arabia the Royalists. Egypt's involvement steadily increased from one Egyptian brigade in Yemen to two divisions – 70,000 soldiers. They withdrew after the 1967 War.

3  The air force party scene is based on interviews with Miriam Eshkol and the memoirs of Yisrael Lior.

4  Anwar el-Sadat, *In Search of Identity: An Autobiography* (New York, 1977), pp. 171-2.

5  *The Jerusalem Post*, 16 May 1967.

6  See 'Soviet Official's Comments on Soviet Policy on the Middle Eastern War – CIA report of conversation with Soviet Official re June War.' LBJ Library, 82-156, doc.8420.

7  Details of this meeting are based mainly on Anwar el-Sadat, *In Search of Identity*, p. 172.

8  On the Egyptian demand that UNEF leave the Sinai see Walter Laqueur, *The Road to War* (London, 1993), pp, 101-2.

9  In an interview for this book with Egyptian General Noufal, it was pointed out that the Straits were not actually closed. But the outside world regarded them as closed from the moment that Nasser said that he would close them.

### Chapter 8

10  This text is based on Eban's memoirs. Also on the 'Memo of conversation between President Johnson and Foreign Minister Eban and

others'. (Secret) National Archives and Records Service, 91-368.

## Chapter 9

11 Minutes of a conversation given to Ahron Bregman by a military-intelligence general.

12 Interview with Ezer Weizman, 17 February 1992, Caesarea.

13 Interview with Yitzhak Rabin, 21 March 1991, Tel Aviv.

14 *Ha'aretz*, 29 May 1967 (Hebrew).

## Chapter 10

15 Interview with Minister of War Shams el-Din Badran, 5 June 1997, London.

16 Interview with Robert McNamara, 21 April 1997, Washington.

17 Interview with Meir Amit, 20 January 1997, Ramat Gan.

## Chapter 11

18 Interview with Yitzhak Rabin, 21 March 1991, Tel Aviv.

19 *The Conversation between Nasser and Hussein* (as recorded by the IDF). Source: Meir Amit (former Head of Mossad).

20 Walter Laqueur, *The Road to War: The Origin and Aftermath of the Arab-Israeli Conflict 1967-8* (London: Reading and Fakenham, 1993), p. 113.

21 Interview with Abba Eban, 29 January 1997, Hertzliya.

22 Shlomo Nakdimon, *Yediot Aharonot*, 30 May 1997 (Hebrew).

23 Rami Tal, 'Moshe Dayan: Soul Searching', *Yediot Aharonot*, 27 April 1997.

24 Brig. Gen. Arie Brown, *Moshe Dayan and the Six Day War* (Tel Aviv, 1997), p. 90 (Hebrew).

25 Interview with Yitzhak Rabin, 21 March 1991, Tel Aviv.

26 The hot line text is based on an interview with Victor Sukhodrev, an operator who was present when the hot line was used in June 1967. Interview, March 1997, Moscow.

27 NEJ 95-157 hot line message from Chairman Kosygin to President Johnson, 10 June 1967 (8.45 a.m).

28 Present were Robert McNamara (Secretary of Defence), Clark Clifford, McGeorge Bundy and Walt Rostow (National Security advisers), Llewellyn Thompson (Ambassador), and Richard Helms (CIA Director) and Katzenbach (Undersecretary).

29 Ambassador Llewellyn E. Thompson's testimony in Memorandum

of conversation, 4 November 1968, LBJ Library, 94-382.

30  Richard Helms, testimony, Memorandum for the record, 22 October 1968.

31  Interview with Walt Rostow, 18 April 1997, Austin, Texas; interview with Robert McNamara, 21 April 1997, Washington DC; Richard Helms, testimony, 22 October 1968.

32  Richard Helms, testimony, 22 October 1968.

33  NEJ 95-157 hot line message from President Johnson to Chairman Kosygin, 10 June 1967 (9.39 a.m).

34  NEJ 95-157 hot line message from Chairman Kosygin to President Johnson, 10 June 1967 (9.44 a.m).

35  NEJ 95-157 hot line message from Chairman Kosygin to President Johnson, 10 June 1967 (11.31 a.m).

## Chapter 12

36  Incoming Telegram, Department of State, Summary of conversation, Secret, June 1967, 3:27, E.O.12356, sec.3.4., NIJ 94.36, NARA Date, 7.18.95.

# PART 3:  Sadat's Historic Quest for Peace

## Chapter 13

1  Henry Kissinger, *Years of Upheaval* (London, 1982), p. 201.

2  Anwar el-Sadat, *In Search of Identity*, (New York, 1977), p. 219.

## Chapter 14

3  Henry Kissinger, *Years of Upheaval*, p. 201.

4  General Saad el-Shazly, *The Crossing of Suez: The October War* (1973) (London, 1980).

5  Hafez M. Ismail, *Amn Misr Al-Kawmy* (Cairo, Ahram, 1987), p. 263 (Arabic).

6  Ibid.

## Chapter 15

7  *The Crossing of Suez*, pp. 121-3.

8  Ibid, p. 123.

9  For meetings between King Hussein and Israeli leaders, see Shimon Peres, *Battling for Peace*, p. 299. Such meetings are also documented in Melman Yoss et al., *A Hostile Partnership: The Secret Relations*

*between Israel and Jordan* (Tel Aviv, Yediot Aharonot, 1987) (Hebrew), see for example, pp. 78-9.

10  Extract from transcript of a recording of this conversation. The source wishes to remain anonymous.

11  Golda Meir, *My Life*, (London, 1975), pp. 357-8.

## Chapter 16

12  The information came from a Mossad agent in Egypt. His mistake was to say that it would start at 6 p.m. It actually started at 2 p.m.

13  Ariel Sharon, *Warrior: The Autobiography of Ariel Sharon* (London, 1989), p. 312.

14  Ibid.

## Chapter 17

15  Walter Laqueur and Barry Rubins (eds), *The Israeli-Arab Reader: A Documentary History of the Middle East Conflict* (London, 1995), pp. 389-97.

## Chapter 18

16  Eliahu Ben Elissar, *No More War* (Tel Aviv, 1995), p. 112 (Hebrew).

17  For extracts from the Sadat-Begin meeting, see Yoel Marcus, *Camp David: The Door to Peace* (Tel Aviv, 1979), pp. 109-15 (Hebrew).

## PART 4: Homelands

### Introduction

1  Although Yemen and Saudi Arabia did not send troops, they supported the Arab effort during the first Israeli-Arab war both morally and financially.

2  Jacques Kano, *The Problem of Land Between Jews and Arabs* (1917-1990), (Tel Aviv, 1992), p. 74 (Hebrew).

### Chapter 19

3  Eitan Haber, *Today War Will Break Out* (Tel Aviv, 1987), pp. 290-1 (Hebrew). More than 100 Palestinian civilians who tried to cross back were shot dead by Israeli forces in the period from the end of the war to mid-September 1967. Prime Minister Eshkol was shocked when he heard that innocent Palestinians returning to their homes were being shot by Israeli soldiers. He ordered this practice to be

stopped.

4   The names of the eight movements that constituted the PLO are: Fatah; PFLP (Popular Front for the Liberation of Palestine); DFLP (Democratic Front for the Liberation of Palestine); Saiga; PFLP-GC (PFLP General Command); ALF (Arab Liberation Front); PLF (Palestine Liberation Front); PPSF (Palestine Popular Struggle Front).

## Chapter 20

5   Both Fatah and the PFLP denied having any hand in the ambush. They claimed it was the work of Jordanian officers acting as agent provocateurs. James Lunt, *Hussein of Jordan* (London, 1989), p. 125.

6   Moshe Dayan, *Story of My Life* (London, 1976), p. 432.

7   Peter Snow et al., *Leila's Hijack War* (London, 1970), pp. 155-6. In telling the story of the conference in Cairo, we have used three main sources: the testimonies of King Hussein and President Numeiry, as well as the above book.

8   Ibid., p. 157.

9   Present were Faisal of Saudi Arabia, El Sabah of Kuwait, Gaddafi of Libya, Numeiry of Sudan, Ladgham of Tunisia, Franjieh of Lebanon, and El Shamy of Yemen.

## Chapter 21

10  The 1932 population census was the last officially taken in Lebanon. Subsequent governments have refused to repeat the exercise. In the 1932 census, the Maronites formed some 29 per cent of the population, the Sunnis 22.5 per cent and the Shi'ites 20 per cent. The country's religion is complex: Muslim 57 per cent; Sunni 20 per cent; Shi'ite 31 per cent; Druze 6 per cent; Christian 43 per cent; Maronite 25 per cent; remainder Greek/Syrian/ Armenian/Latin Catholic and Protestant. From the mid-1970s, the exigencies of the Arab-Israeli situation and the problems arising from the presence of large numbers of Arab armed Palestinians within the country (most of whom had arrived after the defeat of the Palestine Liberation Organization, in Jordan in 1970-1) dealt the Lebanese system another blow.

11  This information was given to the authors by a Mossad agent who cannot be named.

## Chapter 22

12 Dan Margalit, *I Have Seen Them All* (Tel Aviv, 1997), p.90 (Hebrew).

13 Interview with Karim Pakradouni, 21 February 1997, Beirut, Lebanon.

14 Ze'ev Schiff and Ehud Ya'ari, *Israel's Lebanon War* (London, 1985), p. 51.

15 Interview with Karim Pakradouni.

16 Ibid.

## Chapter 23

17 For more information about Abu Nidal and his organization, see Patrick Seale, *Abu Nidal: A Gun for Hire* (London, 1992), p. 67.

## Chapter 24

18 For how Sharon managed to persuade ministers to approve a bigger operation in Lebanon, see Ze'ev Schiff and Ehud Ya'ari, *Israel's Lebanon War* (London, 1985).

19 *Letters from Lebanon* (Israeli television programme), June 1997.

20 Meeting between Philip Habib and Ariel Sharon, 23 June 1982, in Ariel Sharon, *Warrior: The Autobiography of Ariel Sharon* (London, 1989), pp. 478-9.

21 John and Janet Wallach, *Arafat in the Eyes of the Beholder* (London, 1990), p. 34.

## Chapter 25

22 *Israel's Lebanon War*, p. 235

23 Ibid.

24 Thomas Friedman, *From Beirut to Jerusalem* (London, 1990), pp. 157-9.

25 Ibid.

# PART 5: The Road to Peace?

## Chapter 26

1 Walter Laqueur and Barry Rubin (eds), *The Israeli-Arab Reader: A Documentary History of the Middle East Conflict* (London, 1995), pp. 217-18, 310.

2 Shimon Peres, *Battling for Peace* (London, 1995), p. 307. For the

full agreement, see Appendix II, pp. 361-2.
3   Memorandum between Moshe Amirav and Faisel Husseini, Final
     Draft Paper. 25 August 1987.

## Chapter 27
4   Ze'ev Shieff and Ehud Ya'ari, *Intifada* (London, 1990), p. 23.
5   Ibid., p. 128.
6   Parts of this text are based on a book by Dan Raviv and Yossi
     Melman, *Every Spy a Prince* (Boston, 1990), pp. 391-7.

## Chapter 28
7   Because the wording of the resolution said 'territories' and not *the*
     territories, this meant that, in accepting resolution 242, Israel had
     only accepted the principle of withdrawal, and that total withdrawal
     from all the occupied territories remained to be negotiated. In effect,
     in accepting resolution 242, Israel had withdrawn from Sinai (fol-
     lowing its peace treaty with Egypt in 1979) and in 1994 from Gaza,
     and from areas (Jericho) in the West Bank. But it had not withdrawn
     from the Golan Heights, which remained to be negotiated.
8   For statement issued by the Palestine Liberation Organization reject-
     ing UN resolution 242, Cairo, 23 November 1967, see Yehuda
     Luckas, *The Israeli Palestinian Conflict: A Documentary Record
     1967-1990* (Cambridge, 1992).
9   Interview with Abu Mazen, 20 September 1996.
10  George P. Shultz, *Turmoil and Triumph* (New York, 1993).

## Chapter 29
11  Lawrence Freedman and Efraim Karsh, *The Gulf Conflict* (London,
     1994), p. 101.
12  Interview with Abu Mazen, 20 September 1996.
13  *The Gulf Conflict*, p. 168.
14  The Israeli cabinet, fearing that the Iraqis would use non-conven-
     tional weapons and attack them with missiles carrying chemical
     warheads, had taken the precaution of issuing the population with
     gas-masks.
15  This cabinet decision would be reconsidered if the Iraqis used non-
     conventional weapons, such as missiles carrying chemical warheads.
     In this event, Prime Minister Shamir made it clear to the US that
     Israel would retaliate with all the power at its disposal.

## Chapter 30

16 James A. Baker, *Politics of Diplomacy* (New York, 1995), p. 423.
17 Based on interview with Saeb Erekat, 17 February 1997.
18 Based on interview with Faisal Husseini, 12 July 1997.
19 Based on interview with James Baker, 27 March 1997.
20 Based on interview with Hanan Ashrawi, 26 January 1997.
21 *Politics of Diplomacy*, p. 428.
22 Ibid., p. 454.
23 Ibid.
24 Ibid., p. 495.

## Chapter 31

25 Hanan Ashrawi, *This Side of Peace* (New York, 1995), p. 148.
26 Walter Laqueur and Barry Rubin (eds), *The Israeli-Arab Reader: A Documentary History of the Middle East Conflict* (London, 1995), pp. 577-82.
27 As a member of Lehi, also known as 'The Stern Gang', Yitzhak Shamir was wanted by the British who governed Palestine until 1948.

# PART 6: Peace At Last?

## Chapter 32

1 Yitzhak Rabin, *The Rabin Memoirs* (London, 1979).
2 The Red Crescent is an organization in Muslim countries/areas, corresponding to the Red Cross, concerned with the relief of suffering caused by natural disasters and war.
3 Sheikh Yassin was released from jail in October 1997.

## Chapter 33

4 Hanan Ashrawi, *This Side of Peace* (New York, 1995), p. 229.
5 Ibid., p. 241.
6 Yossi Beilin, *Touching Peace* (Tel Aviv, 1997), p. 109 (Hebrew).
7 Ibid., p. 109.
8 Jane Corbin, *Gaza First* (London, 1994), p. 117.
9 August 1993 was a month in which Rabin seriously considered, tested and gave priority to the Syrian option over and above the Palestinian. But even Peres did not know that, during this time, Rabin had actually made a secret offer to the Syrians, and that Assad's reaction to this had been only lukewarm. After that recep-

tion, Rabin put the Syrian option on hold and concentrated on the Palestinian option. For more details, see Part 7 of this book

10  *Gaza First*, p. 175.

11  For the full content of Yasser Arafat's letter, see Shimon Peres, *Battling for Peace* (London, 1995), pp. 377-8.

12  Orly Azoulay-Katz, *Sysiphos' Catch* (Tel Aviv, 1996), p. 205 (Hebrew).

13  Amos Elon, 'The Peacemakers', *The New Yorker*, 20 December 1993, p. 85

14  The story of how the Oslo II agreements were negotiated is fascinating. For the events, as seen through the eyes of Israel's chief negotiator, see Uri Savir, *The Process* (New York, 1998).

## PART 7: Talks with Syria

### Introduction

1  Moshe Dayan in an 1976 interview published in *Yediot Aharonot*, 27 April 1997.

2  This happened in four major border clashes: 17 March 1965, 13 May 1965, 12 August 1965 and 14 July 1966.

3  Israel occupied 485 square miles of the Golan Heights, which, in total, is an area of 675 square miles.

### Chapter 34

4  Alon Pinkas, *The Jerusalem Post*, 17 January 1994.

5  Ze'ev Schiff, 'What did Rabin promise the Syrians?', *Ha'aretz*, 29 August 1997 (Hebrew).

6  Ben Caspit et al., *Committing Suicide: A Party Gives Up Power* (Tel Aviv, 1996), p. 53 (Hebrew).

7  Based on an interview with Walid Moualem.

### Chapter 35

8  Filmed interview with Shimon Peres, 24 January 1997.

9  For more details, see the London Agreement Part 5, Chapter 26.

# Photographic Credits

Key: a – above, m – middle, b – below

Associated Press page 2 (a), p.5 (a), p.6 (a), p.7 (b); Corbis-Bettman/UPI p.1 (b), p.3 (b); Corbis-Bettman p.8 (b); Miriam Eshkol/David Ruringer p.2 (b); Hulton/Getty p.3 (a), p.4 (b), p.5 (b); Popperfoto p.6 (m), p.6 (b); Rex Features p.1 (a), p.7 (a); Abdel Rahman Sadeq p.1 (m); Uri Savir p.7 (m); Sipa/Rex p.8 (a), p.8 (m); Yisrael Tal p.4 (a).

# Index

# A SELECTION OF BOOKS FROM BBC/PENGUIN

### Plato to NATO
Studies in Political Thought

The question 'Why should I obey the state?' forms the basis of all political philosophy from the time of the earliest civilizations to the present day. It has provoked much debate over the centuries on topics including the definition of liberty, the laws of nature and the intervention of divine power. *Plato to NATO* contains fourteen essays on prominent political thinkers that provide a tantalizing introduction to the works of figures as diverse as St Thomas Aquinas, Hobbes, Machiavelli, Rousseau and Russell. *Plato to NATO* contains an introduction by Brian Redhead, and is ideal reading for students of political history.

### Against the State    Janet Coleman
Studies in Sedition and Rebellion

In 399 BC the philosopher Socrates was charged and condemned to death by fellow citizens who believed he had acted against the Athenian democracy. In the seventeenth century Cromwell and the regicides chose the same punishment for Charles I. In *Against the State* Professor Janet Coleman looks at the enduring tradition of rebellion against official authority, studying the violent activities of religious martyrs and terrorists, oppositional movements like feminism, and the radical social analyses of Thomas More, Karl Marx and Sigmund Freud. With an incisive introduction by Brian Redhead, *Against the State* is an excellent companion volume to *Plato to NATO*.

# A SELECTION OF BOOKS FROM BBC/PENGUIN

**Island Race**   John McCarthy and Sandi Toksvig

As a hostage in Beirut, John McCarthy had a dream of sailing on the bow of a classic yacht: to him it was a powerful vision of freedom. In *Island Race* he teams up with his old friend, comedian Sandi Toksvig, to fulfil the dream by sailing around the coast of Britain. In the beautiful *Hirta*, an eighty-year-old wooden cutter, they call in at nearly fifty ports and harbours, and encounter an enormous range of communities – from Buddhist monks on Holy Island in the north to the busy seaside resorts of England's south coast. In this warm-hearted book, by turns thoughtful and hilarious, the gutsy duo make a great many entertaining discoveries and offer two sometimes conflicting but complementary views of Britain from the sea.

**The Making of Pride and Prejudice**   Sue Birtwistle and Susie Conklin

Filmed on location in Wiltshire and Derbyshire, *Pride and Prejudice*, with its lavish sets and distinguished cast, was watched and enjoyed by millions. Chronicling eighteen months of work – from the original concept to the first broadcast – *The Making of Pride and Prejudice* brings vividly to life the challenges and triumphs involved in every stage of production of this sumptuous television series.

Follow a typical day's filming, including the wholesale transformation of Lacock village into the minutely detailed setting of Jane Austen's Meryton. Discover how an actor approaches the character, how costumes and wigs are designed, and how the roles of casting directors, researchers, and even experts in period cookery and gardening, contribute to the series. Including many full-colour photographs, interviews and lavish illustrations, *The Making of Pride and Prejudice* is a fascinating insight into all aspects of a major television enterprise.

# A SELECTION OF BOOKS FROM BBC/PENGUIN

### The Death of Yugoslavia    Laura Silber and Allan Little

While the western world stood by, seemingly paralysed, and international peace efforts broke down, the former Yugoslavia was witnessing Europe's bloodiest conflict for half a century. *The Death of Yugoslavia* is the first account to go behind the public face of battle and into the closed worlds of the key players in the war. Laura Silber, Balkans correspondent for the *Financial Times*, and Allan Little, award-winning BBC journalist, plot the road to war and the war itself.

Drawing on eye-witness testimony, scrupulous research and hundreds of interviews, they give unprecedented access to the facts behind the media stories. Could anything have been done to prevent this terrible tragedy? What will be its lasting effects? The authors consider these questions and assess the present situation and its implications for future international relations.

### States of Terror    Peter Taylor
Democracy and Political Violence

Terrorism is the scourge of most modern democracies, but how can governments fight back without adopting the same terrorist tactics and trampling on those human rights they claim to uphold? In this vivid and disturbing book, based on an acclaimed documentary series, Peter Taylor takes readers inside Irish Cabinet meetings and IRA courts martial. He examines the aims and methods of Palestinian radicals and their Mossad pursuers, and talks to the sons of assassinated enemies who may provide a glimmer of hope. His findings bring fresh insight into one of today's key moral and political issues.